The Intimate Sharing of Friends

Saint Teresa of Ávila on Prayer

The Intimate Sharing of Friends

Saint Teresa of Ávila on Prayer

MARK O'KEEFE, O.S.B.

ICS Publications
Institute of Carmelite Studies
Washington, D.C.

ICS Publications
2131 Lincoln Road NE
Washington, DC 20002-1199
800-832-8489
www.icspublications.org

© ICS Publications, 2024
Published with Ecclesiastical Approval

All rights reserved. No part of this book may be reproduced or transmitted in any form or by any means, electronic or mechanical, including photocopying, recording, or by any information, storage or retrieval system without prior written permission from the publisher.

The Scripture quotations contained herein are from the New Revised Standard Version Bible: Catholic Edition, copyright 1989 by the Division of Christian Education of the National Council of the Churches of Christ in the USA and are used by permission. All rights reserved.

Cover and text design and pagination by Rose Design
Printed in the United States of America

Cover image: Bartolomeo Guidobono (1654–1709), *The Vision of Saint Teresa*, c. 1690, oil on canvas, 117.5 x 92 cm. Public domain.

ISBN: 978-1-939272-96-6 (paperback)
ISBN: 978-1-939272-97-3 (ebook)

Library of Congress Cataloging-in-Publication Data

Names: O'Keefe, Mark, 1956- author.
Title: The intimate sharing of friends : Saint Teresa of Ávila on prayer / Mark O'Keefe, O.S.B.
Description: Washington, D.C. : ICS Publications, Institute of Carmelite Studies, [2024] | Includes bibliographical references and index. | Summary: "Study of the teaching of St. Teresa of Ávila on prayer"-- Provided by publisher.
Identifiers: LCCN 2024016684 (print) | LCCN 2024016685 (ebook) | ISBN 9781939272966 (trade paperback) | ISBN 9781939272973 (ebook)
Subjects: LCSH: Teresa, of Avila, Saint, 1515-1582. | Prayer--Catholic Church. | Spiritual life--Catholic Church.
Classification: LCC BX4700.T4 O45 2024 (print) | LCC BX4700.T4 (ebook) | DDC 248.3/2--dc23/eng/20240531
LC record available at https://lccn.loc.gov/2024016684
LC ebook record available at https://lccn.loc.gov/2024016685

10 9 8 7 6 5 4 3 2

Contents

TRANSLATIONS AND ABBREVIATIONS vii
INTRODUCTION. ix

1 Woman of Prayer and Teacher of Prayer 1
2 Prayer as Friendship 34
3 The First Steps in the Progress of Prayer. 53
4 Prayer as Presence and Recollection 84
5 An Excursus: Acquired Recollection
and Contemporary Contemplative Practice 113
6 Trials and Helps 137
7 Discouragement and Determination 167
8 Prayer and Personal Transformation 182
9 The Gift of Contemplation. 202
10 Deepening Union 222
Epilogue: Is Everyone Called to
Infused Contemplation? 259

SELECT BIBLIOGRAPHY 271
OTHER BOOKS BY THE AUTHOR 275
INDEX 277

Translations and Abbreviations

Scripture quotations are from the *New Revised Standard Version Bible: Catholic edition, Anglicized Text*, copyright ©1999, 1995, 1989, Division of Christian Education of the National Council of Churches of Christ of the United States of America. Used with permission. All rights reserved.

Teresa of Ávila

All quotations from the works of Teresa of Ávila are taken from *The Collected Works of St. Teresa of Avila*, trans. Kieran Kavanaugh, O.C.D., and Otilio Rodriguez, O.C.D., 3 vols. (Washington, D.C.: ICS Publications, 1976–1985, 1987, 2012) and *The Collected Letters of St. Teresa of Avila*, trans. Kieran Kavanaugh, O.C.D., 2 vols. (Washington, D.C.: ICS Publications, 2001, 2007).

The following abbreviations will be used in references to Teresa's works:

C = *The Constitutions*
F = *The Book of Her Foundations*
L = *The Book of Her Life*
SS = *Meditations on the Song of Songs*
W = *The Way of Perfection*
IC = *The Interior Castle*
Ltr = Letters
ST = *Spiritual Testimonies*

In general, when cited in abbreviated form, the first number that follows the title's abbreviation refers to the chapter, and the second number refers to the paragraph. Thus, W 3.5 refers to *The Way of Perfection*, chapter 3, paragraph 5. Regarding *The Interior Castle*, the first number refers to the dwelling places, the second number refers to the chapter, and the third number refers to the paragraph. Thus, IC 3.4.2 refers to the third dwelling places, chapter 4, paragraph 2.

John of the Cross

All quotations from the works of John of the Cross are taken from: *The Collected Works of St. John of the Cross*. 3rd. ed., trans. Kieran Kavanaugh, O.C.D., and Otilio Rodriguez, O.C.D. (Washington, D.C.: ICS Publications, 2017).

The Institute of Carmelite Studies abbreviates John's works as follows:

A = *The Ascent of Mount Carmel*
C = *The Spiritual Canticle*
F = *The Living Flame of Love*
N = *The Dark Night*
SLL = *Sayings of Light and Love*

References to particular texts within these works are indicated in the following way: For *The Ascent of Mount Carmel* and *The Dark Night*, the first number indicates the book, the second number refers to the chapter, and the third number indicates the paragraph. For example: A 2.3.4 would refer to the *Ascent*, book two, chapter 3, and paragraph 4. In a similar manner, for *The Spiritual Canticle* and *The Living Flame of Love*, the first number refers to the stanza and the second number to the paragraph. Thus, C 3.4 is a reference to the commentary on stanza 3, paragraph 4 of *The Spiritual Canticle*.

Introduction

Intimacy . . . sharing . . . friendship . . . presence: these are fundamental elements of St. Teresa of Ávila's experience, understanding, and wisdom on prayer. They are foundations on which this great sixteenth-century mystic and Doctor of the Church builds an accessible, classic, and timeless teaching on prayer. Teresa herself—as her writings and testimonies about her life attest—was a woman with a great capacity for friendship. Her amazing work as a founder and reformer was made possible by her faith, her passion, her drive, her wisdom, and her prudence. But the success of her labors was also a result of her relational skills and the network of friendships that seemed to come so easily to her. It is no surprise that her understanding of prayer should be so fundamentally and essentially interpersonal and even intimate.

Later authors who have alluded to St. Teresa's teaching on prayer have often focused on the stages or grades of prayer that she lays outs, and these have become classic ways of understanding the general progression and deepening of prayer. At the same time, popular attention has often been focused on the extraordinary, mystical experiences that Teresa describes and examines. Bernini's famous statue of St. Teresa in ecstasy, displayed in Rome's Church of Santa Maria della Vittoria, is a classic presentation of the saint. But when we actually read Teresa describe her experience and offer her teaching and counsels about prayer, we see that she is speaking fundamentally of a relationship with a God who has first loved us. Intimate sharing with Christ the divine friend and taking time to be deeply present to him is how she herself understands the act of praying and a life of prayer.

The stages of prayer that Teresa describes simply mark the progression of the deepening of a friendship and of the intimacy of communion with Christ. Unless we see this more fundamental, relational vision, the stages can seem to read like marching orders for a clear, lock-step road map to union with God—which they are not meant to be. All of the extraordinary experiences of prayer that Teresa received and described were an external manifestation of a deeper mutual sharing with the God who calls and invites into union. Unless we recognize their deeper, essential meaning, the mystical phenomena can remain only a fascinating spiritual curiosity or a naïve ideal of what a spiritual tourist sets out to obtain. But Teresa of Ávila is not inviting us to follow a set path with clearly demarcated steps nor to seek particular experiences of encounter with God—no matter how sublime. She invites us into the intimate sharing of friendship with God in Christ that she herself experienced and treasured.

The Intimate Sharing of Friends is a study of St. Teresa's teaching on prayer. It is not a general introduction to her life and thought. But, since prayer is at the heart of how Teresa understood the Christian life, it is a good entryway to a broader understanding of her spiritual and theological vision. In the same way, since Teresa of Ávila was essentially a woman of prayer, we better understand her life and her work as a founder and reformer through the lens of prayer. This becomes clear, for example, in Teresa's first major work, *The Book of Her Life*, which has sometimes been called her autobiography. In fact, in addition to narrating the foundation of the first monastery of her reform, she is using a biographical frame to understand and explain her growth and experience of prayer. In that sense, it is the progression of her prayer, not the chronology of her life, that is central. On the other hand, following what she has to say about her struggles and growth in prayer sheds important light on the unfolding of her life—her priorities, her decisions, and her goals.

Our study will begin with a look at Teresa as a woman and teacher of prayer. We will look at her fundamental definition of prayer (L 8.5) as shared intimacy between friends, unfolding its meaning and implications more generally for a life of prayer. We will then begin to examine the first stages in the growth of prayer as Teresa teaches them. Presence and recollection are two key ideas as we prepare to look at the progression of prayer into true contemplation. At the threshold of that prayer gifted by God is what Teresa calls recollection—at first, a kind of wordless, imageless prayer acquired by our own efforts aided by grace. It has recently been understood by some as a parallel to contemporary contemplative practices such as Centering Prayer. After looking at what Teresa means by recollection—as both acquired by our own effort and later infused by God's gift—we will try, by way of a kind of excursus, to offer more insight into her meaning by comparing her teaching with the more contemporary discussions of wordless prayer. Teresa was a mystic of profound and extraordinary experiences, but her own prayer journey was long and sometimes challenging. She therefore has helpful insights to offer about obstacles and aids to our prayer and especially about discouragement about our prayer and the corresponding need for a determined perseverance. For Teresa, deepening prayer is built on our graced work of ongoing conversion. At the same time, personal transformation is the fruit of more profound prayer. Finally, we will look at Teresa's teaching on contemplative prayer and union with God in this life. In the epilogue, we will ask the question whether Teresa believed that everyone is called to contemplation. Throughout the study, prayer as the intimate sharing of friends will provide a constant reference for our reflections.

As in my previous studies of Teresa of Ávila and John of the Cross,[1] it is my hope in this book to introduce English speakers to some of the riches of Spanish scholarship on St. Teresa. There are many fine introductions and studies of Teresian thought and spirituality available in English, but there is also a whole world of studies available from Discalced Carmelite scholars in her native land and language. My bibliography does not seek to provide an exhaustive look at what is written about Teresa of Ávila but rather to indicate important works in English and especially in Spanish that examine her experience and teaching about prayer. I found the work of Maximiliano Herráiz particularly useful in my consideration of Teresa's writings on prayer, and my bibliography will show that he, too, has used friendship as a guiding image to understand her teaching (though Teresa's generally acknowledged "definition" of prayer in chapter eight of the *Life* easily directs any reader to the same image, as we shall see). Herráiz has a distinctive gift, in my opinion, in taking a broad view of Teresa's writing and drawing out helpful categories by which to understand her thought as it unfolds in sometimes less than well-organized ways. In the chapters that follow, I will lay out my own understanding of Teresa's magisterial teaching on prayer, but I will indicate occasions in which Herráiz's categories have benefited my way of organizing Teresa's thought—and hopefully that of my readers. This will be especially true in chapters one and three, in which I am laying some broader foundations for Teresa's teaching on prayer. For those who are able, I encourage the reader to look especially for the works of Herrráiz and Daniel de Pablo Maroto as they relate to prayer in the works of St. Teresa.

A note on the use of quotations: In the pages that follow, the reader will find that I have often decided to include a fairly large

---

1. See the bibliography for a list of my previous studies of St. Teresa's life.

number of quotations from the works of Teresa of Jesus (as she called herself after the beginning of her reform)—many of them rather long. In fact, I discourage this practice when receiving papers from my students. The frequent use of quotes can suggest that writers have failed to really incorporate the topic of the quoted material into their own reflection. And the use of long quotations can suggest that writers are not really providing a focus on the central point or points being made by the inclusion of the quoted material. But in this context, I want the reader to get an immediate sense of Teresa's own voice and thereby encourage firsthand reading of her works in their entirety. In my comments introducing or concluding the quotations, I will try to bring out what I consider to be the relevant point being made—while, at the same time, give the reader the opportunity to "hear" Teresa make the point in her own unique voice and often colloquial style.

I want to thank Sister Anne Brackmann, O.C.D., and Sister Mary Clare Trolley, O.C.D., who reviewed the whole or parts of the text. St. Teresa is a saint and teacher of prayer for the entire church, but she was also, fundamentally, the founder of the Discalced Carmelite reform. I am privileged to serve as chaplain for the nuns of the Carmel of Saint Joseph in Terre Haute, Indiana. I am certain that any understanding of Teresa of Ávila that I have gained has been aided by my occasional conversations with the nuns and observation of their life and prayer. With great respect and affection, I dedicate this book to them.

1

Woman of Prayer and Teacher of Prayer

St. Teresa of Ávila (1515–1582)—or Teresa of Jesus, as she called herself after she began her Carmelite reform—was, by any measure, an extraordinary woman of her time and really of any time. She was an exceptional person of faith, a church reformer, a founder, as well as a friend and counselor to nuns and friars, lay people, priests, and bishops. She is a well-known saint, her life and example held up by the church as a model for Christian living. Proclaimed a Doctor of the Church in 1970 (the first of only four women among the thirty-six doctors), her teaching has been upheld as reliable and worthy of study for every Christian. All of her remarkable accomplishments were realized in a time and a culture that devalued women, denied them opportunities for higher education and even of literacy, and doubted any contribution that they could make outside the home or cloister. She worked and wrote in a church vigilant and ready to crush any sign of heresy, false mysticism, or Reformation ideas, and in a time in which travel was arduous and dangerous and in which means of communication were slow and unreliable. And still, Teresa of Jesus—this extraordinary woman in so many ways—was preeminently and principally a person, a master, and a teacher of prayer.

Before we proceed in the chapters that follow to unfold Teresa's understanding of prayer as the intimate sharing of friends, we take a broader look in this chapter at what she says about her own prayer and about prayer in general. And so, we will set the stage by surveying prayer as a focus of all of her major published works, her own personal journey of prayer, the challenges that the young Teresa experienced as she struggled to remain faithful and to grow in prayer, and some general characteristics of her prayer. This background will inform and provide context for the chapters that follow.

Writing about Prayer

To read the writings of Teresa of Jesus is to read about prayer. All of her major works and many of her other writings are or include expositions of prayer. Her *Life* was written to clarify for her spiritual director ("confessor," as she often referred to her directors) her own experience and growth in prayer. In the Prologue of the work, she writes: "My confessors commanded me and gave me plenty of leeway to write about the favors and the kind of prayer the Lord has granted me" (L Prol.1). Looking back on the *Life* in a later work, she says of it: "Not long ago I was ordered to write a certain account of my life, in which I also dealt with some things about prayer" (W Prol.4). And in the midst of what is otherwise a chronological unfolding of her experience, she includes several chapters of what can only be called a little treatise on prayer (L 11–22). It is not, however, a digression, since it helps to explain to the reader the rich spiritual experiences that she will be describing.

The Way of Perfection is intended as a primer, a kind of textbook, on prayer and especially contemplative prayer. In the Prologue, she writes: "I received permission from . . . my confessor to write some things about prayer. It seems I might be able to meet with success in doing this because I have discussed prayer with many spiritual and holy persons" (W Prol.1). In *The Interior Castle*, the product of her full spiritual maturity, she writes that she is reluctantly writing again under obedience about prayer (IC Prol)—though, in the Epilogue, she reports how much happiness she has found in her task (IC Epil.1). Even in *The Book of Her Foundations*, a narrative of her work of establishing new monasteries of her reform, she writes in the Prologue: "They also are ordering me, if the occasion offers itself, to deal with some things about prayer and how, by being deceived, those who practice it could be kept from making progress" (F Prol.5). The fifth chapter of the *Foundations* offers an important and very insightful chapter on what many sincere people of prayer experience—the tension between prayer and a life of busy activity.

More than simply writing *about* prayer, Teresa's writings often include her own prayers. She often breaks into prayer as she is narrating or explaining some experience of prayer. Her *Life* is her only explicitly autobiographical work, but all of her works, in fact, give the reader a window into her own rich life of prayer. And so, implicitly but powerfully and insistently, her writings are always inviting the reader into prayer—to begin prayer, to remain faithful to it, and always to go deeper by responding to the divine invitation and self-offer. All of this is presented in a personal and colloquial style that sometimes almost disguises the profound realities that she is addressing. In reading Teresa, the reader can sense a real encounter with this great woman of faith and of prayer whose living message is a call and a challenge to pray. Those who knew her personally testified for her beatification that her voice and spirit live in her works. They are, one author concludes,[1] the most authentic relics of St. Teresa.

1. Daniel de Pablo Maroto, *Dinámica de la oración: acercamiento del orante moderno a Santa Teresa de Jesús* (Madrid: Editorial de Espiritualidad, 1973), 45–48.

Teresa of Jesus writes about prayer because she was most often directed to do so by her directors or asked to do so by the nuns of her reform. In fact, her books have the spirit of being extended letters to her nuns, her directors, and other readers, meant to explain to them what she has learned about prayer.[2] She writes because she believes that there was a real need for writings about contemplative prayer, especially during a time in which the Spanish Inquisition had prohibited almost every book in the vernacular about advanced prayer. She writes by a kind of inner compulsion to tell others what God's merciful grace had accomplished in her and to invite others to learn to embrace the same divine gifts. But Teresa writes because she is firm in a belief that prayer is utterly central and essential to every Christian life. Prayer is the expression of a relationship—a shared intimacy—with Christ that is at the heart of what it means to be a Christian. For her, growth in prayer is the measure of a deepening relationship with God, of an advancing Christian spirituality, and of the maturing of Christian life and discipleship. For her, prayer is "the royal road to heaven" (W 21.1). She writes: "Well, believe me; and don't let anyone deceive you by showing you a road other than that of prayer" (W 21.6). The necessity of growth in prayer is crystal clear in the progression laid out in *The Interior Castle*.

Even more fundamentally, Teresa believes that prayer is essential to every authentically lived human life—because the life of human persons can only be fully lived in relationship with God in Christ. It is in deepening prayer and encounter with God in whose image we are created that the person of prayer attains a true self-knowledge and enters into the path to an authentic transformation in Christ. It is no accident that her

2. Maroto, *Dinámica*, 18.

"primer" on prayer is called *The Way of Perfection*—"perfection," not in the sense of being free of human flaws and foibles, but in the sense of an authentic human fulfillment that she believes is only possible with prayer.

Teresa believed that "in this life there could be no greater good than the practice of prayer" (L 7.10) and that "to give up the practice of prayer was the greatest evil" (L 19.10). It is the remedy for all of life's ills, and to abandon it is to lose one's way (L 19.3). She writes: "Not long ago a very learned man told me that souls who do not practice prayer are like people with paralyzed or crippled bodies; even though they have hands and feet they cannot give orders to these hands and feet" (IC 1.1.6).

Books about the beginnings of prayer were abundant in sixteenth-century Spain. Books about meditation and manuals for daily meditation were widely available. Teresa recognized the value of such books and recommended them. But few books were available on deeper contemplative prayer. Teresa herself was greatly aided early in her spiritual journey by being given a book on the "prayer of recollection"—a type of wordless prayer meant to prepare for true contemplation (discussed below in a later chapter), being promoted especially by the Franciscans of her time. But such books were soon banned by the Inquisition—at the same time that the nuns of her reform were hungry for teaching about growth in the type of prayer experienced and taught by their founder. As Teresa's prayer expanded to include various extraordinary phenomena (visions, locutions, ecstasies, and the like), she felt the need to provide some counsel to others who might have similar experiences and find themselves confused by them, even as she had been. As she writes early in the progression of prayer laid out in *The Interior Castle*: "We always hear about what a good thing prayer is, and our constitutions oblige us to spend so many hours in prayer. Yet only what we ourselves can do in prayer is explained to us; little is explained about what the Lord does in a soul, I mean about the supernatural" (IC 1.2.7). She intended to fill that vacuum. And so, she devotes only five chapters to the first three dwelling places of *The Interior Castle* (which deal with earlier stages of prayer), three chapters to the fourth dwelling places (that mark the transition from the predominance of human effort in prayer to the inflow of divinely gifted prayer), and nineteen chapters to the remaining three dwelling places (which address contemplative prayer and the progress of union with God).

To learn to pray, one must pray. Anyone can read about prayer and explain what he or she has read. But to truly understand prayer, one must be a person of prayer. And this is especially true of deeper, more profound encounters with God.[3] And Teresa of Jesus was essentially a person of prayer. But, as she herself writes: "It is one grace to receive the Lord's favor; another, to understand which favor and grace it is; and a third, to know how to describe and explain it" (L 17.5). And Teresa was abundantly and uniquely endowed with all three: profound experience of God, the ability (and, for her, really the need) to reflect on and understand her experience, and the ability to explain and teach it—as is evident in her classic writings on prayer.

As Teresa reveals, especially in the *Life*, she knew the struggles of prayer—the experience of having her mind and imagination run wild in seemingly endless distractions (L 4.8–9). She herself experienced the painful awareness of an incongruence between her prayer and her actual manner of living, tempting her to discouragement (L 7.17). She tells her readers that she felt the temptation to simply give up on prayer, and during the

3. Maximiliano Herráiz Garcia, *La oración, historia de amistad*, 6th ed. (Madrid: Editorial de Espiritualidad, 2003), 1–2.

year and a half that she did so, she felt lost (L 19.4; 19.10; 7.1). She knew the struggles of beginning in prayer and establishing a habit of prayer, and she knew herself blessed by divine gifts in prayer without her deserving. She recognized the blessing of having been able to encounter books, theologians, and people of prayer to help her to understand what she was experiencing and to give her vocabulary to explain it. She came to feel a responsibility to write for the sake of others who were in danger of falling into discouragement or error (IC 1.2.7).

Teresa clearly possessed a gift for writing about prayer. In fact, she credited God for any true insight that she offered: "for many of the things I write about here do not come from my own head, but my heavenly Master tells them to me" (L 39.8; see also L 38.22). Especially in the *Life*, she often tells her readers that God has inspired her as she tries to explain what are really ineffable experiences in prayer: "God enlightened my intellect: sometimes with words, at other times showing me how to explain this favor, as He did with the previous prayer. His Majesty, it seems, wanted to say what I neither was able nor knew how to say" (L 18.8). In another place, she informs us: "He put before me these comparisons, taught me the manner of explaining it, and what the soul must do here" (L 16.2). She noted that she really lacked time to write with care, but God made up for it by providing her with what to write:

> I should like to have time, because when the Lord gives the spirit, things are put down with ease and in a much better way. Putting them down is then like copying a model you have before your eyes. But if the spirit is lacking, it is more difficult to speak about these things than to speak Arabic, as the saying goes, even though many years may have been spent in prayer. As a result, it seems to me most advantageous to

> have this experience while I am writing, because I see clearly that it is not I who say what I write; for neither do I plan it with the intellect nor do I know afterward how I managed to say it. This often happens to me. (L 14.8)

In prayer, Teresa received graces to understand and to explain what otherwise might remain completely ineffable.

Teresa of Jesus's descriptions of her experience in prayer and her explanation of the process of growth in prayer are classics of Western Christian spirituality. But Teresa was also a true theologian of prayer. In fact, she never formally studied theology or spirituality in an academic sense. Much of that world was closed to her, as a woman of her time. But she was widely read, hungry for knowledge and for understanding, and she consulted regularly and deeply with some of the best theologians of sixteenth-century Spain. But, most profoundly, she was reflecting on her own experience of prayer—using the resources available to her to reflect prayerfully on how God was acting in her life and prayer. With each new encounter and deeper experience of union with God, she came to a deeper—and ultimately, mystical and profoundly intuitive—knowledge of God.

Although preeminently a teacher of prayer, Teresa was not so concerned about offering particular methods of prayer. She was by no means opposed them. She was aware that many books were available to her readers to help with making prayerful meditations. She recommended such books, especially for beginners at prayer and as a means of attaining a more stable and mature prayer. In a later chapter, we will see that in *The Way of Perfection* she does offer a kind of method—what she calls her "manner of prayer"—for entering into a form of wordless prayer ("acquired recollection"). We will examine to what extent it is a parallel to contemporary teachings on Centering Prayer and similar methods. But her real focus is the effort to encourage her readers to give themselves completely and faithfully to prayer and thus to grow in a relationship—an ever-deepening friendship—with God. Her attention is therefore less focused on the *act* of praying and its how-tos and more on a *life* of prayer—which always means, for her, a life of relationship with God in Christ.

Her Own Prayer Journey

Teresa's first book, *The Life*, is a chronological unfolding of her experience of deepening prayer in which she describes three periods in her spiritual journey: (1) the discovery and youthful enthusiasm for prayer of her early years; (2) followed by about twenty years of ups-and-downs, alternations of special graces with periods of half-heartedness and distraction; and (3) finally her mature years of sustained contemplative prayer and deepening union with God.

Youthful Enthusiasm for Prayer

Teresa describes herself as a child filled with youthful enthusiasm for her faith and for prayer. After a thwarted childhood attempt with her younger brother to run away to seek martyrdom by the Moors, she says of herself:

> When I saw it was impossible to go where I would be killed for God, we made plans to be hermits. And in a garden that we had in our house, we tried as we could to make hermitages piling up some little stones which afterwards would quickly fall down again. And so in nothing could we find a remedy

> for our desire. It gives me devotion now to see how God gave me so early what I lost through my own fault.
>
> I gave what alms I could, but that was little. I sought out solitude to pray my devotions, and they were many, especially the rosary, to which my mother was very devoted; and she made us devoted to it too. When I played with other girls I enjoyed it when we pretended we were nuns in a monastery, and it seemed to me that I desired to be one, although not as much as I desired the other things I mentioned. (L 1.5–6)

The adult Teresa presents a picture of her earlier self as idealistically devoted to prayer and even to solitude.

After passing through a period of adolescent frivolity, she entered the monastery. Not long after, a pious uncle gave her a book that would become an essential tool and foundation for the development of a more mature prayer, leading to the divinely given gift of true contemplation: *The Third Spiritual Alphabet* by Francisco de Osuna (L 4.7). Having begun the practice of the prayer of recollection as taught in the book, she advanced quickly and was blessed with many graces in prayer:

> At the end of this time that I mentioned there, the Lord, as I was saying, began to favor me by means of this path; so much so that He granted me the prayer of quiet. And sometimes I arrived at union, although I did not understand what the one was or the other, or how much they were to be prized—for I believe it would have done me great good to have understood this. True, this union lasted for so short a time that I do not know if it continued for the space of a Hail Mary. But I was left with some effects so great that, even though at this time I was no more than twenty, it seems I trampled the world under foot. And so I pitied those who went following after it, even though in permissible things. (L 4.7)

But her youthful enthusiasm and early experience of deep prayer gave way to a longer period of back-and-forth, ups-and-downs, in her life of prayer.

A Long Period of Back-and-forth

Although it might have seemed that Teresa was sailing along on the path of deepening prayer, she did not arrive at consistent contemplative prayer and union with God without a long struggle. She alternated between periods of fervor and half-heartedness—often feeling anguish about her distraction and lack of devotion. The call to pray remained strong in her even in times when she did not pursue it as she wanted and felt called to do. She tried to remain faithful with the "very determined determination" that she would later recommend to her nuns and readers. But, in fact, she once went for a whole year and a half without prayer, except for common liturgical prayer (which, in fact, required significant time for the nuns of her monastery) and simple vocal prayers (L 7.11;19.4). She describes how, during that time, she found herself ashamed in speaking to her own father after he had become devoted to prayer through her encouragement. Accompanying him in his dying, she decided to speak to his confessor who urged her to take up prayer again. And, from then, she never gave it up again:

> This Dominican father who was very good and God-fearing profited me a great deal. For I went to confession to him, and he took it upon himself with care to do good for my soul and make me understand the perdition that I was bringing on myself. He had me receive Communion every fifteen days [frequent for that time]. And, little by little, in beginning to talk to him, I discussed my prayer with him.

> He told me not to let it go, that it could in no way do me anything but good. I began to return to it, although not to give up the occasions of sin; and I never again abandoned it. (L 7.17)

Still, the period of struggle continued for eighteen to twenty years (L 4.9; 8.2–3)—practically from the time of her entrance to the monastery in 1535 until her mature "conversion" in 1554—despite her earlier discovery of the prayer of recollection and her experience of special graces.

Although much of what Teresa will describe about the final period of her prayer journey may seem foreign to many of us and even seemingly beyond our grasp, it is precisely the description of these first two periods that make clear that Teresa's prayer journey is not so different from ours. Many of us experience youthful enthusiasm and special moments of grace as well as years of struggle and ups-and-downs, fits and starts. It is important for the readers of her works not to become so fascinated or captivated by her descriptions of her mature prayer, forgetting the years that required her "very determined determination" and willingness to get up and set out again. Teresa of Ávila was indeed an extraordinary mystic, but she passed through years of plodding that may not seem too distant from our own. On the one hand, the remembrance of that simple truth may serve as the reality check for our hopes of a single moment when our prayer will suddenly and miraculously "come together" into advanced mystical prayer; but, on the other, it gives us renewed hope—even as we plod along—that the depths of prayer and relationship with God that Teresa attained in this life are not, with the help of God, beyond our reach, too. This is certainly the hope and the help that Teresa very much intended to offer her readers in her writings.

In the ups-and-downs of our efforts to remain faithful and to grow in the depth of our prayer, Teresa urges us not to give up:

> These labors take their toll. Being myself one who endured them for many years (for when I got a drop of water from this sacred well I thought God was granting me a favor), I know that they are extraordinary. It seems to me more courage is necessary for them than for many other labors of this world. But I have seen clearly that God does not leave one, even in his life, without a large reward; because it is certainly true that one of those hours in which the Lord afterward bestowed on me a taste of Himself repaid, it seems to me, all the anguish I suffered in persevering for a long time in prayer. (L 11.11)

Ultimately, Teresa of Jesus became a great mystic, but she arrived at that height by God's immense grace and by her own willingness to persevere in the face of the common difficulties of a sustained life of prayer.

Mature of Years of Contemplative Prayer and Union

The transition into her mature experience of prayer was marked by a kind of adult spiritual conversion, precipitated by an encounter with an image of the wounded Christ and by her reading of the *Confessions* of St. Augustine (L 9). This conversion was not, however, from a life of sin to a life of virtue but rather a kind of spiritual awakening and of radical openness to the communication and inflow of God. The little treatise on prayer that takes up chapters eleven through twenty-two of *The Life* initially seems like a digression, but it explains the new world of prayer that opens up for Teresa when she takes up again the narrative of her prayer journey in chapter twenty-three.

After her mature conversion, Teresa's prayer became increasingly directed by divine action—"supernatural," as she calls it. God's action becomes progressively more dominant, as Teresa describes her passage beyond her acquired recollection, through a contemplative prayer of quiet and then through deepening and more encompassing stages of union with God. In her little treatise on prayer in the *Life*, Teresa describes this progression as four different ways of watering a garden—moving from "first manner of watering the garden," where graced human effort is predominant, into the remaining three manners where God is the principal agent. From the perspective of *The Interior Castle*, this passage into spiritual maturity is described as movement through the seven dwelling places of the castle of the soul. What she was describing in the *Life* was the passage through the fourth dwelling places into the fifth and beyond. We will examine her images of the progression of prayer in a later chapter.

Challenges to Her Growth in Prayer

Especially in the *Life*, Teresa addresses the challenges that she herself experienced in the years of struggle in her prayer:[4] her inability to pray discursively by using her imagination and intellect in traditional meditation; the incoherence that she felt existed between her prayer and her actual living; the absence of a spiritual director; and a community ambience that did not favor or support the deepening of prayer. A closer examination of these challenges will help us to see the root of some of the main elements of her teaching and counsels on prayer—as well as, again, to humanize her prayer and help us to see ourselves in her journey and struggles.

4. See Herráiz, *La oración*, 22–32.

Her Inability to Engage in Traditional Meditation

Meditation, at the time of Teresa, was generally understood to mean a type of prayer in which one actively used the intellect or the imagination.[5] A person would reflect prayerfully on a biblical text or on a mystery of the faith (such as the crucifixion or resurrection). Or one might use the intellect to ponder, in faith, the mystery of God, the divine attributes, or the wonder of the Trinity. On the other hand, one might use the imagination to place oneself in the scene, imagining the self as a participant in a gospel story, listening to Jesus or receiving his teaching or healing power. In addition to promoting a spirit of devotion and personal engagement with God and the saints, the meditation might conclude with identifying resolutions for action or changes in one's daily living. This was often called "discursive" meditation—that is, it involves the intellect or imagination moving from point to point, as in Ignatian meditation. Meditating on the mysteries of the rosary or praying the Stations of the Cross can be one form of such prayer. *Lectio divina*, associated with the Benedictine tradition, teaches a four-part process that includes meditation as an important element (reading, meditation, prayer, contemplation). At the time of Teresa, books teaching a particular method of meditation or containing helps or points for meditation were widely available. And she accepted the value of such meditation and recommended it to those who could practice it fruitfully. It would be a natural next step for someone who wanted to move beyond the recitation of established

---

5. In contemporary discussions, the word *meditation* can sometimes be used to mean some form of contemplative prayer. Indeed, for some, the two words can be used interchangeably. But in Teresa's time and in her usage, *meditation* refers to an active form of prayer that involves reflection or the use of the imagination—as distinct from the gifted, infused prayer of wordless, imageless contemplation.

written prayers, to establish a helpful routine for prayer, and thus to grow in one's life of faith.

Teresa, however, found that, as much as she tried, she could not profitably use her intellect or imagination in the manner that such meditation assumed. She says of herself: "God didn't give me talent for discursive thought or for a profitable use of the imagination" (L 4.7; see also L 9.4). Elsewhere, she writes: "I had such little ability to represent things with my intellect that if I hadn't seen the things my imagination was not of use to me, as it is to other persons who can imagine things and thus recollect themselves. I could only think about Christ as He was as man, but never in such a way that I could picture Him within myself no matter how much I read about His beauty or how many images I saw of Him" (L 9.6).

Her principal problem was the constant distractions that "tormented" her in her efforts (L 9.4), an inability to keep her mind or imagination focused on the point of meditation: "I suffered many years from the trial—and it is a very great one—of not being able to quiet the mind in anything" (W 26.2; see also W 31.8). Her mind sometimes seemed to her to be like a "madman": "But this intellect is so wild that it doesn't seem to be anything else than a frantic madman no one can tie down; nor am I master of it long enough to keep it calm for the space of a Creed. Sometimes I laugh at myself and know my misery, and I look at this madman and leave it alone to see what it does" (L 30.16). Although books by prominent spiritual writers to aid meditation were widely available and helpful to many people, Teresa found that she could not profitably engage in that form of prayer.

Because of her inability to keep her mind focused, she turned to books, to images of Christ, and to quietly attending to nature in order to keep her mind at rest. But the silver lining in her inability to engage in discursive meditation is that she turned to and developed a manner of praying that involved simply being attentive and present to Christ—the prayer of recollection that we will examine in a later chapter. She didn't try to imagine or think about Christ but simply tried to be attentive and present to him with and within her.

Christian spiritualities and especially mystics are often understood to be "kataphatic" or "apophatic"—that is, embracing the use of images as a doorway to divine encounter or striving to move beyond any images. The spirituality of St. Ignatius of Loyola is often given as the classic example of a kataphatic spirituality since it involves active meditation on gospel scenes and mysteries. On the other hand, St. John of the Cross is often portrayed as a classic example of an apophatic spirituality since he urges his readers to pass beyond the use of images, concepts, and ideas in prayer. Neither form is, of course, good or bad, right or wrong, or mutually exclusive. People of prayer must find the manner of prayer that draws them and is fruitful for them. Teresa of Ávila is difficult to classify according to these categories.[6] She is sometimes identified as a kataphatic mystic since her prayer of recollection involves "representing Christ" or attending silently to an image of Christ. She experienced, and described at some length, visions of Christ. She heard divine words (locutions) spoken to her. Ultimately, there is no need to "classify" her spirituality at all, but it is important to see that her focus is not on any form of active meditation. Again, she did not recommend against it and even encouraged meditation for those who could do so profitably; but she herself could not. And so, she turned to a form

6. See differing viewpoints offered by Peter Tyler and Edward Howells in *Teresa of Avila: Mystical Theology and Spirituality in the Carmelite Tradition* (New York: Routledge, 2017).

of prayer that did not really involve either the intellect or the imagination—at least beyond the possible use of a stationary image in order to hold one's focus in a form of wordless, imageless prayer.

A Lack of Congruence between Prayer and Living

For Teresa, a life of deepening prayer must be consistent with good moral living. One cannot have an authentic relationship with God manifest in prayer if one's life is not consistent or conformed to God's will as revealed in the church's tradition and teaching. Even if we are unable to live perfectly good lives at every moment, growth in prayer and in good moral living must generally go hand-in-hand. A life of virtue and good deeds serves as the foundation for a sound relationship with God manifest in prayer, and prayer bears fruit in growth in virtue. Teresa is clearest about her firm conviction of this connection in *The Way of Perfection*, in which she identifies three virtues which are essential to our preparation for contemplation. At the same time, she shows how every encounter with God bears fruit in the development of a more authentic Christian living. We will look more closely at this relationship in a later chapter.

Especially in her period of struggle and alternation between fervor in prayer and distraction and half-heartedness, Teresa felt acutely that this congruence was often absent in her life. She understood prayer to be a friendship with God, but her way of living was not always consistent with the One who offered her friendship. She believed that God wanted to give the divine self to her, but her manner of life often did not reflect a willingness to really give herself completely in return. God was inviting her into communion, but her attention was too often focused on what, by comparison, she called vanities and superficialities. She writes of herself: "Although in this matter of desires I have always had great ones, I strove for what I have mentioned: both to practice prayer and to live for my own pleasure" (L 13.6). Teresa felt herself to be caught between two attractions: "I should say that it is one of the most painful lives, I think, that one can imagine; for neither did I enjoy God nor did I find happiness in the world. When I was experiencing the enjoyments of the world, I felt sorrow when I recalled what I owed to God. When I was with God, my attachments to the world disturbed me. This is a war so troublesome that I don't know how I was able to suffer it even a month, much less for so many years" (L 8.2). Teresa realized that growth in intimate sharing with the divine friend required a life, values, and the use of time consistent with that relationship.

In fact, Teresa did not feel that she had fallen into serious sin, but nonetheless she felt the pull of a worldly life expressed in silly distractions. She liked to spend time in the visiting parlors of the monastery where lay friends and family members could come and share the local gossip. She liked being liked, and she enjoyed the attention of others. Teresa liked people, she had many friends, and there was a part of her that enjoyed being seen as both charming and prayerful at the same time. None of this rises to the level of moral evil, but Teresa felt acutely that she had a call to religious life and an invitation to deeper prayer. She had already been blessed, as we have seen, even in her youth, with special graces in prayer. Nothing that she was doing was a violation of a commandment, but in comparison to the self-offer of God, to the relationship to which she was invited, and the graces and helps that she had already received, all of it was superficiality and vanity.

Teresa felt tormented by her alternation between seeking superficialities and seeking deeper friendship with God. She felt pulled by two worlds:

> I was living an extremely burdensome life, because in prayer I understand more clearly my faults. *On the one hand God was calling me; on the other hand I was following the world.* All the things of God made me happy; those of the world held me bound. It seems *I desired to harmonize these two contraries—so inimical to one another—such as are the spiritual life and sensory joys, pleasures, and pastimes.* In prayer I was having great trouble, for my spirit was not proceeding as lord but as slave. And so I was not able to shut myself within myself (which was my whole manner of procedure in prayer); instead, I shut within myself a thousand vanities. Thus I passed many years, for now I am surprised how I could have put up with both and not abandon either the one or the other. Well do I know that to abandon prayer was no longer in my hands, for He held me in His, He who desired to give me greater favors. (L 7.17, emphasis added)

She continues:

> I should say that it is one of the most painful lives, I think, that one can imagine; for *neither did I enjoy God nor did I find happiness in the world. When I was experiencing the enjoyments of the world, I felt sorrow when I recalled what I owed to God. When I was with God, my attachments to the world disturbed me.* This is a war so troublesome that I don't know how I was able to suffer it even a month, much less for so many years. (L 8.2, emphasis added; see also L 6.4)

In the sixth dwelling places of *The Interior Castle*, Teresa will describe the exquisite pain of being caught between ordinary human living and the yearning instilled by deepening union with God. But what she describes in the *Life* is the painful tension caused by our own choices in the face of the allure of worldly goods—even while experiencing the desire for deeper relationship with God.

Teresa's sense of the inconsistency of her life and her prayer led to what she later realized was the greatest mistake: the temptation of believing that she was not worthy of prayer. She was tempted to abandon prayer because she thought she was unworthy of it. This was, in fact, the reason that she had given up prayer around the time of her father's death. She writes: "Since I thus began to go from pastime to pastime, from vanity to vanity, from one occasion to another, to place myself so often in very serious occasions, and to allow my soul to become so spoiled by many vanities, I was then ashamed to return to the search for God by means of a friendship as special as is that found in the intimate exchange of prayer" (L 7.1). Only later did Teresa realize how terribly mistaken it was to abandon prayer. It was, as she saw it, a temptation of the devil:

> It doesn't seem to me that I underwent any danger as bad as with this invention the *devil taught me under the pretext of humility. He put the thought in my head to question how, since I was so wretched and had received so many favors, I could engage in prayer*; and the thought that it was enough for me to recite, like everyone else, my obligatory vocal prayers; and the question about how I could pretend to do more since I didn't even say my vocal prayers well; *he suggested that engaging in prayer showed a lack of reverence and little esteem for the favors of God.* It was right to think about and understand these things; *but to give up the practice of prayer was the greatest evil.*

> May You be blessed, Lord, who came to my rescue. (L 19.10, emphasis added)

She writes that she had continued to feel the call to pray, and she sensed that she would never fully give up on it. But she says: "I never thought . . . I would cease being determined to return to prayer—but I was waiting to be very purified of sin. Oh, how wrong was the direction in which I was going with this hope! The devil would have kept me hoping until judgment day and then have led me into hell" (L 19.11). Later, her experience during this time would lead her to challenge her nuns and readers never to give up on prayer, never to be tempted to think that one has to be worthy or pure in order to pray, and always to remain firm in that very determined determination.

Finally, Teresa was forced to decide: to truly be the friend of God that her prayer required or to continue to live halfhearted and distracted. Her father's confessor convinced her to return to faithful prayer, and her mature conversion led to a deeper surrender to God and openness to grace. All of it, she was sure, was God's merciful love at work in her.

Lack of Adequate Spiritual Direction

Teresa believed that good spiritual direction was important in developing and deepening one's prayer.[7] Although she knew that the Holy Spirit remains the true spiritual director, a human guide can help the person of prayer to understand the paths of

7. For a closer look at Teresa's understanding of spiritual direction, see Mark O'Keefe, *Learned, Experienced, and Discerning: St. Teresa of Avila and St. John of the Cross on Spiritual Direction* (Collegeville, Minn.: Liturgical Press, 2020).

prayer, to recognize the movements of the Spirit, and to avoid pitfalls and the danger of self-deceit. She felt that she would have benefited greatly from sound direction. This was especially true as her prayer deepened.

She writes that her discovery of the book *The Third Spiritual Alphabet* by Francisco de Osuna helped her greatly; but, even so, she would have benefited from someone to accompany and guide her:

> When I was on the way, that uncle of mine I mentioned who lived along the road gave me a book. It is called *The Third Spiritual Alphabet* and endeavors to teach the prayer of recollection. And although during this first year I read good books (for I no longer desired to make use of the others, because I understood the harm they did me), I did not know how to proceed in prayer or how to be recollected. And so I was very happy with this book and resolved to follow that path with all my strength. Since the Lord had already given me the gift of tears and I enjoyed reading, I began to take time out for solitude, to confess frequently, and to follow that path, taking the book for my master. For during the twenty years after this period of which I am speaking, I did not find a master, I mean a confessor, who understood me, even though I looked for one. This hurt me so much that I often turned back and was even completely lost, for a master would have helped me flee from the occasions of offending God. (L 4.7)

The journey of prayer—like any long and sometimes difficult passage through unknown territory—is aided by an experienced and knowledgeable guide.

Especially in the years before her mature conversion, Teresa suffered from directors who lacked the knowledge, the skills, or the spiritual experience to be of real help in providing counsel for authentic growth in prayer. Some of them failed to see the important connection of the coherence of daily life with the effort to grow in prayer: "And I think that with God's help it would have been so if I had had a master or person who would have counseled me about fleeing occasions at the beginning and made me turn away quickly when coming upon them" (L 4.9). She adds later: "The whole trouble lay in not getting at the root of the occasions and with my confessors who were of little help. For had they told me of the danger I was in and that I had the obligation to avoid those friendships, without a doubt I believe I would have remedied the matter" (L 6.4; see also L 7.20).

For Teresa, an able spiritual director is an important help for growth in prayer, but it is important that the spiritual companion possess certain characteristics. First, in her view, a good director must be "learned"—that is, knowledgeable of the Scriptures and of the church's teaching and spiritual tradition—in order to offer sound resources to the person of prayer and to help her or him to remain securely within the Christian faith. Second, the director must be experienced in the ways of prayer and in discerning the ways of the Spirit, able to recognize common pitfalls and obstacles. Third, the sound guide must be discerning—that is, attentive to the actual state of the person, knowing when to push a little or hold back. But the director must also be able to help the person of prayer to discern how the Spirit is moving in the events of daily life and in the often subtle unfolding of prayer.

An Unfavorable Environment

Early biographies of St. Teresa often presented the Monastery of the Incarnation in which Teresa first became a Carmelite and in which she lived for twenty years as a community of decadent observance. This picture provided a convenient contrast to the Discalced Carmelite reform that Teresa inaugurated with the foundation of her first monastery, Saint Joseph. But this portrayal of the Incarnation and of the Spanish Carmelites of Teresa's time is inaccurate.[8] In fact, the Incarnation was a monastery with a careful liturgical life, established piety, and sound morality. At the same time, it was overcrowded, populated by holy nuns devoted to the service of God but also by women for whom joining religious life was an escape from the expectations or restrictions of the time and culture. The monastery did not have strict enclosure—that is, the nuns could come and go. They had many opportunities to enjoy social visits with family and friends. Teresa did not find it an environment conducive to the development of real contemplative prayer, at odds with her sense that the Carmelites should return to the more contemplative and even eremitical roots of their founders.

In fact, Teresa herself had enjoyed the freedoms offered by the monastery of her first profession, but she came to feel the tension of embracing such freedoms and the call to deeper, wordless prayer. Careful not to judge any of the other nuns, Teresa writes that ultimately it was not an ambience helpful to her personally: "That's why it seems to me it did me great harm not to be in an enclosed monastery. For the freedom that those who were

---

8. For an examination of the spiritual state of the Carmelites and of the Incarnation at the time of Teresa, see my *In Context: Teresa of Avila, John of the Cross, and Their World* (Washington, D.C.: ICS Publications, 2020), 75–112.

good were able to enjoy in good conscience (for they were not obligated to more since they did not make the vow of enclosure) would have certainly brought me, who am so wretched, to hell, if the Lord with so many remedies and means and with His very special favors had not drawn me out of this danger" (L 7.3). She makes clear that the fault was principally her own: "The only real excuse could be that the convent was not founded on a strict observance. I, miserable creature that I was, followed after what I saw wrong and left aside the good" (L 5.1).

Teresa writes as a nun, largely addressing other nuns of her reform. Her focus is therefore on the environment provided by the life of a religious community and the supports (or hindrances) to deepening prayer that it can provide. But Teresa is making an important point about the need for support and encouragement of the life of prayer and of a way of life that is consistent with and conducive to growth in prayer for any state in life. She believed that God calls all people to deeper prayer, recognizing that outside cloistered contemplative life, the real demands of life can create greater challenges to finding such support. We can be sure that she would agree that when God calls, God provides. Meanwhile, we must aim high while living our reality as we find it—with trust that God will provide.

Characteristics of Teresa's Prayer

Maximiliano Herráiz has published several helpful studies of Teresa of Ávila's teaching on prayer, suggesting a number of characteristics of her prayer that can help us to see it in broad, summary form. In one work, he concludes that, for Teresa, prayer is personal, transformative, and dynamic.[9] We will

9. Herráiz, *La oración*, 41–99.

examine all three of these characteristics in the course of chapters that follow: a chapter on prayer as friendship (personal), another on virtues and transformation (transformative), and a third on the language and itinerary of prayer (dynamic). In another work, Herráiz expands the characteristics that he believes mark the prayer of Teresa of Jesus.[10] For her, he argues, prayer is all-encompassing, personal, realistic, committed, and ecclesial. Other ways of characterizing Teresa's prayer are possible.[11] But, by way of introducing the discussion to follow, it may be helpful to the reader to expand on the characteristics identified by Herráiz as they shed light on topics to be addressed in our study.

Prayer Is All-Encompassing

For Teresa, prayer is not so much about *doing* but, rather, about *being*—being in relationship with God and attending to the divine presence in all of our doing. Certainly we can speak of times of prayer and the activity of prayer, but it is more fundamentally a matter of being attentive to God in all of the moments and activities of our lives: "Moreover, the true lover loves everywhere and is always thinking of the Beloved! It would be a thing hard to bear if we were able to pray only when off in some corner. I do realize that prayer in the midst of occupations cannot last many hours; but, O my Lord, what power over You a sigh of sorrow has that comes from the depths of

10. Maximiliano Herraíz García, "Características de la oración teresiana," in *A zaga de tu huella: escritos teresiano-sanjuanistas y de espiritualidad* (Burgos, Spain: Editorial Monte Carmelo, 2004), 143–56.

11. Martín del Blanco, for example, concludes that Teresa's prayer is affective (without denying the intellectual), dynamic, grounded in the Word of God, Christocentric, ecclesial, and apostolic. *Catecismo de la oración según Santa Teresa de Jesús* (Burgos, Spain: Editorial Monte Carmelo, 2014), 35.

our hearts on seeing that it isn't enough that we are in this exile but that we are not even given the chance to be alone enjoying You" (F 5.16). Even in natural loving, Teresa is reminding us, there are *acts* of loving expressed at discrete *times*, but there is more fundamentally the reality of *being in* love that naturally expresses itself in action.

As we will see, prayer is grounded essentially in friendship with God that encompasses all of life. A person of prayer lives a life in reference to God—a life progressively centered in God. To give up on prayer is to give up on an essential element of the Christian life. Moreover, being a friend of God means being a particular kind of person—in conformity and consistent with the divine ways as revealed in Christ. Teresa opens her little treatise on prayer in the *Life* by saying: "Well, let us speak now of those who are beginning to be servants of love. This doesn't seem to me to mean anything else than to follow resolutely by means of this path of prayer Him who has loved us so much" (L 11.1). To be a person of prayer is to be a "servant of love." Particular moments of prayer are an expression of this deeper reality.

Prayer Is Personal and Interpersonal

Prayer involves relationship between the human person and the Divine Person most especially in Christ. We do not pray to a concept, an abstraction, a nebulous presence, or an impersonal Someone out in the cosmos. God is not a passive spectator or observer of our prayer. God is active—indeed, the first and principal actor—in our prayer. God is profoundly and intimately present to us at every moment, gazing at us with love—even as, most fundamentally, prayer for our part is our simple gazing at God. At the same time, the loving gaze of God invites, offers, gives, calls, and entices our response especially in explicit times of prayer but also in our daily living. And, for Teresa, the face of the God who is present is preeminently Christ Jesus, divine and human. We can add, then, that Teresa's prayer is consistently and even insistently Christocentric. It is grounded in a personal and interpersonal relationship with Christ.

Prayer Is Realistic

For all of Teresa's descriptions of contemplation and extraordinary mystical phenomena, she understands that prayer must be grounded in life as we find it, in our state in life, and according to our vocations and their particular demands. Famously, she reminds her nuns that the Lord "walks among the pots and pans" (F 5.8). They must not complain that they are called from prayer if there is work that must be done, if someone needs a hand, or if obedience or charity demands it. The acceptance of such demands—even at the cost of time spent in prayer—does not in itself impede prayer, since it involves response to God's will at a particular moment: "Observe, sisters, whether leaving the pleasure of solitude is not well repaid. I tell you that it is not because of a lack of solitude that you will fail to dispose yourselves to reach this true union that was mentioned, that is, to make your will one with God's. This is the union that I desire and would want for all of you, and not some absorptions, however delightful they may be, that have been given the name 'union'" (F 5.13). Friendship with God grows not only in prayer but also in living as "servants of love" in daily life.

When Teresa comes to teach about the kind of wordless prayer that came to be called "acquired recollection" (as distinct from its infused, gifted form), she tells her readers that they must come as they are. It is not the time for active talking to God—though her writings make clear that she herself often had such active conversations with God. Rather, even when the person's prayer has reached the threshold of contemplative prayer, they must always come as they are, with life as they experience it. Recollected prayer is not the time we give to actively talk to God, nor the time we give to actively imagine or think about God. But people must nonetheless come to such prayer as they find themselves because it is simply the present reality of their lives:

> If you are experiencing trials or are sad, behold Him on the way to the garden: what great affliction He bore in His soul; for having become suffering itself, He tells us about it and complains of it. Or behold Him bound to the column, filled with pain, with all His flesh torn in pieces for the great love He bears you; so much suffering, persecuted by some. spit on by others, denied by His friends, abandoned by them, with no one to defend Him, frozen from the cold, left so alone that you can console each other. Or behold Him burdened with the cross, for they didn't even let Him take a breath. He will look at you with those eyes so beautiful and compassionate, filled with tears; He will forget His sorrows so as to console you in yours, merely because you yourselves go to Him to be consoled, and you turn your head to look at Him. (W 26.5)

The intimate sharing of true friends requires coming "as we are."

Prayer Is Committed

Perhaps there are times that we might be tempted to think that St. Teresa and other great people of prayer arrived at deep prayer in one sudden and miraculous moment—in the hope that the same might happen to us. Or, on the other hand, we might be tempted to dismiss Teresa and others, thinking that their journey of prayer was easy and quick—not at all like our own. But Teresa testifies that her own journey was a long one that demanded of her a firm commitment not to give up:

> And very often, for some years, I was more anxious that the hour I had determined to spend in prayer be over than I was to remain there, and more anxious to listen for the striking of the clock than to attend to other good things. And I don't know what heavy penance could have come to mind that frequently I would not have gladly undertaken rather than recollect myself in the practice of prayer. It is certain that so unbearable was the force used by the devil, or coming from my wretched habits, to prevent me from going to prayer, and so unbearable the sadness I felt on entering the oratory, that I had to muster up all my courage (and they say I have no small amount of that, and it is observed that God has given me more than women usually have, but I have made poor use of it) in order to force myself; and in the end the Lord helped me. (L 8.7)

Prayer requires commitment, she writes, but God helps and rewards our efforts:

> Now, then, if the Lord put up with someone as miserable as myself for so long a time, and it seems clear that by this means all my evils were remedied, who, no matter how bad they may be, has reason to fear? For no matter how bad they may be, they will not be bad for as many years as I was after having received so many favors from the Lord. Who can lose confidence? For the Lord endured so much with me only because I desired and strove to have some place and time in order that He might be with me. And this I often did without eagerness

> but through my own great struggles or through the strength the Lord Himself gave me. For if those who do not serve Him but offend Him derive so much good from prayer and find it so necessary—and no one can truly discover any harm that prayer can do, the greatest harm being not to practice it—why do those who serve God and desire to serve Him abandon it? I, indeed, cannot understand why, unless it is that they want to undergo the trials of life with greater trial and close the door on God so that He may not make them happy. I certainly pity those who serve the Lord at their own cost, because for those who practice prayer the Lord Himself pays the cost since through their little labor He gives them delight so that with the help of this delight they might suffer the trials. (L 8.8.)

We must be committed to our prayer in a determined way, but this is only possible and fruitful because it is God who is first committed to the growth of the relationship expressed in prayer.

Commitment and fidelity to prayer is a fruit of prayer. A greater openness to God's presence—whether consciously experienced or not—bears fruit in empowerment to stay the course. But commitment and fidelity are also a necessary precondition to growth in prayer. And Teresa insists, as we shall see in a later chapter, that we must have a "very determined determination" (*muy determinada determinación*) in our faithfulness to prayer. But always prior to our effort, God is faithful and active in the relationship that is at the heart of prayer.

Prayer Is Ecclesial

The focus of Teresa's writing is personal prayer. She is writing especially for nuns of her reform who were eager to grow in prayer. She is therefore able to presuppose the regular common prayer of her nuns and their participation in the Eucharist. Being a person of the sixteenth century, her ecclesiology was not exactly the same as an understanding of the church that we have today. Still, she was very aware that the contemplative life is important for the life of the whole church. When, in the first chapters of *The Way of Perfection*, she describes the reasons for the beginning of her reform, it is very much in her mind that the prayer of the nuns will touch the life of the whole church. In the same way, early in *The Book of Her Foundations* (F 1.7–8), she describes her reaction to the description of the American missions offered by a visiting Franciscan friar. She regretted deeply that she could not take an active role in the work of evangelization, but God helped her to realize that she and her nuns were doing their part without leaving their cloisters. Centuries later, in 1927, her cloistered spiritual daughter, St. Thérèse of Lisieux, was named by Pope Pius XI as copatron of the church's missions, testifying to the ecclesial character of all authentic contemplative prayer.

2

Prayer as Friendship

Teresa of Jesus was a prolific letter writer. Almost five hundred of her letters are extant, addressed to a wide variety of people—nuns, friars, bishops, wealthy benefactors, and family and other lay people (including the king of Spain).[1] We can be sure that far more of her letters were lost. In these letters, Teresa discusses the business of the reform and founding of monasteries, offers advice and spiritual counsel, directs business affairs, expresses her frustrations and joys. Her tone can be stern, consoling, challenging, chatty, and teasing. What the letters reveal—really, like all of her writings—is that Teresa was a profoundly relational person. She had many friends in different states of life, and she clearly valued these relationships and strove to nurture them. She tells us that, early in her life in the monastery, she was tempted by opportunities for frivolous visits with people who came to the monastery's visiting parlors. She liked to be liked. She was aware of what so many people who knew her said of her: she was blessed with charm and the ability to win people over. It is no surprise, then, that Teresa fundamentally understands prayer as rooted in relationship. Prayer is grounded in friendship with God in Christ.

1. Teresa of Avila, *The Collected Letters of St. Teresa of Avila*, trans. Kieran Kavanaugh, 2 vols. (Washington, D.C.; ICS Publications, 2001, 2007).

Christ as Friend

Teresa's prayer and her entire view of faith and spirituality are radically Christocentric. Christ, for her, is central in the Christian life and prayer from its beginnings to its heights—Christ in his glorified divinity and but also and distinctively in his humanity. For Teresa, Christ is both "His Majesty" and the very best of friends—both transcendent Lord and intimate companion. Sometimes, this is evident in the same sentence: "His Majesty wants this determination, and He is a friend of courageous souls if they walk in humility and without trusting in self" (L 13.2). But when she speaks about prayer, she focuses especially on the nearness of Christ and identifies him as friend.

Before offering her famous definition of prayer, Teresa urges her reader to take up prayer and never give it up because: "if one perseveres, I trust then in the mercy of God, who never fails to repay anyone who has taken Him for a friend" (L 8.5). When she comes to speak of the quiet, attentive form of prayer that she will call recollection, she urges the person of maturing prayer: "Believe me, you should remain with so good a friend as long as you can. . . . Do you think it's some small matter to have a friend like this at your side?" (W 26.1). Many more examples can be offered that demonstrate the central place that Christ as friend plays in Teresa's spirituality and prayer—each of which, on its own, could be the basis of a fruitful meditation:

> "Oh, what a good friend You make, my Lord! How You proceed by favoring and enduring. You wait for the others to adapt to Your nature, and in the meanwhile You put up with theirs! You take into account, my Lord, the times when they love You, and in one instant of repentance You forget their offenses." (L 8.6)

"Whoever lives in the presence of so good a friend and excellent a leader, who went ahead of us to be the first to suffer, can endure all things. The Lord helps us, strengthens us, and never fails; He is a true friend." (L 22.6)

"What more do we desire than to have such a good friend at our side, who will not abandon us in our labors and tribulations, as friends in the world do? Blessed are they who truly love Him and always keep Him at their side!" (L 22.7)

"He loves whoever loves Him; how good a beloved! How good a friend!" (L 22.17)

"O my Lord, how You are the true friend; and how powerful! When You desire You can love, and You never stop loving those who love You! All things praise You, Lord of the world! Oh, who will cry out for You, to tell everyone how faithful You are to Your friends! All things fail; You, Lord of all, never fail!" (L 25.17)

"And I know some persons for whom I have felt quite sorry—and I've seen what I'm speaking about—because they have turned away from One who with so much love wanted to be their friend and proved it by deeds." (IC 4.3.10)

"Oh, great dignity, worthy of awakening us that we might try diligently to please this Lord and King of ours! But how badly these persons repay this friendship since they turn so quickly into mortal enemies! Indeed, how great is the mercy of God. Where would we find a friend so patient? And even if a friend commits one fault, it is never erased from the other's memory, nor do the two manage to have a friendship as trusting as before. Now then, how often will souls similarly fail in their friendship with our Lord, and how many years He waits for us in this way." (MSS 2.19)

At the end of the present chapter, we will examine Teresa's insistence on maintaining a constant focus on the humanity of Christ. But first, we examine her definition of prayer as friendship and its implications.

The Definition of Prayer and Its Implications

Teresa's fundamental understanding of prayer appears in the definition that she offers in the *Life* (L 8.5): "For mental prayer in my opinion is nothing else than an intimate sharing between friends; it means taking time frequently to be alone with Him who we know loves us" (L 8.5).[2] The term *mental prayer* can mean a number of things, including active forms of meditation. But here Teresa uses *mental* simply to mean attentive: prayer in which the person is not simply repeating phrases vocally without attention. As we will see, when she speaks of the progression of maturing prayer, she will begin with vocal prayer—the repetition, aloud or silently, of words addressed to God, whether established or spontaneous. But, she says, in order to truly be prayer, the words must be said with attention and devotion. Thus, vocal prayer must, at the same time, be mental prayer in order to be authentically prayer. Although the definition is brief, it is dense and rich. We can draw from it a number of important implications about prayer that we will continue to unfold in the chapters that follow.

---

2. Because the definition is so central, we recall, too, the Spanish original: "no es otra cosa oración mental, a mi parecer, sino tratar de amistad, estando muchas veces tratando a solas con quien sabemos nos ama." In addition to the ICS translation of Teresa's work being used here, the earlier English translation by E. Allison Peers remains highly regarded. He translates the definition in this way: "Mental prayer, in my view, is nothing but friendly intercourse, and frequent solitary converse, with Him Who we know loves us."

(1) Prayer is more about relationship than about individual acts or moments of prayer.

Sometimes we speak with complete strangers, perhaps asking for directions or making small talk while we wait in line. Such conversation creates a kind of temporary relationship but ultimately the conversation makes no impact on us except for some useful information we may have gathered. We can also talk with people whom we see frequently, such as coworkers with whom we might share workspace or some common task. Again, this represents a kind of relationship but not what we would necessarily call friendship at any real level, and the conversation between us, although perhaps frequent and even prolonged, is not really impactful in our lives. Sometimes, prayer can seem like such conversations—sometimes useful if we are asking for something, sometimes courteous if we are expressing thanks, but not necessarily a reflection of our lives and deep feelings and not necessarily an expression or deepening of a real relationship.

Conversation between friends is different. Such dialogue, too, can be useful and practical. Still, it has a different character. Speech between friends is both an expression of their relationship and, at the same time, nurtures it. Often there is a deeper level of communication. But beyond what is being specifically communicated, there is a connection between the friends that is not fully expressed by the words shared between them. Their interaction is deeper than the words that a third party might read in a transcript of a conversation. Regular conversation is essential to friendship, and, at least sometimes, these dialogues must be deeper than just the weather, politics, sports, or fashion.

Prayer—"mental prayer," as Teresa says—is an intimate sharing between friends. Sometimes it must be like talking or dialogue—especially at the beginning and during the maturing of prayer—but her definition encompasses and presupposes that what is occurring between friends is more than the words expressed. Authentic praying is certainly more than talking *at* God and even more than *talking* with God. It cannot be reduced simply to discreet moments or acts of prayer, although there must be frequent and faithful interactions with God. Prayer, for Teresa, is a manifestation, an expression, a fruit of friendship with God. At the same time, it is a savoring, a nurturing, and a deepening of that friendship. Human friendship is more than the explicit moments of interaction, but, at the same time, it requires such interactions—frequently and faithfully. For Teresa, true Christian prayer cannot be understood apart from friendship with God in Christ, and friendship with God is not possible without a *life* of prayer rather than just *acts* of prayer. For her, the Christian life is friendship with Christ, and prayer is central and essential to it.

(2) Prayer is more about relationship than about technique/method.

Teresa is not in any way opposed to looking for methods of prayer that can promote its growth and our fidelity to it. Different methods can be helpful to different people at different periods of their life of prayer. In the history of the Christian tradition, different religious families have been associated with certain manners or techniques of prayer, such as, for example, Benedictine *lectio* or Ignatian meditation. The Carmelite tradition, after Teresa and John of the Cross, would develop a kind of method drawn from their teaching. But Teresa's focus is not on methods or techniques of prayer. The closest that she comes to offering a method is in the description of her "manner of prayer" that she recommends for developing a wordless form of prayer as preparation for the desired gift of contemplation. We will devote a later chapter to that topic.

Teresa does not write about methods, because there were many books available to her first readers to teach and support a practice of prayer. Furthermore, her main focus was to teach her readers about more advanced forms of prayer in which the divine action is prevalent—and thus beyond any real method, except as setting the stage for contemplation. But Teresa did not devote attention to techniques because her principal concern was the promotion of the friendship with Christ that is fundamental to all prayer. She will insist: be present to Christ; attend to Christ in the Scriptures; take time frequently to be with the one who loves us; and be attentive at the Eucharist. Most broadly and fundamentally, promote friendship with Christ; make each period of prayer, as much as possible, an "intimate sharing" with Christ; use whatever method is useful to you; and prayer will grow and deepen. In other words, what is ultimately important is not so much *how* we are praying or *what* we might be praying about. It is, rather, *to whom* we are praying and *with whom* we are sharing intimately in the context of friendship.

(3) Prayer is personal, involving a real personal engagement.

There is an important place for thinking in the growth of prayer. Especially in forms of meditation, we use the intellect and the imagination to reflect and ponder, perhaps to arrive at resolutions for change or ongoing conversion, and as a springboard to a vocal response or petition to God or to resting in quiet in order to savor and attend to the divine presence in silence. But friendship is not fundamentally about thinking about one's friend—no matter how fondly. Prayer requires a deeper foundation than thinking alone, which can leave one focused on self rather than being a real reaching out to God. Prayer narrowly focused on thinking, then, would isolate from God rather than really bringing us into deepening encounter—when true prayer is meant to pull us out of ourselves toward Another (and toward others). Prayer must be more than thinking—even if it is devoted, focused, and insightful thinking. We must bring ourselves to prayer and be present and attentive to Christ as we are. This is essential to the real personal engagement and intimate sharing with Christ the friend that is at the heart of prayer.

Teresa recognized that, for some people, using the intellect and imagination actively in prayer is a helpful foundation for prayer. This was not the case for her personally. But whatever one's preferred form of prayer, she insists that it is more about loving than about thinking. This is already implied by defining prayer in terms of friendship. Not everyone can use the intellect profitably in prayer, but, she says, "all souls are capable of loving" (F 5.2). Therefore, she continues, "the soul's progress does not lie in thinking much but in loving much." Since everyone is capable of loving, everyone is capable of prayer. Just as human persons have an innate capacity to love, they have an inherent capacity to pray. Elsewhere, Teresa writes: "The important thing is not to think much but to love much; and so do that which best stirs you to love" (IC 4.1.7). Reflection on God—even the loftiest theological musing on sublime doctrine—cannot in itself grasp the truth of God as God is. The human intellect, on its own, will never attain to God. It is love—and the knowledge born of love—that brings personal encounter and ultimately union with God. To speak of prayer fundamentally as friendship focuses prayer away from merely or only thinking about God and directs it to that love of God that is the heart and the fruit of friendship with God.

As we will have occasion to repeat many times, for Teresa, God dwells within the depths of each person—at the "center of the soul." Certainly, God transcends each of us and all of us together. God is present in the sacraments, in the Word of God, in other persons, and in creation—and God transcends all. And still, God dwells in the deepest core of every person. The journey that Teresa will lay out in *The Interior Castle* is precisely the journey within to the inmost core of the soul where God dwells. From superficial prayer over transitory things, we must grow in ever deeper personal engagement with God. The deepest prayer is the most profound personal engagement with God—deeper than thinking, imagining, conceptualizing, words, or images.

(4) Prayer is interpersonal and mutual.

To conceive of prayer as friendship emphasizes that it is interpersonal and mutual. The God to whom we pray and with whom we share intimately is actively engaged in our prayer as well. God is not some far distant Being, not simply the "Unmoved Mover" of some religious philosophy, not a stern judge, or an impassive listener to what we might say in prayer. God is not simply a spectator, an observer, or merely the recipient of our prayer. The God of Christian prayer is the God of Jesus Christ as revealed in the Good News of the Scriptures. Jesus Christ is the human face of God, and, as we have said, Christ is central to Teresa's vision of the Christian life and prayer. When we catch a glimpse of Teresa of Jesus at prayer in the context of her writing and when she teaches us about prayer, she clearly demonstrates a fundamental belief that God is an active and interested dialogue partner and friend. To think of Christ as essentially a friend makes evident that we are not praying to a Distant and Unmoved Being.

But God is not merely engaged in our prayer. God is its principal participant and its source and beginning. As Teresa's definition says, in prayer, we are sharing intimately "with Him who we know loves us." While speaking of friendship clearly implies a two-way relationship, the emphasis is firmly on God who loves us. As St. John says: "In this is love, not that we loved God but that he loved us" (1 Jn 4:10). It is God's love at work in us that makes friendship possible between the divine and human. It is God who initiates it. Jesus—his message and his incarnation, death, and resurrection—are the perfect manifestation of the divine invitation. It is the saving action of Christ that makes our response possible. It is the presence of the Spirit of the risen Christ that grounds our friendship and sharing.

"Prayer," says Teresa, "is an exercise in love" (L 7.12). But it is an exercise made possible, initiated, sustained, and nurtured first by God's love for us. She expresses God's desire for communication between us in an astonishing way, saying that God takes "particular care . . . in communicating with us and beseeching us to remain with Him" (IC 7.3.9). All authentic prayer, therefore, is an exercise in *mutual* loving.

(5) Prayer is essential to growing in self-knowledge.

Through prayer and our friendship with God, we come to a true knowledge of ourselves. Teresa was profoundly aware that we are created in the image of God (IC 1.1.1). In the very first chapter of *The Interior Castle*, she marvels at the beauty of the human soul created in the divine image. But in the second chapter, she notes that this beauty is marred by the reality of sin. These two fundamental truths of human existence reveal the deepest truth of who we are in the world. And it is in our deepening encounter with God that we come to know this truth and grow in self-knowledge. Each experience of intimate sharing with God in Christ reveals to us what we are meant to be and how we are meant to live. But each of these encounters with the Holy God reveals again the distance caused by our sin. Holding together the truth of the beauty of being created in God's image with the truth of our sin constitutes the foundation of self-knowledge.

Teresa tells us that the doorway that leads into the interior castle of our souls consists of "prayer and reflection" (IC 1.1.7). The context makes clear that "reflection" here refers to knowing the God with whom we are entering into relationship and knowing ourselves properly in relation to this God. Kieran Kavanaugh concludes that the first dwelling places of the interior castle "consist in entering the castle, which means beginning the process of knowing oneself and entering into relationship with God."[3] Teresa insists that the pursuit of self-knowledge must never be abandoned at any stage of the journey that leads to union with God in our deepest center. We can and must deepen and enrich our grasp of who and what we are and are meant to be. It is only by looking on Jesus, divine and human, and growing in our intimate sharing with God in Christ that we can grow in our knowledge of the truth of ourselves.

(6) Prayer, like friendship, is meant to grow and deepen.

Relationships are dynamic. They grow or they weaken and die. We can slowly kill a friendship by neglect or end it quickly by betrayal. Or it can grow through frequent contact and deeper sharing. Conceiving of prayer as an intimate sharing suggests not only the possibility for friendly conversation but also for deeper communication and even for a wordless exchange in communion. Friendships grow, and prayer, too, is meant to grow. Indeed, friendship with God cannot grow without deepening prayer.

---

3. Teresa of Avila, *The Interior Castle: Study Edition*, 2nd ed., ed. Kieran Kavanaugh (Washington, D.C.: ICS Publications, 2020), 64.

Teresa always writes about prayer with the expectation that it is meant to mature and deepen, and her writing is oriented to helping her readers in that process. Her *Life* is an exposition of the growth of her own prayer. It includes her well-known image of the four ways to water a garden, which is an image for how prayer progresses. *The Way of Perfection* teaches the reader how to grow in prayer beyond its beginnings into contemplation with God's help. *The Interior Castle*, most especially, explicitly lays out the growth of prayer through the image of this journey into the interior castle of the soul to reach God who dwells in its inmost chamber.

(7) Prayer must be faithful and frequent.

As Teresa defines prayer, "it means *taking time frequently* to be . . . with Him who loves us." She is not simply offering counsel about how to grow in prayer. She says, rather, that prayer *means* a desire and especially a commitment to seek out intimate sharing with God in Christ. This is usually the nature of friendship. There are times and reasons for human friends to be apart and unable to be present to one another face-to-face, but when it is possible, frequent interaction is generally the norm. And so it is in our relationship with God.

Any person of prayer knows from experience that growth and fidelity in prayer—developing a life of prayer—requires its frequent practice. And this is the case whether or not we feel like devoting ourselves to prayer at particular moments. We cannot simply and only pray when we feel like it—at least not if we hope to grow in prayer. Frequency is interrelated with fidelity. And we will see in a later chapter that Teresa is insistent on faithfulness in our prayer—never giving up and pursuing growth in prayer with a steady determination.

(8) Prayer requires solitude.

"Taking time frequently *to be alone* with Him who we know loves us"—solitude is essential to prayer. This, too, is the nature of friendship. We can enjoy the company of a close friend within a larger gathering of friends in shared activities. In fact, Teresa wanted the nuns in each of her communities to be a community of friends: "all must be friends, all must be loved, all must be held dear, all must be helped" (W 4.7). Lack of such openness to others, as Teresa warns in the same text, can signal an unhealthy relationship, especially in the context of community life. But friends also enjoy their time alone. Intimate sharing requires it.

Prayer requires time alone. As prayer deepens, we naturally seek out solitude and quiet. Teresa wanted to assure that, in her communities, the nuns should have private cells and the general expectation of working individually in order to provide such solitude (C 8). But the solitude that is most important to Teresa is not exterior aloneness; it is an inner solitude and quiet that we might call a spirit of attentiveness. As we will see, Teresa speaks of the spirit of recollection that strives to keep one constantly attentive to the presence of Christ. It can be difficult to form and maintain such inner solitude, especially in the midst of noise and activity. Still, it is a comfort and goal for people who do not live in cloisters with rules and places of silence to promote this inner spirit of quiet and solitude wherever they might find themselves.

(9) Prayer requires becoming like our divine friend.

Authentic prayer is intimately related to our manner of living. We will look at the relationship between prayer and life in a later chapter. Here, it is important to pay attention to the sentence that immediately follows Teresa's definition of prayer: "In order that love be true and the friendship endure, the wills of the friends must be in accord" (L 8.5). Human friends can have differing opinions and interests, but, at the same time, there must common interests and goals that bring them together and nurture their growth in friendship. The ancient and medieval world assumed that authentic friends must be united by the pursuit of the good. Their wills, therefore, would have to be "in accord."

For Teresa—as for the Christian tradition in general—the goal of the Christian life is the conformity and communion of our will with the always-loving will of God. She saw clearly that such adherence to the divine will was more important than even the highest mystical experiences in the most profound prayer. Prayer, for Teresa, requires a lived commitment on our part to unite our will with God's in our daily actions. And authentic prayer, in which we share intimately with Christ our Friend, bears fruit in deeper conformity of our actions with God's loving will.

(10) Formation for and growth in prayer is formation for and growth in the Christian life.

Defining prayer in terms of friendship suggests the fact that growth in authentic prayer is virtually synonymous with growth in the Christian life. Without prayer, there is no Christian life—at least in the sense of an authentic, vibrant, and maturing Christian discipleship. And formation in service to others, in the truths of the Christian faith, and in Christian life that builds up community is the essential context of prayer. In order to grow and mature as a Christian, we must grow in prayer; conversely, in order to grow in prayer, we must grow in our authentic living of the Christian life each day.

Focus on the Humanity of Christ

Prayer, for Teresa of Jesus, is friendship—and specifically friendship with Christ, divine and human. Her perspective and her teaching on prayer are radically Christocentric. Her focus on Jesus Christ is not simply an element of her teaching, not just an important aspect, but its very core.[4] He is not a vague presence to the Christian who prays, not a spectator or mere recipient of prayer; Christ is the initiator and the principal partner in prayer. And this is true not only at the beginnings of prayer but also at its heights.

Teresa engaged in the "intimate sharing" of prayer with Christ whom she knew to be both divine and human—both His Majesty and a friend. Christ, both God and human, is the place of encounter, the meeting point, the entry and the way into the divine life. But Teresa's distinctive emphasis was especially on the "sacred humanity." It is common in the tradition of Christian prayer—and especially in the religious culture during Teresa's life—to encourage active meditation on the life of Christ and on gospel scenes from his birth to his resurrection and ascension. Often, particular attention was focused on his passion and death. Many books of meditation were available during Teresa's time to teach and guide such prayer. For herself, Teresa found it fruitful instead to try to make herself simply present—not engaging in an active meditation but rather in simply being present to Christ in whatever scene was the focus of her prayerful attention.

Teresa tells us that, before she embraced a consistent life of contemplative prayer, she liked especially to imagine herself present with Christ suffering in the garden (L 9.4). She had a

---

4. Maximiliano Herráiz Garcia, *La oración, historia de amistad*, 6th ed. (Madrid: Editorial de Espiritualidad, 2003), 104.

great devotion to Mary Magdalene (L 9.2) and to the story of the Samaritan woman at the well (Jn 4), and she frequently asked Christ to give her the living water to drink—which for her became an image of contemplative prayer (L 30.19; cf. MSS 7.6). In receiving Holy Communion, she liked to picture Jesus entering into her soul and she entering into his life—noting that this communion was not simply a matter of imagining his presence (W 34.7–8). This focus on the humanity of Christ continued as her prayer matured. In the *Life*, she tells us that, as she began to receive extraordinary experiences in prayer, she rediscovered her youthful focus on the human Christ, and this became an essential grounding for her prayer thereafter: "I started again to love the most sacred humanity. Prayer began to take shape as an edifice that now had a foundation" (L 24.2).

For Teresa, focus on the humanity of Christ makes the divine more approachable to people who know themselves to be sinners. It makes possible the acceptance of the divine invitation to enter into intimate sharing and friendship. She writes: "Christ is a very good friend because we behold Him as man and see Him with weaknesses and trials—and He is company for us" (L 22.10). Later in the *Life*, she adds: "A much greater love for and confidence in this Lord began to develop in me when I saw Him as one with whom I could converse so continually. I saw that He was man, even though He was God; that He wasn't surprised by human weaknesses; that He understands our miserable makeup, subject to many falls on account of the first sin which He came to repair. I can speak with Him as with a friend, even though He is Lord" (L 37.5).

Christ played a central role in the major moments of Teresa's own prayer. Her mature "conversion," which ushered in her mystical prayer, came with a chance encounter with an image of the suffering Jesus (L 9.1). When the Inquisition banned almost all books in the vernacular on contemplative prayer—many of which had supported and helped her in making sense of her advancing prayer—Christ personally assured her that he would himself be the living book that she needed (L 26.5). Many of her mystical experiences are specifically experiences of Christ (see, for example, L 27.4; 28.1). It was with a vision of Christ that Teresa entered into the spiritual marriage or transforming union (IC 7.2.1–5). But even the vision of the Trinity does not displace the humanity of Christ: "The imaginative visions have ceased, but it seems this intellectual vision of these three Persons and of the humanity of Christ always continues" (ST 65.3).

Teresa was insistent that the person of prayer must never leave behind the sacred humanity of Christ, even in advanced prayer. It appears that some authors during her time were arguing that, at a certain point in prayer, one must move beyond any focus on the human Christ. They reasoned that the wordless and quiet prayer of contemplation could not coexist with continued attention to Christ in his humanity. In response, Teresa acknowledges that, when God draws the person into contemplative prayer, one passes beyond—for the time of such prayer—any kind of active reflection or imagining of Christ. But, at the same time, the person of prayer ought not leave behind a deeper contemplative, nonreflective awareness of Christ in his humanity as the foundation of all prayer (IC 6.7.12). She firmly believed that she would never have advanced in the prayer of union if she had tried to do so (L 22.2), and she points to the witness of saints of great prayer such as Sts. Paul, Bernard, Francis of Assisi, and Catherine of Siena, whose prayer was centered on Christ (L 22.7). Her reaction against the idea of moving beyond Christ's humanity was emphatic:

> They give strong advice to rid oneself of all corporeal images and to approach contemplation of the Divinity. They say that in the case of those who are advancing, these corporeal images, even when referring to the humanity of Christ, are an obstacle or impediment to the most perfect contemplation. . . . They think that since this work is entirely spiritual, any corporeal thing can hinder or impede it, that one should try to think of God in a general way, that He is everywhere, and that we are immersed in Him. This is good, it seems to me, sometimes; but to withdraw completely from Christ or that this divine Body be counted in a balance with our own miseries or with all creation, I cannot endure. (L 22.1; cf. IC 6.7.6)

In her later work, she repeats this insistence on remaining attentive to the humanity of Christ even at the most advanced stages of prayer:

> How much more is it necessary not to withdraw through one's own efforts from all our good and help which is the most sacred humanity of our Lord Jesus Christ. I cannot believe that these souls do so, but they just don't understand; and they will do harm to themselves and to others. At least I assure them that they will not enter these last two dwelling places. For if they lose the guide, who is the good Jesus, they will not hit upon the right road. It will be quite an accomplishment if they remain safely in the other dwelling places. The Lord Himself says that He is the way; the Lord says also that He is the light and that no one can go to the Father but through Him, and "anyone who sees me sees my Father." They will say that another meaning is given to these words. I don't know about those other meanings; I have got along very well with this one that my soul always feels to be true. (IC 6.7.6)

For Teresa, prayer from its beginnings to its heights must be centered on Christ.

Chapter twenty-two of the *Life* is devoted to the same topic. Its title is: "Treats of how safe a path it is for contemplatives not to raise the spirit to high things unless the Lord raises it and of how the humanity of Christ must be the means to the most sublime contemplation. Tells about a mistaken theory she once tried to follow." She returns to the topic in her mature work, *The Interior Castle*, when describing the penultimate sixth dwelling places. The title of chapter seven of these dwelling places includes the following: "Tells what a great mistake it is, however spiritual one may be, not to practice keeping the humanity of our Lord and Savior Jesus Christ present in one's mind; also His most sacred Passion and life, His glorious Mother, and the saints." Teresa reasons that, being human, we benefit from not losing attention to our Savior as human like us. It is true that God sometimes absorbs our consciousness, making it impossible to think actively about anything. If that happens, we should surrender to the divine initiative, but beyond those moments, any effort to leave aside a focus on the humanity of Christ is ultimately counterproductive: "The soul is left floating in the air, as they say; it seems it has no support no matter how much it may think it is full of God. It is an important thing that while we are living and are human we have human support" (L 22.9).

For Teresa of Jesus, Jesus Christ remains the true friend who loves us and with whom we enter into intimate sharing—whatever the depths of that communication—and we must never allow ourselves to leave aside loving attention to him.

3

The First Steps in the Progress in Prayer

That there is a progression in the life and practice of prayer is evident in traditional metaphors for prayer such as a journey, a path, a way, or a process. Teresa allows us to see the development of her own prayer throughout her writings—in a more explicitly autobiographical way in the *Life* and in a more systematic way in *The Interior Castle*. Teresa's teaching on the progress of prayer—"grades" or stages of prayer—has become classic, and subsequent writings on prayer in the Christian tradition have frequently drawn on her images and schemas.

Prayer is Dynamic

For Teresa of Ávila, prayer, like friendship, is a dynamic relationship and process. Friendships grow; friends become closer; their love matures; their sharing becomes deeper, even as words between the friends become less needed for communication. Prayer is not just an action or a technique learned once and for all. Dynamism is an essential aspect of prayer.

In this chapter, we will be looking more closely at how Teresa understands this development through its first stages, but it is critical at the outset to see that what is essential in her teaching is not the exact "steps" that she describes. Rather, she is offering us ways of understanding a deepening of relationship with Christ and of the intimacy of sharing between friends. What she seeks to promote is a deeper interiorization of prayer, a more complete receptivity to the divine action, a greater simplification, a more profound immersion in Christ—that is, prayer focuses more on God who is present in the depths of our being; the person of prayer increasingly surrenders to the divine action; prayer becomes less wordy and more quiet; and the person enters more deeply into communion with Christ.[1] There is not an endpoint, a moment when we will have "arrived" and "accomplished" our growth in prayer, once and for all. Our friendship with Christ, our intimate sharing with an infinitely transcendent God, begins in this life and extends into eternity. For Teresa, our progress in prayer can be understood in terms of a progression in interiorization, receptivity, simplification, and immersion in Christ.

Interiorization: Prayer grows by making us more present to—more attentive toward—our divine friend, listening and responding. It is true that we communicate with God in heaven; we become more attuned to the divine presence all around us, "outside" of us. But Teresa's focus in her teaching on prayer is especially on the presence of God who dwells in the inmost depths of the human soul. The deepening of prayer involves a more profound interior encounter with and personal presence to God—a more profound receiving and self-giving between friends at the deepest level of our being. We are created to be an infinite capacity to receive the divine life and love, and, as we enter into the inner silence of prayer, we enter into our own depths—apart from the activities and bustle of daily life—to be more truly present to our God. This deepening of prayer, at

1. Maximiliano Herráiz offers an insightful overview of the dynamism of prayer in Teresa's teaching, moving to greater interiorization, receptivity, and simplification. See his *La oración, historia de amistad*, 6th ed. (Madrid: Editorial de Espiritualidad, 2003), 79–86.

times, may be accompanied by the felt experience of the divine presence, an inner sense of serenity and equilibrium, a sensation of light and lightness, but its essence is not found in any felt experience of it but rather in the depth of encounter, presence to, and mutual giving and receiving. And, with the deeper interiorization of prayer, there comes a deeper self-knowledge.

It should be noted at the same time that Teresa is not speaking of prayer as if it were simply private, interior, and individual. It is fair to say, though, that she sets out principally to address the issue of personal prayer, because she believes that other resources about growth in prayer were lacking for her readers. Her confessors and nuns asked her to write about personal prayer. Further, it must be noted that the immediate audience for her writings was principally the nuns of her Discalced communities. She could presume on the substantial common liturgical and sacramental prayer of the nuns. Especially in *The Way of Perfection*, she devotes a great deal of attention to virtues that are essential not only to prayer but also to the life of community. Teresa has a profound sense of the place of her monasteries within the life of the broader church. She knew from experience that authentic encounter with God always directed the person out to the needs of others. A humble and practical love for others is always a fruit of authentic prayer, because it is the fruit of an encounter with a God who is love.

Receptivity: The stages of prayer, as Teresa will describe them, can also be understood as a movement from the predominance of our own action to a greater receptivity to divine presence and action. The beginnings of a life of prayer are marked by effort and inner activity: talking to God, telling God our needs, bringing petitions to God, making sure that we also offer prayers of thanksgiving for blessings received. Meanwhile, at first, we must actively decide to pray, and we must carve out time for prayer and work to develop a regular habit and pattern of prayer. Perhaps we choose and practice a particular technique or method of prayer. We know, of course, that every decision to pray and every act of prayer is really the working of grace in us. God, in fact, is always—at every step—the principal actor in our prayer. But, as prayer matures, our activity subsides, and we begin to let go in prayer so that God can become yet more active. We move from talking to more listening. We feel a call into a greater silence—just being with our God—open to the movements and whisperings of the Spirit. As prayer matures, the person becomes simply present with and to God, an intimate sharing that involves attentiveness, a simple loving awareness, and which is content simply to listen and wait on God. The person of maturing prayer becomes more receptive to God at more profound levels of consciousness and being. And when we consent to let God be more active, a greater transformation in our lives becomes possible, and there is more abundant fruit in daily living.

Simplification: More interior and more receptive, deepening prayer, as Teresa describes it, becomes simpler. There are less words and more silence, less effort and more resting, less dispersion in attention and more simple attentiveness, more depths of presence and awareness. As Teresa will make clear in her description of the spiritual journey in *The Interior Castle*, a greater simplicity in life is the essential context for this inner simplification, but the simplifying of prayer yields a greater spirit of letting go in daily living as well. In *The Life*, as she describes the effects of a vision, she describes a manifestation of this simplifying of prayer:

> I think that just as in heaven you understand without speaking (which I certainly never knew until the Lord in His goodness desired that I should see and showed Himself to me in a rapture), so it is in this vision. For God and the soul

> understand each other only through the desire His Majesty has that it understand Him, without the use of any other means devised to manifest the love these two friends have for each other. It's like the experience of two persons here on earth who love each other deeply and understand each other well; even without signs, just by a glance, it seems, they understand each other. This must be similar to what happens in the vision; without our knowing how, these two lovers gaze directly at each other, as the Bridegroom says to the Bride in the *Song of Songs*—I think I heard that it is there. (L 27.10)

Growth in prayer, for Teresa, means a movement from many words, concepts, and images to a prayer of a simple, loving gaze.

Deeper Immersion in Christ: Prayer is an intimate sharing with Christ the friend who we know loves us. For Teresa, prayer is always an encounter with Christ, even in advanced stages when one is not consciously thinking about Christ during the time of prayer. Beginning with this foundational understanding of prayer, progress in prayer necessarily involves growth in relationship with Christ and the deepening of our intimate sharing with him. As we saw in the text just quoted above, Teresa teaches that maturing through "stages" of prayer is, more fundamentally, growth in friendship.

In the advanced prayer that Teresa describes especially in the final three of the seven dwelling places of *The Interior Castle*, the person of mature and gifted prayer enters into deeper and more frequent union with Christ. The relationship and communion with Christ in prayer becomes a deeper immersion in Christ. In a striking reversal of the primary image of moving through the interior rooms of the soul to encounter Christ within, Teresa observes that we can also think of ourselves as immersed in the palace that is God's own life (IC 6.10.3).

There Is More Than One Path

Although Teresa teaches about general patterns of progress in prayer and lays out stages of prayer, she does not believe that she is teaching a one-size-fits-all roadmap. It is true that later commentators often seemed to interpret her to be saying that any real persons of prayer must move from one defined step to another, experiencing each stage in exactly the way that Teresa describes it. But this was not Teresa's intent or message. She writes to help especially those people who are seeking and experiencing advanced forms of prayer—people who often lacked the resources to guide them and help them to avoid pitfalls. She offers to her reader a general pattern of development, based on her own experience, her many conversations with people of prayer, her consultations with learned and holy people, and her knowledge of the spiritual wisdom of the tradition.

Teresa's writings offer many examples of her belief in many authentic paths and ways of prayer. In *The Life*, she writes: "For just as there are many mansions in heaven, there are many paths" (L 13.13). A chapter on prayer in *The Book of Her Foundations* is titled "Gives some counsels on matters concerning prayer." (Teresa seems unable to resist talking about prayer even in a book explicitly devoted to the narrative of her work as a founder of religious communities!) She opens the chapter with these words: "It is not my intention or thought that what I say here be taken for certain and as an infallible rule, for that would be foolish in things so difficult. Since there are many paths along this way of the spirit, it could be that I will manage to say certain useful things about some of them. If those who do not walk along the path of which I'm speaking do not understand what I am saying, it will be because they are walking by another" (F 5.1). *The Interior Castle* describes the spiritual journey as a progressive journey through a series of dwelling places, and subsequent authors repeated that teaching as if Teresa intended to suggest a definitive road map. But she writes early in the text:

> *You mustn't think of these dwelling places in such a way that each one would follow in file after the other*; but turn your eyes toward the center, which is the room or royal chamber where the King stays, and think of how a palmetto has many leaves surrounding and covering the tasty part that can be eaten. *So here, surrounding this center room are many other rooms; and the same holds true for those above.* The things of the soul must always be considered as plentiful, spacious, and large; to do so is not an exaggeration. The soul is capable of much more than we can imagine, and the sun that is in this royal chamber shines in all parts. It is very important for any soul that practices prayer, whether little or much, not to hold itself back and stay in one corner. *Let it walk through these dwelling places which are up above, down below, and to the sides,* since God has given it such great dignity. (IC 1.2.8, emphases added)

In the sixth dwelling places, Teresa writes firmly that people of prayer come to find that they can no longer engage in active meditation, but she tempers her certainty: "I hold that one who has advanced further along cannot practice this discursive reflection. It could be that one can, for God leads souls by many paths" (IC 6.7.12).

"Grades" or "Stages" of Prayer

Each of Teresa's three major works offers a view of the general progression of prayer. In *The Life*, she devotes several chapters (L 11–22) to an important little treatise on prayer. She suggests that there are four degrees or stages in the ongoing growth and development of prayer.[2] To understand this process of growth, she offers an image that she has found helpful: the four degrees of prayer are like four different ways of watering a garden:

> It seems to me the garden can be watered in four ways. You may draw water from a well (which is for us a lot of work). Or you may get it by means of a water wheel and aqueducts in such a way that it is obtained by turning the crank of the water wheel. (I have drawn it this way sometimes—the method involves less work than the other, and you get more water). Or it may flow from a river or a stream. (The garden is watered much better by this means because the ground is more fully soaked, and there is no need to water so frequently—and much less work for the gardener). Or the water may be provided by a great deal of rain. (For the Lord waters the garden without any work on our part—and this way is incomparably better than all the others mentioned). (L 11.7)

Water is a frequent image in the writings of Teresa of Jesus, and the manners of obtaining water—from the more rigorous to the most passive—are a natural way for her to explain the growth of prayer to herself and her contemporary readers.

Teresa then proceeds in the next several chapters to unfold her teaching about each degree of prayer. At first, this little treatise appears to be a digression in the narrative telling of her own

2. In the discussion that follows, we will be using the terms "stages," "degrees," and "grades" interchangeably. In the Spanish original, Teresa refers to *grados* (see, for example, the titles of L 16, L 18, and ST 59). Kavanaugh translates *grados* as "degrees," but it is easy to see why other authors would translate *grados* as "grades." But Teresa also refers to *estados* which Kavanaugh sometimes translates as "stages" (e.g., titles of L 12 and IC 3.1) and, in other places, as "states" (e.g., L 13.2; 19.13, 15). The Spanish title of L 18 refers to both *grado* and *estado* which Kavanaugh translates as "degree" and "stage." In reference to progress in prayer, it is evident that Teresa is often using *grado* and *estado* synonymously.

progress in prayer. In fact, it helps to set the stage for the forms of advanced prayer that she will describe when she picks up the narrative in chapter twenty-three. The emphasis here, then, is on the more advanced degrees of prayer. Only the first way of watering the garden—through the hard labor of manually drawing water from a well and carrying it to the garden—describes active prayer (that is, our efforts to practice and grow in prayer). The remaining three ways of watering the garden concern degrees of contemplative, gifted prayer—in which God's action begins more and more to predominate in prayer while the person becomes more receptive and less active. Only the first manner, then, is immediately helpful to the beginner in prayer—and, in fact, to those who are still practicing any form of active prayer.

In her *Spiritual Testimony* 59, Teresa offers a rather summary description of the degrees of infused prayer, beginning with interior (infused) recollection. Since in this text Teresa is intentionally focused on growth in true contemplative, divinely gifted prayer, she does not offer any description of earlier forms of active prayer.

The entire structure of *The Interior Castle* involves movement. The central image invites the reader to view the Christian life as a movement inward through deeper dwelling places and rooms in order to enter into union with Christ who dwells in the inmost chamber. Degrees of prayer are not the singular focus of her description of the movement, which also involves deeper freedom from superficialities and attachments, a greater discovery of our interior depths, and thus growth in self-knowledge, a deeper transformation of the person, a greater enlightenment from the light that radiates out from the center of the soul, and deepening communion and union with Christ. Nonetheless, through the image of movement through the rooms, Teresa is offering a description of growth in prayer. In the *first* dwelling places are the basic beginnings of prayer, such as the saying of vocal prayer. One is talking with and especially to Christ the friend. In the *second* dwelling places, we find the beginning of a practice of meditation (we will describe her definition of meditation below). The person begins to think and reflect prayerfully about Christ. In the *third* dwelling places, meditation becomes sustained and steady. The *fourth* dwelling places describe the transition from acquired to infused prayer. Meditation becomes simpler, the person begins some active form of wordless prayer by which the person seeks simply to rest in the presence of God, and God begins to introduce the gift of contemplation, which alternates for a time with the active practices of prayer. The person's intimate sharing with Christ becomes largely wordless—a simple presence and gazing—first by our action and later by God's action drawing one into interior quiet. In the *fifth* dwelling places, the person begins to experience true union with God, though only in a passing sort of way. In the *sixth* dwelling places, more regular, longer, and deeper times of union can result in extraordinary experiences as the person becomes adjusted or accommodated to union with God. Teresa describes here the spiritual betrothal: the image of friendship passes to the image of marital unity. And in *seventh* dwelling places, the person enters into full or transforming union, which Teresa calls the spiritual marriage.

All of Teresa's major works offer some teaching on progression in prayer, but it is *The Way of Perfection*—intended as a primer or textbook on prayer—that offers the most focused presentation of the stages of growth from its beginnings. It is for this reason that we will examine Teresa's description of the forms that advancing prayer can take: vocal prayer, mental prayer, meditation, and acquired recollection—followed by truly contemplative experiences of prayer: infused recollection, the further experiences of true contemplation, and deepening experiences of union with God.

Vocal Prayer

Vocal prayer is simply the saying or recitation of prayer.[3] This can include the saying of established prayers such as the Our Father and Hail Mary, reading from a book of compiled prayers, recitation of the psalms, or simply spontaneous personal prayers of petition, thanksgiving, or repentance. In order to be prayer, vocal prayer must be done with attention: "A prayer in which a person is not aware of whom he is speaking to, what he is asking, who it is who is asking and of whom, I do not call prayer however much the lips move" (IC 1.1.7). She offers a similar challenge in another work: "Here you see, friends, what it means to pray vocally with perfection. It means that you be aware of and understand whom you are asking, who it is that is asking, and what you are asking for" (W 42.4).

Although in Teresa's schema, vocal prayer is usually a beginning form of prayer, she does not disparage or belittle it. In the context of a well-lived Christian life, people can attain holiness even if they never really pass beyond vocal prayer: "I know an elderly person who lives a good life, is penitential and an excellent servant of God, who has spent many hours for many years in vocal prayer, but in mental prayer she's helpless;[4] the most she can do is go slowly in reciting the vocal prayers. There are a number of other persons of this kind. If

3. For an overview of Teresa's teaching on vocal and mental prayer, see María José Pérez, "La oración vocal y mental: La religiosidad en la escuela de Teresa de Jesús," in Francisco Javier Sancho Fermín, ed., *Meditación y contemplación: Caminos hacia la paz (Budismo Theravada y mística teresiana)* (Burgos, Spain: CITeS/Grupo Editorial Fonte [Monte Carmelo], 2019), 235–54.

4. In this context, *mental prayer* probably refers to some form of discursive meditation.

humility is present, I don't believe they will be any the worse off in the end but will be very much the equals of those who receive many delights" (W 17.3).

Although the gift of contemplation is only usually given by God to those whose prayer is advanced beyond vocal prayer, Teresa notes that such prayer, said sincerely and faithfully, can be the foundation for receiving contemplation:

> It may seem to anyone who doesn't know about the matter that vocal prayer doesn't go with contemplation; but I know that it does. Pardon me, but I want to say this: I know there are many persons who while praying vocally, as has already been mentioned, are raised by God to sublime contemplation [without their striving for anything or understanding how. It's because of this that I insist so much, daughters, upon your reciting vocal prayer well.] I know a person who was never able to pray any way but vocally, and though she was tied to this form of prayer she experienced everything else. And if she didn't recite vocal prayer her mind wandered so much that she couldn't bear it. Would that our mental prayer were as good! She spent several hours reciting a certain number of Our Fathers, in memory of the times our Lord shed His blood, as well as a few other vocal prayers. Once she came to me very afflicted because she didn't know how to practice mental prayer nor could she contemplate; she could only pray vocally. I asked her how she was praying, and I saw that though she was tied to the Our Father she experienced pure contemplation and that the Lord was raising her up and joining her with Himself in union. And from her deeds it seemed truly that she was receiving such great favors, for she was living a very good life. So I praised the Lord and envied her for her vocal prayer. (W 30.7; see also W 17.3)

Vocal prayer might seem elementary to those experienced and practiced in prayer, but, said with attention, fidelity, and devotion, it can be the fruitful ground for receiving the divine gift of contemplation.

Teresa's teaching on prayer in the second half of *The Way of Perfection* is structured by a kind of commentary on the Our Father. She marvels that we can draw such wisdom from such a simple vocal prayer:

> We ought to give great praise to the Lord for the sublime perfection of this evangelical prayer. Each of us, daughters, can apply the prayer to her own needs since it was composed by such a good Master. I marvel to see that in so few words everything about contemplation and perfection is included; it seems we need to study no other book than this one. Up to now the Lord has taught us the whole way of prayer and of high contemplation, from the beginning stages to mental prayer, to the prayer of quiet, and to that of union; so much so that, if I knew how to explain the matter, a large book on prayer could be written based on this genuine foundation. (W 37.1)

But, more than simply teaching us about prayer, the attentive recital of the Our Father can be the doorway to receive contemplation:

> To keep you from thinking that little is gained through a perfect recitation of vocal prayer, I tell you that it is very possible that while you are reciting the Our Father or some other vocal prayer, the Lord may raise you to perfect contemplation. By these means His Majesty shows that He listens to the one who speaks to Him. And it is His grandeur that speaks to the soul, suspending one's intellect, binding one's imagination,

> and, as they say, taking the words from one's mouth; for even though the soul may want to do so, it cannot speak unless with great difficulty. (W 25.1)

We do our part in prayer. Meanwhile, we can be sure that God is attentive and ready to advance our prayer according to the divine wisdom and mercy.

Teresa warns that one should not be so focused on getting through one's vocal prayer—reciting all of the prayers that one had intended—that one misses the subtle introduction of the gift of contemplation:

> But there are persons—and I have been one of them—who make themselves deaf when the Lord, taking pity on them, gives them holy inspirations and light concerning the nature of things, and, in sum, gives this kingdom and places them in this prayer of quiet. For they are so fond of speaking and reciting many vocal prayers very quickly, like one who wants to get a job done, since they oblige themselves to recite these every day, that even though, as I say, the Lord places His kingdom in their hands, they do not receive it. But with their vocal prayers they think they are doing better, and they distract themselves from the prayer of quiet. Do not do this, sisters, but be on your guard when the Lord grants you this favor. Consider that you are losing a great treasure and that you do much more by saying one word of the Our Father from time to time than by rushing through the entire prayer many times. (W 31.12–13)

Vocal prayer can sometimes be the doorway to contemplation, but only if we do not allow our focus on the words and the prayers to prevent us from discerning the gentle and often subtle invitation to contemplation.

Mental Prayer

Teresa uses the term *mental prayer* rather broadly. Most generally, it simply refers to prayer with intention and attention, though it can also be used to mean any form of prayer—such as meditation—that principally involves our graced efforts. Vocal prayer must, at the same time, be mental prayer. In a chapter titled "How vocal prayer must be recited with perfection, and mental prayer joined with it," she writes: "You are right in saying that this vocal prayer is now in fact mental prayer. But I tell you that surely I don't know how mental prayer can be separated from vocal prayer if the vocal prayer is to be recited well with an understanding of whom we are speaking to. It is even an obligation that we strive to pray with attention" (W 24.6). She teaches elsewhere: "Realize, daughters, that the nature of mental prayer isn't determined by whether or not the mouth is closed. If while speaking I thoroughly understand and know that I am speaking with God and I have greater awareness of this than I do of the words I'm saying, mental and vocal prayer are joined. If, however, others tell you that you are speaking with God while you are reciting the Our Father and at the same time in fact thinking of the world, then I have nothing to say" (W 22.1).

We must be truly present to God in any form of prayer. Even in ordinary daily interactions with other people, we know that you can be speaking with someone while your mind is "a thousand miles away" or your eye is wandering to some activity or person unrelated to the person with whom you are speaking. Prayer is an intimate sharing with the divine friend, and we must remember with whom we are sharing: "Here you see, friends, what it means to pray vocally with perfection. It means that you be aware of and understand whom you are asking, who it is that is asking, and what you are asking for" (W 42.4). Evoking the common experience of dialogue with another person, she writes: "But if you are to be speaking, as is right, with so great a Lord, it is good that you consider whom you are speaking with as well as who you are, at least if you want to be polite" (W 22.1).

Meditation

The development of a solid habit of prayer generally involves the use of some form of what is traditionally called "discursive meditation"—the word *discursive* in this context meaning moving from point to point, topic to topic. As Teresa notes: "This is the method of prayer with which all must begin, continue, and finish; and it is a very excellent and safe path until the Lord leads one to other supernatural things" (L 13.12). In meditation, one uses the imagination, for example, to picture a biblical scene and perhaps one's own involvement in it. Or someone might use their intellect to reflect prayerfully over a scriptural text, its meaning, and the challenge or solace that it offers to one's life at the moment. Or it might involve a combination of both. Understanding prayer as a sharing with a friend, it is a means by which we come to know Christ by quietly pondering his life and saving deeds as well as its meaning to us personally. In the monastic tradition of *lectio divina* (classically formulated in the twelfth century by the Carthusian Guigo II), the person moves from the attentive reading of the text (*lectio*) to reflection or meditation (*meditatio*) on it, to a prayerful response (*oratio*), and finally to quietly allowing God to speak a yet deeper word in silence (*contemplatio*). St. John of the Cross refers to this tradition in his *Sayings of Light and Love* (158): "Seek in reading and you will find in meditation; knock in prayer and it will be opened to you in contemplation."

Teresa, following a long spiritual tradition, recommends the practice of meditation in order to grow in a habit of prayer and as a foundation for receiving the gift of contemplation: "This kind of reflection is an admirable and very meritorious prayer" (IC 4.1.6). She defines it in the following way:

> By meditation I mean much discursive reflection with the intellect in the following way: we begin to think about the favor God granted us in giving us His only Son, and we do not stop there, but go on to the mysteries of His whole glorious life; or we begin to think about the prayer in the garden, but the intellect doesn't stop until He is on the cross; or we take a phase of the Passion like, let us say, the arrest, and we proceed with this mystery considering in detail the things there are to think of and feel about the betrayal of Judas, the flight of the apostles, and all the rest; this kind of reflection is an admirable and very meritorious prayer. (IC 6.7.10)

She speaks of it in a general way in all three of her major works (L 11–13; W 20–26; IC 1–3). She does not, however, devote a great deal of attention to it. She notes that there are many books available to teach and guide the practice of meditation, and her focus is on contemplative prayer, about which little was available for her nuns to read. She concludes:

> There are so many good books written by able persons for those who have methodical minds and for souls that are experienced and can concentrate within themselves that it would be a mistake if you paid attention to what I say about prayer. As I say, there are books in which the mysteries of

> the Lord's life and Passion are divided according to the days of the week, and there are meditations about judgment, hell, our nothingness, and the many things we owe God together with excellent doctrine and method concerning the beginning and end of prayer. There is nothing for me to say to anyone who can form the habit of following this method of prayer, or who has already formed it, for by means of so good a path the Lord will draw him to the haven of light. And through such a good beginning the end will be reached. All who are able to walk along this path will have rest and security, for when the intellect is bound one proceeds peacefully. (W 19.1)

Although Teresa herself found that she lacked the ability to use her intellect and imagination fruitfully in prayer in discursive meditation, she did not doubt its value for others.

Subjects or Themes for Meditation

Books of meditation at the time of Teresa usually provided, beyond an explanation of a technique for its practice, specific points for meditation, whether a biblical scene or presentation of an important Christian mystery of faith, often quite detailed and directive. Teresa herself does not offer much specific direction. Following traditional practice and in keeping with her own focus on Christ and deepening friendship with him, she recommends especially meditating on the life and humanity of Christ: "Let us begin to think about an episode of the Passion, let's say of when our Lord was bound to the pillar. The intellect goes in search of reasons for better understanding the great sorrows and pain His Majesty suffered in that solitude and many other things that the intellect if it works hard, can herein deduce" (L 13.12).

Teresa herself reports that she found particular help from pondering the scene of Jesus in the Garden of Gethsemane:

> The scene of His prayer in the garden, especially, was a comfort to me; I strove to be His companion there. If I could, I thought of the sweat and agony He had undergone in that place. I desired to wipe away the sweat He so painfully experienced, but I recall that I never dared to actually do it, since my sins appeared to me so serious. I remained with Him as long as my thoughts allowed me to, for there were many distractions that tormented me. Most nights, for many years before going to bed when I commended myself to God in preparation for sleep, I always pondered for a little while this episode of the prayer in the garden. (L 9.4)

The practice of such meditation can increase devotion and a sense of personal relationship with Christ:

> For in thinking about and carefully examining what the Lord suffered for us, we are moved to compassion; and this sorrow and the resulting tears bring delight. In thinking about the glory we hope for, the love the Lord bore us, and His resurrection, we are moved to a joy that is neither entirely spiritual nor entirely of the senses. But the joy is virtuous and the sorrow very meritorious. Virtue and merit are found in all the things that cause the devotion acquired partly by the intellect, even though this devotion could not be merited or obtained if God did not give it. (L 12.1)

Such prayer fosters a growth in friendship—not simply in the time of prayer but in an abiding sense of Christ's presence: "The soul can place itself in the presence of Christ and grow accustomed to being inflamed with love for His sacred humanity. It can keep Him ever present and speak with Him, asking for its needs and complaining of its labors, being glad with Him in its enjoyments and not forgetting Him because of them, trying to speak to Him, not through written prayers but with words that conform to its desires and needs" (L 12.2).

As important as it is to meditate on the life and mysteries of Christ, there are many other possible aspects of our faith on which we might profitably and prayerfully reflect:

> There are many souls that benefit more by other meditations than those on the sacred Passion. For just as there are many mansions in heaven, there are many paths. Some persons find it helpful to think about hell, others about death; some if they have tender hearts experience much fatigue if they always think about the Passion, and they are refreshed and helped by considering the power and grandeur of God in creatures—and the love He bore us, and its manifestation in all things. This is an admirable method of procedure as long as one often reflects on the Passion and life of Christ from which has come and continues to come every good. (L 13.12–13)

Meditation helps to keep us in right relationship with Christ and to find new reason to remain faithful to the Christian path: "For anyone, who reflects discursively on what the world is, and what one owes God, and how much God suffered, and on how little one serves Him, and what God gives to anyone who loves Him, deduces doctrine to defend oneself from thoughts, occasions, and dangers" (L 4.8).

Meditation and Self-knowledge

For Teresa, attaining a deeper knowledge of ourselves is also an important focus of meditation. She tells us in the first two chapters of the first dwelling places of *The Interior Castle* that we must hold together two fundamental truths: that we are created in the image of God and thus fundamentally beautiful and precious to God, and that we are sinners in constant need of divine mercy. We must ponder prayerfully this reality: what we are created to be and become as well as how far we are from where God calls us to be. We must come to a deeper recognition of our sin and its roots, and we must recognize with wonder and gratitude that we are called into the intimacy of friendship with the God who first loves us.

Self-knowledge, for Teresa, is critical at every step on the Christian journey. In this life, we will never arrive at a point that we can pass beyond its cultivation:

> This path of self knowledge must never be abandoned, nor is there on this journey a soul so much a giant that it has no need to return often to the stage of an infant and a suckling. And this should never be forgotten. Perhaps I shall speak of it more often because it is very important. There is no stage of prayer so sublime that it isn't necessary to return often to the beginning. Along this path of prayer, self knowledge and the thought of one's sins is the bread with which all palates must be fed no matter how delicate they may be; they cannot be sustained without this bread. (L 13.15)

Created in the image of God, we can only come to a true knowledge of our self by knowing God as revealed in Christ, and, meditating on God in Christ, we see ourselves as we truly are:

> Knowing ourselves is something so important that I wouldn't want any relaxation ever in this regard, however high you may have climbed into the heavens. While we are on this earth nothing is more important to us than humility. So I

> repeat that it is good, indeed very good, to try to enter first into the room where self-knowledge is dealt with rather than fly off to other rooms. This is the right road, and if we can journey along a safe and level path, why should we want wings to fly? Rather, let's strive to make more progress in self-knowledge. In my opinion we shall never completely know ourselves if we don't strive to know God. By gazing at His grandeur, we get in touch with our own lowliness; by looking at His purity, we shall see our own filth; by pondering His humility, we shall see how far we are from being humble. (IC 1.2.9)

Regular meditation on the life and teaching of Christ, on the God revealed by Christ and taught by the church, and on the example of the saints can shine a mirror on our own manner of living, yielding a greater, critical knowledge of ourselves.

Meditation: Importance of the Intellect

Teresa places great value on the use of the intellect in the spiritual life. She herself, in addition to her own avid personal study of books on prayer, consulted theologians widely and frequently. She wanted her nuns to be able to think and read so that their prayer would be grounded in Christian truth and not simply in subjective feeling. The regular practice of discursive meditation helps to build an important foundation for the further development of prayer, insuring that wordless and imageless prayer remains truly Christian prayer. The possession of a sound intellect was to be a criterion for admission to her communities:

> When a nun with good intelligence begins to grow attached to good, she takes hold of it with fortitude because she sees that

> doing so is most appropriate. And if her intelligence doesn't help her to attain a high degree of spirituality, it will be useful for giving good counsel and for many other services without being a bother to anyone. If this good intelligence is lacking, I don't know how she can be of any use to the community, and she could be the cause of much harm. This lack of intelligence is not so quickly noticed. For many speak well but understand poorly; others speak little and without polish but they have the intelligence for a great deal of good. In fact, there is a holy simplicity that knows little about the affairs and style of the world but a lot about dealing with God. Hence much information is necessary before accepting new members and a long probation before admitting them to profession. (W 14.2)

Here, Teresa is not talking about formal learning—which she valued highly—but rather about the importance of the ability to engage in critical thinking, whether for one's own spiritual life or for the life of a community.

Teresa seeks to teach and promote a life of prayer, including the most profound contemplation, that is grounded in and guided by the use of the intellect, focused on the model and teaching of Christ, and in line with the church's faith. This requires the use of the intellect to serve as a check on our experience—as Teresa herself did by her reading and by her consultation with theologians. The description of her own struggles to understand and feel secure in her own experiences of prayer makes this abundantly clear. Christ is the focus of her prayer, and he is the model and teacher of the virtues that are the foundation of growth in prayer and its authentic fruit.[5]

---

5. Secudino Castro, *Ser cristiano según Santa Teresa: teología y espiritualidad*, 2nd ed. (Madrid: Editorial de Espiritualidad, 1985), 73–74.

But Meditation Is More Than Thinking

Discursive meditation, although it is an exercise of intellect and imagination, is not meant to be a purely intellectual exercise—not just about thinking, Teresa cautions. Even meditation, as a form of prayer, is meant to be a kind of intimate sharing with Christ. It requires our conscious presence to Christ and our attention to the divine presence to us. As we grow in the practice of meditation, we must also take time to let the intellect rest and simply be present to Christ even in the midst of our meditation:

> But returning to those who practice discursive reflection, I say they should not pass the whole time thinking. For, although discursive reflection is very meritorious, they don't seem to realize that since their prayer is delightful there should ever be a Sunday or a time in which one is not working; but they think such time is lost. I consider this loss a great gain. But, as I have said, they should put themselves in the presence of Christ and, without tiring the intellect, speak with and delight in Him and not wear themselves out in composing syllogisms; rather, they should show Him their needs and the reason why He doesn't have to allow us to be in His presence. The discursive reflection they can do at one time, and the other acts at another. (L 13.11)

Even in thinking about Christ and the ways of God, the person must be attentive to the deeper reality of the personal presence of Christ.

In the next chapter, we will address Teresa's firm belief that, whatever our form of prayer, we must attend to the presence of Christ the friend. Meditation, practiced with that admonition in mind, opens out to a deeper prayer in which we are simply resting in the presence of Christ.

> Now returning to what I was saying about Christ bound at the pillar; it is good to reflect awhile and think about the pains He suffered there, and why, and who he is, and the love with which He suffered them. But one should not always weary oneself in seeking these reflections but just remain there in His presence with the intellect quiet. And if we are able we should occupy ourselves in looking at Christ who is looking at us, and we should speak, and petition, and humble ourselves, and delight in the Lord's presence, and remember that we are unworthy of being there. When we can do this, even though it may be at the beginning of prayer, we will derive great benefit; and this manner of prayer has many advantages—at least my soul derived them. (L 13.22)

Meditation is not an end in itself. It is a tool to a deeper communion. Thinking about a friend or trying to understand a friend is not a substitute for an intimate sharing between friends.

During the practice of meditation, if one becomes conscious of a feeling of devotion or love for Christ, the person should leave aside the thinking and imagining and savor the experience and attend to the divine presence. In a period of prayer, moments of active meditating can alternate with moments of savoring a felt devotion and a quiet resting in Christ. Meditation has attained its purpose if it is laid aside, at least for a time, because one has entered into a deeper, quieter experience of prayer.

> For the most part, the souls in the previous dwelling places [of the interior castle] are the ones who have these devout feelings, for these souls work almost continually with the intellect, engaging in discursive thought and meditation. And they do well because nothing further has been given them; although they would be right if they engaged for a

> while in making acts of love, praising God, rejoicing in His goodness, that He is who He is, and in desiring His honor and glory. These acts should be made insofar as possible, for they are great awakeners of the will. Such souls would be well advised when the Lord gives them these acts not to abandon them for the sake of finishing the usual meditation. (IC 4.1.6)

It is the whole person who prays. As useful as the intellect can be, prayer must go deeper and be broader than reflection.

In the end, for Teresa, prayer is more about loving than about thinking. She adhered to the belief that ultimately God could not be grasped by the ordinary function of the intellect and imagination, no matter how learned or deep. God can finally only be grasped by love. Prayer, even with an important place for the intellect and imagination, is primarily about sharing with a friend "who we know loves us." It is fundamentally an exercise in love—a loving, personal engagement with Christ: "For I have run into some for whom it seems the whole business lies in thinking. If they can keep their minds much occupied in God, even though great effort is exerted, they at once think they are spiritual. . . . Hence, the soul's progress does not lie in thinking much but in loving much" (F 5.2). Elsewhere, she teaches: "I only wish to inform you that in order to profit by this path and ascend to the dwelling places we desire, the important thing is not to think much but to love much; and so do that which best stirs you to love" (IC 4.1.7). Authentic prayer, in all of its forms, should set us to the service of love: "Well, let us speak now of those who are beginning to be servants of love. This doesn't seem to me to mean anything else than to follow resolutely by means of this path of prayer Him who has loved us so much" (L 11.1).

Not Everyone Can Meditate

Although Teresa recognizes the importance of and recommends the practice of meditation, she found that she herself was unable to do so profitably. Her mind could not focus for long periods of time, moving from point to point in prayer. While she found images helpful to her prayer and in that way used her imagination, she found that she could not engage in a focused exercise of imagining biblical scenes. She found that she was not alone in her inability to pray in that otherwise laudable form of prayer. Some people can meditate, while others simply cannot. As useful as meditation can be for many people, each person of prayer must find what works for them. She says of herself and others who cannot meditate: "I spent fourteen years never being able to practice meditation without reading. There will be many persons of this sort, and others who will be unable to meditate even with the reading but able only to pray vocally, and in this vocal prayer they will spend most of their time. There are minds so active they cannot dwell on one thing but are always restless, and to such an extreme that if they want to pause to think of God, a thousand absurdities, scruples, and doubts come to mind" (W 17.3; see also L 9.4–6; 13.11). She struggled through this inability to meditate until she learned the prayer of recollection (which we will examine in a later chapter).

For those who find that they are able to meditate, its practice can open the door to the beginning of contemplative prayer:

> Yet this favor of the Lord remains with them in such a way that afterward they cannot engage as before in discursive thought about the mysteries of the Passion and life of Christ. I don't know the reason, but this inability is very common, for the intellect becomes less capable of meditation. I believe the reason must be that since in meditation the whole effort

> consists in seeking God and that once God is found the soul becomes used to seeking Him again through the work of the will, the soul doesn't want to tire itself by working with the intellect. Likewise, it seems to me that since this generous faculty, which is the will, is already enkindled, it wants to avoid, if it can, using the other faculty; and it doesn't go wrong. But to avoid this will be impossible, especially before the soul reaches these last two dwelling places; and the soul will lose time, for the will often needs the help of the intellect so as to be enkindled. (IC 6.7.7)

The four traditional steps of *lectio divina* (reading, meditation, prayer, and contemplation) assume this type of possible progression from meditation to contemplation.

The Prayer of Recollection: from Acquired to Infused

The prayer of recollection is a movement away from words and images in prayer into a simple attentiveness to the presence of God. Again, following the metaphor of friendship, the intimate sharing of prayer moves to a communication that requires very few words. For Teresa and those like her who find that they cannot engage in discursive meditation, recollection is an important step in the progress of prayer. But even for those who can and do practice meditation, Teresa argues that it is important for them, too, to leave aside the use of the intellect and imagination and spend time in simple presence with Christ. Prayer moves from quiet reflection into a simple gaze, a loving attention to Christ. Even in the midst of meditation, people of prayer may find that they are drawn beyond into a quiet attentiveness:

> The intellect represents them [mysteries of Christ] in such a way, and they are so stamped on the memory, that the mere sight of the Lord fallen to the ground in the garden with that frightful sweat is enough to last the intellect not only an hour but many days, while *it looks with a simple gaze at who He is* and how ungrateful we have been for so much suffering. Soon the will responds even though it may not do so with tender feelings, with the desire to serve somehow for such a great favor and to suffer something for One who suffered so much, and with other similar desires relating to what the memory and intellect are dwelling upon. *I believe that for this reason a person cannot go on to further discursive reflection on the Passion, and this inability makes him think that he cannot think about it.* (IC 6.7.11, emphasis added)

Meditation should be allowed to unfold into a prayer of simple gazing at the one who we know loves us.

Teresa herself found that, after receiving Communion at the Eucharist, her prayer of thanksgiving moved frequently into this simple beholding. Speaking of herself in the third person, she writes:

> But I know that for many years, when she [i.e., Teresa] received Communion, this person, though she was not very perfect, strove to strengthen her faith so that in receiving her Lord it was as if, with her bodily eyes, she saw Him enter her house. Since she believed that this Lord truly entered her poor home, she freed herself from all exterior things when it was possible and entered to be with Him. She strove to recollect the senses so that all of them would take notice of so great a good, I mean that they would not impede the soul from recognizing it. (W 34.7)

For Teresa, her time of post-Communion meditation could be the doorway to a deeper spiritual communion with her divine friend.

The prayer of recollection, as taught by Teresa of Jesus, begins primarily as our own human action. We make the effort to draw in our attention—"re-collect" our senses, as she will say. But, in time, the person finds that it becomes God who quietly draws our attention, our consciousness, into quiet. This "infused" recollection (as distinct from its earlier form, "acquired" recollection) is the beginning of true contemplative prayer. In the fourth dwelling places of *The Interior Castle*, which address the transition from acquired to infused forms of prayer, Teresa says of this divinely given form of recollection: "Once the great King, who is in the center dwelling place of this castle, sees their good will, He desires in His wonderful mercy to bring them back to Him. Like a good shepherd, with a whistle so gentle that even they themselves almost fail to hear it, He makes them recognize His voice and stops them from going so far astray so that they will return to their dwelling place. And this shepherd's whistle has such power that they abandon the exterior things in which they were estranged from Him and enter the castle" (IC 4.3.2). Meditation has made the person familiar with God and the divine ways. It has helped to deepen one's friendship with God and self-knowledge. In this way, the person of prayer is better disposed to respond to the gentle and subtle invitation to silent communion.

Progress into Contemplation and Union

Teresa, following a traditional definition of terms, believed that true contemplation is always a gift of God. It cannot be acquired by our own efforts, no matter how diligent and sincere.

In acquired recollection, we can grow in an inner quiet and in a silent gazing at Christ. But the gift of true contemplation is God's gift and action. God can give it to whomever God wills and whenever God wills it, but generally it is a gift given after a long period of preparation. The person has grown in prayer, coming to know Christ intimately in prayer, meditation, and sacramental participation. One has conformed one's life to God's will through the uprooting of sin and growth in virtue. Once given, there is the possibility of yet deeper encounter, a more intimate sharing and communion, and ultimately true union with God, even in this life. This progression in the experience of infused prayer is described in a more focused way beginning with the fourth dwelling places of *The Interior Castle* and continuing into the seventh.

Before we examine these forms of infused prayer, we will, in the chapters that follow, look more broadly at growth in acquired forms of prayer, particularly what Teresa calls the prayer of recollection.

4

Prayer as Presence and Recollection

In the previous chapter, we examined the earlier stages of prayer as Teresa of Jesus described them. But wherever we find our prayer, she invites us to attend to the presence of Christ. Every true act of prayer is an exercise in being present, and the deepening of prayer involves being more deeply and silently attentive to the divine friend.

Prayer as Presence

Fundamentally, for Teresa of Jesus, true prayer means being present to Christ who is always fully present to us. We are always in his presence, but we are not always present to him in the sense of being attentive and aware—just as it is possible to be in the physical presence of a human friend and yet have one's attention focused elsewhere. It is not a matter of inviting Christ to be present, trying to produce his presence, or even having active thoughts or reflections on Christ; rather, Teresa is inviting us to make ourselves aware of—or really, let ourselves become awake to—what is always true: Christ our friend is with us, always looking at us with love.

Christ is the true friend, prayer is an intimate sharing with him, and this sharing is most basically being attentive to his constant presence and being present ourselves to him. In prayer, Teresa sought to draw near to Christ and to allow his presence and love to recollect, center, and integrate her.[1] Kieran Kavanaugh says of Teresa's prayer: "Her method is one of presence, of being fully present to God in our prayer, for he is fully present to us at all times. . . . Centering the attention within, being fully present to him, look at, gazing upon; these are the expressions that fit her method."[2] The same author concludes later in the same work: "The personal presence, intimacy between friends, is what Teresa emphasizes as she begins to teach us about recollection. Her method has more to do with relationship than technique."[3]

Describing her early efforts at a serious life and habit of prayer, Teresa tells us: "I tried as hard as I could to keep Jesus Christ, our God and our Lord, present within me, and that was my way of prayer" (L 4.7). Later, writing about how she had tried to live a life of deep prayer even while enjoying silly pastimes, she reports: "I was not able to shut myself within myself (which was my whole manner of procedure in prayer); instead, I shut within myself a thousand vanities" (L 7.17). She was being present to superficialities rather than to Christ.

"Representing" Christ

Teresa often wrote of developing an awareness of the presence of Christ as "representing" Christ: "This is the method of prayer I then used. . . . I strove to represent Christ within me, and

1. Maximiliano Herráiz Garcia, *La oración, historia de amistad*, 6th ed. (Madrid: Editorial de Espiritualidad, 2003), 37.

2. Teresa of Avila, *The Way of Perfection: Study Edition*, ed. Kieran Kavanaugh (Washington, D.C.: ICS Publications, 2000), 24.

3. Teresa of Avila, *The Way of Perfection: Study Edition*, 285.

it did me greater good—in my opinion—to represent Him in those scenes where I saw Him more alone. It seemed to me that being alone and afflicted, as a person in need, He had to accept me" (L 9.4). It may seem that she was speaking of imagining or meditating on Christ, but she is really speaking of "re-presenting" Christ—of making him present again in our consciousness and awareness. In an important passage in the *Life*, Teresa explains her own experience of "representing Christ," which did not involve the intellect or imagination but rather was like knowing someone present even though one is blind or in darkness:

> I had such little ability to represent things with my intellect that if I hadn't seen the things my imagination was not of use to me, as it is to other persons who can imagine things and thus recollect themselves. I could only think about Christ as He was as man, but never in such a way that I could picture Him within myself no matter how much I read about His beauty or how many images I saw of Him. I was like those who are blind or in darkness; they speak with a person and see that that person is with them because they know with certainty that the other is there (I mean they understand and believe this, but they do not see the other); such was the case with me when I thought of our Lord. (L 9.6)

Gospel scenes and physical images of Christ became access roads or entry ways in the awareness of Christ's constant presence, ways of "re-presenting" him or making ourselves aware of his presence again.[4] Kavanaugh concludes: "When she speaks of representing

4. Tomás Álvarez, *Prayer: Journeying to God with St. Teresa*, trans. Anne Harriss (Oxford, England: Teresian Press, 2019), 31.

Christ within her, she is referring to a kind of activity in which she would bring into her awareness the presence of Christ, the person to whom she was about to relate in friendship. A detailed picture in her imagination was unnecessary for her communion with the Lord."[5]

In Every Stage of Prayer

Teresa offers to beginners in prayer the traditional advice to meditate on the life and especially the passion of Christ, but she also encourages them to a deeper attentiveness. With such attention to his presence, they will find that their prayer will deepen:

> It is good to reflect awhile and think about the pains He suffered there, and why, and who he is, and the love with which He suffered them. But one should not always weary oneself in seeking these reflections but just remain there in His presence with the intellect quiet. And if we are able we should occupy ourselves in looking at Christ who is looking at us, and we should speak, and petition, and humble ourselves, and delight in the Lord's presence, and remember that we are unworthy of being there. When we can do this, even though it may be at the beginning of prayer, we will derive great benefit; and this manner of prayer has many advantages—at least my soul derived them. (L 13.22)

Prayer at its beginnings and in its maturing is aided by the effort to remain aware and attentive to the personal presence of Christ.

5. Kieran Kavanaugh, "How to Pray: From the Life and Teachings of Saint Teresa," in *Carmel and Contemplation: Transforming Human Consciousness*, Carmelite Studies 8, ed. Kevin Culligan and Regis Jordan (Washington, D.C.: ICS Publications, 2000), 121.

Recollection as an Awareness of Presence

Later in the present chapter, we will look at the prayer of recollection as a kind of (in contemporary terms) contemplative practice—a manner or method of growing in a wordless, imageless prayer. But before Teresa's recollection can be called a particular method of prayer at all, it must first and most basically be understood as a foundational attitude or stance in prayer of whatever kind—and really in the daily living of a person of serious prayer. It can be said that simply being present to Christ was her fundamental method of prayer.[6] For Teresa, Christ is an always-loving presence, inviting us into deeper friendship. What she describes as stages of prayer can be understood as levels of the deepening of our loving awareness of the divine presence—at first, by our own graced efforts but increasingly by the divine action of drawing us in. Recollecting oneself—gathering in one's attention and consciousness—is an essential stance in every form of prayer, even in vocal prayer, if it is to be authentic.

In the *Life*, as she describes the beginnings of prayer as the first way of watering the garden, Teresa insists on the importance of attending to the presence of Christ as a most fruitful path to grow in prayer:

> *The soul can place itself in the presence of Christ* and grow accustomed to being inflamed with love for His sacred humanity. *It can keep Him ever present* and speak with Him, asking for its needs and complaining of its labors, being glad with Him in its enjoyments and not forgetting Him because of them, trying to speak to Him, not through written prayers but with words that conform to its desires and needs. *This is*

6. Francisco Javier Sancho Fermín, *Orar con Santa Teresa de Jesús* (Bilbao, Spain: Editorial Desclée Brouwer, 2014), 38.

> *an excellent way of making progress, and in a very short time. I consider that soul advanced who strives to remain in this precious company* and to profit very much by it, and who truly comes to love this Lord to whom we owe so much. As a result, we shouldn't care at all about not having devotion—as I have said—but we ought to thank the Lord who allows us to be desirous of pleasing Him, even though our works may be weak. *This method of keeping Christ present with us is beneficial in all stages and is a very safe means of advancing in the first degree of prayer, of reaching in a short time the second degree, and of walking secure against the dangers the devil can set up in the last degrees. Keeping Christ present is what we of ourselves can do.* Whoever would desire to pass beyond this point and raise the spirit to an experience of spiritual consolations that are not given. (L 12.2–4, emphases added)

Christ is always present to us, and we must try to be present to him in our awareness, especially during times of prayer.

When Teresa speaks of the prayer of recollection in *The Way of Perfection*, she invites us to simply "behold" Christ. Depending on our own life experience at a particular moment, we might choose to picture him in a particular scene, but, in the prayer of recollection, the point is not to think about him, imagine him, or meditate on him, but simply to behold him:

> If you are experiencing trials or are sad, *behold Him* on the way to the garden: what great affliction He bore in His soul; for having become suffering itself, He tells us about it and complains of it. Or *behold Him* bound to the column, filled with pain, with all His flesh torn in pieces for the great love He bears you; so much suffering, persecuted by some. spit on by others, denied by His friends, abandoned by them, with no one to defend Him, frozen from the cold, left so alone that you can

> console each other. Or *behold Him* burdened with the cross, for they didn't even let Him take a breath. He will look at you with those eyes so beautiful and compassionate, filled with tears; He will forget His sorrows so as to console you in yours, merely because you yourselves go to Him to be consoled, and you turn your head to look at Him. (W 26.5, emphasis added)

Reflecting on this passage, Tomás Álvarez concludes: "The advice to 'look at Him' is the definitive centre of her whole exposition, her intention clearly being to contain the whole grasp of his presence in this intuitive act."[7]

Presence as a Contemplative Attitude in Life

Teresa's written works are focused on teaching particularly about prayer. As such, her encouragement of maintaining a stance or attitude of presence toward the Other is foundational for growth in prayer. But her teaching also encourages a basic stance in life that we might call a spirit of recollection, a contemplative attitude, or even heartfulness (to emphasize that it is not primarily an intellectual consciousness).[8] Even in the midst of activity, we should try to be attentive to God's inner presence: "We must, then, disengage ourselves from everything so as to approach God interiorly and even in the midst of occupations withdraw within ourselves. Although it may be for only a moment that I remember I have that Company within myself, doing so is very beneficial" (W 29.5). Keith Egan concludes: "Teresa's prayer

---

7. Álvarez, *Prayer*, 88.

8. Luis Jorge González, *Mindfulness y Santa Teresa: estar con Quien sabemos nos ama* (Mexico City: Ediciones Duruelo, 2017); Peter Tyler, "Oración Mental, Mindfulness, and Mental Prayer: The Training of the Heart in the Iberian School of Abbot García de Cisneros of Montserrat and St. Teresa of Avila," *Buddhist-Christian Studies* 38 (2008): 253–66.

of recollection is a way of life, of living with a consciousness of Christ within, a way of walking in the presence of Christ."[9] This life stance is reflected in the well-known book by Teresa's seventeenth-century spiritual son, Brother Lawrence of the Resurrection, *The Practice of the Presence of God.*[10]

God Within

Central to Teresa's teaching on the prayer of recollection is the insight that God dwells within every human soul. This is a fundamental premise of *The Interior Castle,* in which God is sought in the inmost chamber of the soul where God always remains. Even sin and unbelief do not drive God away—though they cut us off from this center and source of life. These are some of the important truths with which Teresa opens *The Interior Castle.* The prayer of recollection, then, is a gathering in of our senses—our consciousness and awareness—away from the world outside of us in order to make ourselves attentive and present to the divine presence at the core of our being:

> Those who by such a method can enclose themselves within this little heaven of our soul, where the Maker of heaven and earth is present, and grow accustomed to refusing to be where the exterior senses in their distraction have gone or look in that direction should believe they are following an excellent path and that they will not fail to drink water from the fount; for they will journey far in a short time. Their situation is like that of a person who travels by ship; with a little wind he

9. Keith J. Egan, *Teresa, Teach Us to Pray: Study Guide* (CD lecture series) (Rockville, Md.: Know You Know Media, 2011), 26.

10. Brother Lawrence of the Resurrection [Nicolas Herman], *The Practice of the Presence of God,* ed. Conrad de Meester, trans. Salvatore Sciuba (Washington, D.C.: ICS Publications, 1994).

> reaches the end of his journey in a few days. But those who go by land take longer. (W 28.5)

The personal discovery that God dwells within provided Teresa with a focus for her own prayer that she urges others to discover for themselves.

Ignorance of this divine presence within each of us at every moment is a source of harm, a hindrance to growth in deep prayer and in intimate friendship with Christ: "All the harm comes from not truly understanding that He is near, but in imagining Him as far away. . . . This alone is what I want to explain: that in order to acquire the habit of easily recollecting our minds and understanding what we are saying, and with whom we are speaking, it is necessary that the exterior senses be recollected and that we give them something with which to be occupied. For indeed we have heaven within ourselves since the Lord of heaven is there" (W 29.5).

At first, the presence of God deep within her had come to her as a new insight,[11] and it filled her with wonder when she came to realize it:

> I understood well that I had a soul. But what this soul deserved and who dwelt within it I did not understand because I had covered my eyes with the vanities of the world. For, in my opinion, if I had understood as I do now that in this little palace of my soul dwelt so great a King, I would not have left Him alone so often. I would have remained with Him at times and striven more so as not to be so unclean. But what a marvelous thing, that He who would fill a thousand

11. Although the presence of God within the center of the soul was Teresa's predominant sense, she was also aware that we can also understand ourselves to be held within God. In one of her *Spiritual Testimonies*, she writes: "I also heard the words: 'Don't try to hold Me within yourself, but try to hold yourself within Me'" (ST 14).

> worlds and many more with His grandeur would enclose Himself in something so small! (W 28.11)

While the prayer of recollection itself may have been introduced to her by her reading of Osuna's *The Third Spiritual Alphabet*, she credits St. Augustine with providing her with the recognition that the quiet attention to the divine presence must be directed within:

> I think this vision is advantageous to recollected persons, in teaching them to consider the Lord as very deep within their souls; such a thought is much more alluring and fruitful than thinking of Him as outside oneself, as I mentioned at other times. And some books on prayer tell about where one must seek God. Particularly, the glorious St. Augustine speaks about this for neither in the market place nor in pleasures nor anywhere else that he sought God did he find Him as he did when he sought Him within himself. Within oneself, very clearly, is the best place to look; and it's not necessary to go to heaven, nor any further than our own selves; for to do so is to tire the spirit and distract the soul, without gaining as much fruit. (L 40.6; see also IC 4.3.3)

She gives the same attribution in *The Way of Perfection*. All we have to do is enter into an inner solitude and find Christ present within us:

> Consider what St. Augustine says, that he sought Him in many places but found Him ultimately within himself. Do you think it matters little for a soul with a wandering mind to understand this truth and see that there is no need to go to heaven in order to speak with one's Eternal Father or find delight in Him? Nor is there any need to shout. However softly we speak, He is near enough to hear us. Neither is there

> any need for wings to go to find Him. All one need do is go into solitude and look at Him within oneself. (W 28.2)

The fact that God dwells within us means that we can say that God has made the human soul an outpost of heaven:

> You already know that God is everywhere. It's obvious, then, that where the king is there is his court; in sum, wherever God is, there is heaven. Without a doubt you can believe that where His Majesty is present, all glory is present. Consider what St. Augustine says, that he sought Him in many places but found Him ultimately within himself. Do you think it matters little for a soul with a wandering mind to understand this truth and see that there is no need to go to heaven in order to speak with one's Eternal Father or find delight in Him? Nor is there any need to shout. However softly we speak, He is near enough to hear us. Neither is there any need for wings to go to find Him. All one need do is go into solitude and look at Him within oneself, and not turn away from so good a Guest. (W 28.2)

She goes on to marvel at the truth: "But what a marvelous thing, that He who would fill a thousand worlds and many more with His grandeur would enclose Himself in something so small!" (W 28.11). In fact, knowing that God dwells deep within each of us, we can picture the human soul as beautiful palace built to house the divine presence:

> Well, let us imagine that within us is an extremely rich palace, built entirely of gold and precious stones; in sum, built for a lord such as this. Imagine, too, as is indeed so, that you have a part to play in order for the palace to be so beautiful; for there is no edifice as beautiful as is a soul pure and full of virtues. The greater the virtues the more resplendent the jewels.

> Imagine, also, that in this palace dwells this mighty King who has been gracious enough to become your Father; and that He is seated upon an extremely valuable throne, which is your heart. (W 28.9)

God chose to create us in the divine image and to dwell in every soul, thus providing us with a special locus to seek and rest in the divine presence.

Recollection as a Manner of Prayer

"Recollection," as we have seen, is an important concept in the teaching of Teresa of Jesus on prayer and the spiritual life more generally. We must strive, with God's help, to practice and develop a habit of "gathering in" our attention in order to maintain an abiding awareness of the presence of Christ. This is the spirit that should permeate all of our prayer. But the word *recollection*, in Teresa's writings, also refers to a distinct manner or method of prayer that moves beyond discursive meditation and lays the groundwork for the reception of the divine gift of true contemplation.[12] Recollection, in this sense, is an active (or "acquired") form of prayer (i.e., we are its principal agent, with the help of grace) that serves as preparation to receive the infused prayer of contemplation that can only come from God according to the divine plan for us.

---

12. This interpretation of Teresa's intention to speak of recollection as a specific stage or method of prayer is widely accepted. For an opposing view, see Venancio dello Spirito Santo, "Oración y virtudes según Santa Teresa de Jesús," *Revista de Espiritualidad* 18 (1959): 490. The author argues that recollection is not a higher step or distinctive method of prayer but rather a special manner of attention in discursive meditation. The article is cited by Daniel de Pablo Maroto in *Teresa en oración: historia, experiencia, doctrina* (Madrid: Editorial de Espiritualidad, 2004), 364n20. In the text above, we have acknowledged recollection as a "manner of attention" in other forms of prayer, but we concur with other contemporary authors who interpret Teresa also to be speaking, in some places, of a distinctive method of prayer—even though it is not clearly defined nor extensively addressed in her writings.

In fact, Teresa is not always consistent in her use of the term *recollection*, and her teaching develops from the *Life*, through *The Way of Perfection*, to *The Interior Castle*. But she comes to distinguish an acquired form from an infused form of recollection, which is the first experience of true contemplation. Acquired recollection itself is an active form of prayer. We ourselves "gather in the senses." In that sense, we are (with the help of grace) its principal agents: "This recollection is not something supernatural, but that it is something we can desire and achieve ourselves with the help of God—for without this help we can do nothing, not even have a good thought. This recollection is not a silence of the faculties; it is an enclosure of the faculties within the soul" (W 29.4). In infused recollection, if God chooses to give it, it is God who gathers in our senses.

In traditional works on prayer after St. Teresa, this development in the life of prayer that seeks a wordless advance beyond meditation has been called the "prayer of simplicity," "prayer of simple regard/gaze," "prayer of simple presence," "simple vision of faith,"[13] or (in a term which would have seemed incongruent to St. Teresa though used by later Carmelite authors) "acquired contemplation."[14] These later authors refer to St. Teresa and her

---

13. Adolphe Tanquerey, *The Spiritual Life: A Treatise of Ascetical and Mystical Theology*, 2nd rev. ed., trans. Herman Branderis (Charlotte, N.C.: Tan Books, 2000 [1930]), 637–47. See also Antonio Royo Marín and Jordan Aumann, *The Theology of Christian Perfection* (Dubuque, Iowa: The Priory Press, 1962), 524–27; Reginald Garrigou-Lagrange, *The Three Ages of the Interior Life: Prelude to Eternal Life*, trans. M. Timothea Doyle (St. Louis, Mo.: B. Herder, 1948), II: 286–87n32. For a Carmelite discussion of "simplified prayer," see Marie-Eugène of the Child Jesus [Henri Grialou], *I Want to See God*, 2nd English ed., trans. M. Verda Clare (Washington, D.C.: Christian Classics, forthcoming), t° 269–73.

14. In the early seventeenth century, the influential Carmelite Tomás de Jesús (1564–1627) distinguished three stages of prayer in his reading of the teaching of Sts. Teresa and John of the Cross: ordinary meditation, acquired contemplation, and infused contemplation. See his *Suma y compendio de los grados de oración por donde sube un alma a la perfección de la contemplación* (Rome: Iacomo Mascardo, 1610). For a twentieth-century Carmelite author, see Doroteo de la Sagrada Familia, *Guía espiritual de la contemplación adquirida según la doctrina del Doctor de la Iglesia San Juan De La Cruz y sus discípulos* (Barcelona, Spain: Luis Gili, 1942).

"acquired recollection," though their understanding of this particular form of prayer may not be fully equivalent. But possible differences between and among authors need not concern us here. Some contemporary authors have found parallels between Teresian recollection and Centering Prayer as well as other similar contemporary contemplative practices. In the next chapter, we will examine that claim. Doing so will allow us to emphasize some distinctive aspects of Teresa's teaching on recollection as a manner of prayer.

"Discovering" the Prayer of Recollection

Although Teresa does not generally offer specific methods of prayer, she does speak of recollection as a "manner" or "method" of prayer.[15] She did not invent the method. It was being taught in sixteenth-century Spain by groups of Franciscans as a manner of inviting priests, religious, and laity into contemplative prayer through learning to rest in quiet awareness of God's inner presence.[16] Teresa recognized in it a method and a spirit of prayer that could guide her through her own struggle with discursive meditation and the use of the imagination in prayer.[17] Her first encounter with teaching on recollection was probably in her fateful reception of Francisco de Osuna's *Third Spiritual Alphabet* (L 4.6–8), heightened by her reading of St. Augustine's

15. In the ICS translation of *The Way of Perfection*, Teresa writes about recollection as a "manner" of prayer (W 28.8; 29.6) but also as a "method" of prayer (W 26.title; 28.5; 29.6–8). The English text is translating the original Spanish words *manera* or *modo*. In both texts, the specific words seem interchangeable in meaning.

16. Although Teresa's reading of Osuna was critical for her appropriation of the prayer of recollection, it can be argued that she clarified it, corrected it, simplified it, and made it more accessible. See Nicolás Caballero, *Cómo enseñaba a orar Santa Teresa* (Burgos, Spain: Editorial Monte Carmelo, 2003), 37–38, 46.

17. Maroto, *Teresa en oración*, 365–66.

Confessions, in which he recounts that he had discovered and learned to seek God within himself (L 9.7; W 28.2; IC 4.3.3). But ultimately Teresa credits God with having led her to this form of prayer: "May the Lord teach this recollection to those of you who don't know about it, for I confess that I never knew what it was to pray with satisfaction until the Lord taught me this method. And it is because I have always found so many benefits from this habit of recollection that I have enlarged so much upon it" (W 29.7).

Teresa embraced recollection for herself especially because she found it difficult to reflect prayerfully or to use her imagination in discursive meditation. It offered her a method for simply gazing silently at the Lord whom she had discovered was dwelling within her, as God dwells in the center of every human soul. But, without disparaging discursive meditation for those who could do so fruitfully, she urges everyone to practice recollection as an enhancement or as a doorway to deeper, contemplative prayer. She writes (in a text cited previously):

> For, although discursive reflection is very meritorious, they don't seem to realize that since their prayer is delightful there should ever be a Sunday or a time in which one is not working; but they think such time is lost. I consider this loss a great gain. But, as I have said, they should put themselves in the presence of Christ and, without tiring the intellect, speak with and delight in Him and not wear themselves out in composing syllogisms. . . . The discursive reflection they can do at one time, and the other acts at another, so that the soul may not grow tired of always eating the same food. These acts are very delightful and helpful if one's taste becomes accustomed to them. They contain a great amount of sustenance giving the soul life and many benefits. (L 13.11; see also L 12.2; W 26.1–3)

Even those who profitably engage in discursive meditation should, at least at times, simply place themselves in the presence of Christ. She repeats this advice later in the same chapter of the *Life*: "But one should not always weary oneself in seeking these reflections but just remain there in His presence with the intellect quiet. And if we are able, we should occupy ourselves in looking at Christ who is looking at us" (L 13.22).

The "Method"[18]

Teresa addresses the practice of acquired recollection in chapters twenty-six through twenty-nine of *The Way of Perfection*. She reminds her readers to make an adequate transition into a time of quiet prayer: "As is already known, the examination of conscience, the act of contrition, and the sign of the cross must come first" (W 26.1). The person should then try to gently gather the senses—to re-collect one's attention—to rest in Christ who dwells within: "They do what they can during that time to get free from it by recollecting their senses within. . . . There is a withdrawing of the senses from exterior things and a renunciation of them in such a way that, without one's realizing it, the eyes close so as to avoid seeing them and so that the sight might be more awake to things of the soul. So, anyone who walks by this path keeps his eyes closed almost as often as he prays" (W 28.6).

The basic movement of the prayer itself is simply to make oneself present to the divine friend: "Represent the Lord Himself as close to you and behold how lovingly and humbly He is teaching you. Believe me, you should remain with so good

18. See the pamphlet "The Prayer of Recollection" (Washington, D.C.: ICS Publications, 2012), which provides a nice summary of the concept and method.

a friend as long as you can" (W 26.1). In this context, *represent* (the Spanish verb is *representar*) means a simple making present in one's awareness, attending to the presence of the friend, being mindful of Christ's presence. Christ is, in fact, always present to us, but we are not present to him—that is, attentive and mindful of him. And so, we must re-collect our attention in order to "behold" him—gaze at the One who is always looking at us in love: "Just remain there in His presence with the intellect quiet. And if we are able we should occupy ourselves in looking at Christ who is looking at us [*mire que le mira*]" (L 13.22). Teresa's counsel is not so much to make oneself empty and solitary within; rather, she is suggesting that we should draw near to Christ the friend. It is his presence and the knowledge of his love for us that centers and draws our awareness into a silent receptivity.[19]

Teresa is clear that "representing Christ" does not mean thinking about Christ or imagining him. Recollection is not a form of discursive meditation: "I'm not asking you now that you think about Him or that you draw out a lot of concepts or make long and subtle reflections with your intellect. I'm not asking you to do anything more than look at Him" (W 26.3). The prayer consists in gently returning one's attention to Christ whenever the mind wanders—to return one's gaze to the One who is gazing at us with love. There is no real thinking or active imagining involved. It is an "intimate sharing" with a friend that does not involve words or conversation. Rather, it is an attentive being with.

Teresa seems to contradict herself when she adds: "If you are joyful, look at Him as risen. Just imagining how He rose from the tomb will bring you joy. . . . If you are

19. Herráiz, *La oración,* 37.

experiencing trials or are sad, behold Him on the way to the garden. . . . Or behold Him bound to the column. . . . Or behold Him burdened with the cross." (W 26.4–5). It may appear that she is recommending a traditional discursive meditation on the life of Christ. But she is urging her reader to just "look" and "behold." If meditation could be conceived as watching a video, with the "characters" moving and speaking, recollection is like keeping one's gaze fixed on a still scene, largely unfocused in the consciousness. Teresa is saying that we can bring ourselves to prayer as we find ourselves and, without actively thinking about our current mood or about a parallel scene in the life of Christ, simply be present to Christ who, ever the good friend, understands our experience. In recollection, we can share intimately in prayer with him without talking to him or thinking actively about him. "The important thing," she writes, "is not to think much but to love much" (IC 4.1.7; see also F 5.2).

In the prayer of recollection, the place of encounter with Christ is not outside ourselves. It is within, in the deepest core of our being where God dwells. It is therefore a kind of centering: "This prayer is called 'recollection,' because the soul collects its faculties together and enters within itself to be with its God. And its divine Master comes more quickly to teach it and give it the prayer of quiet than He would through any other method it might use. For centered there within itself, it can think about the Passion and represent the Son and offer Him to the Father and not tire the intellect by going to look for Him on Mount Calvary or in the garden or at the pillar" (W 28.4).

Here again, it might seem, on initial reading, that Teresa is talking about active thinking ("think about the Passion"), but the context makes clear that she is not speaking of making a reflection; she is speaking about recollection and "entering into oneself" to be with God. It is a potential gateway to the infused gift of the prayer of quiet; one is to "represent" Christ, without "tiring the intellect."

Teresa teaches, from her own experience, that the practice of recollection can be helped at its beginnings by reading from a good spiritual book: "It is also a great help to take a good book written in the vernacular in order to recollect one's thoughts and pray well vocally, and little by little accustom the soul with coaxing and skill not to grow discouraged" (W 26.10; see also L 9.5). Such reading can dispose one to enter into a spirit of recollection and begin the practice of moving from the concepts and words of the book to quiet awareness of the Presence. Likewise, a physical image of Christ can help one to maintain one's focus in recollection and call an overactive mind back to silent gazing: "What you can do as a help in this matter is try to carry about an image or painting of this Lord that is to your liking" (W 26.9). But the point, during the recollection, is not the physical image itself. Speaking specifically of post-Communion recollection, she writes: "If you have to pray to Him by looking at His picture, it would seem foolish. You would be leaving the Person Himself in order to look at a picture of Him. Wouldn't it be silly if a person we love very much and of whom we have a portrait came to see us and we stopped speaking with him to carry on a conversation with the portrait?" (W 34.11). As we will see in the next chapter, teachers of Centering Prayer urge people to silently repeat a brief prayer word in order to gently return one to quiet prayer. But another possibility, they teach, is using an image—physical or held gently in one's awareness—as a kind of instrument. This latter is parallel to Teresa's thought.

Accepting Distractions

The prayer of recollection can coincide with distractions—that is, there can be a deep being present to Christ even while random thoughts and images are passing through the mind. It is critical to realize this truth. Otherwise, as Teresa herself experienced, one can be tempted to abandon the prayer of recollection, wrongly believing that distractions indicate failure. Teresa addresses this issue in the first chapter of the fourth dwelling places of *The Interior Castle*—the dwelling places in which the transition from acquired to infused prayer can happen. In that context, she offers a distinction between the intellect and mind (equivalent, as she notes, with the imagination) as a key to understanding how authentic recollection can coincide with the presence of distractions. In sum, there can be a part of ourselves held in silent awareness of God even while the imagination—images, ideas, random thoughts—can run wild in the form of distractions. In part, the chapter title reads: "Tells of her happiness on learning the difference between the mind and the intellect. This knowledge is very beneficial for anyone who is greatly distracted in prayer." She writes:

> A little more than four years ago I came to understand through experience that the mind (or imagination, to put it more clearly) is not the intellect. I asked a learned man and he told me that this was so; which brought me no small consolation. For since the intellect is one of the soul's faculties, it was an arduous thing for me that it should be so restless at times. Ordinarily the mind [imagination] flies about quickly, for only God can hold it fast in such a way as to make it seem that we are somehow loosed from this body. I have seen, I think, that the faculties of my soul were occupied and recollected

> in God while my mind [imagination] on the other hand was distracted. This distraction puzzled me. (IC 1.1.8)

In more advanced stages of prayer, God may, for a time, absorb or "suspend" our consciousness ("faculties" and "senses") and dispel any distraction, but this cannot be produced by our own effort.

As spiritual authors have consistently taught, there are distractions that come about because of our own fault, such as: we do not take time to calm and relax ourselves before beginning prayer; we allow ourselves to bring our stresses into our prayer rather than either putting them aside or beginning our prayer by gently asking God to take them, at least for the time of prayer; we have not tried to develop a consistent habit of prayer that would bring stability and peace to our prayer; or our lives more generally are not really consistent with prayer (i.e., in Teresa's terms, we are not acting consistently as God's friends outside of our effort to enter into intimate sharing with our friend in times of prayer). And yet, there are distractions that simply come upon us without apparent cause on our part. It is the human condition. If we are awake, our minds are nearly always active. Such distractions must be accepted, even in the time of the quiet prayer of recollection:

> Just as we cannot stop the movement of the heavens, but they proceed in rapid motion, so neither can we stop our mind [imagination]; and then the faculties of the soul go with it, and we think we are lost and have wasted the time spent before God. But the soul is perhaps completely joined with Him in the dwelling places very close to the center while the mind [imagination] is on the outskirts of the castle suffering from a thousand wild and poisonous beasts, and meriting by

> this suffering. As a result we should not be disturbed; nor should we abandon prayer, which is what the devil wants us to do. For the most part all the trials and disturbance come from our not understanding ourselves. (IC 4.1.9)

Teresa's advice is acceptance and endurance: "And so it isn't good for us to be disturbed by our thoughts, nor should we be concerned. If the devil causes them, they will cease with this suspension. If they come, as they do, from one of the many miseries inherited through the sin of Adam, let us be patient and endure them for the love of God" (IC 4.1.11).

It is ineffective and indeed counterproductive to try to make the mind a blank—"suspend the intellect," as Teresa says (L 12.5; 23.2; IC 4.3.7). This was an ideal that some contemporary authors were apparently recommending. The human mind is constantly at work. Ideas, images, random thoughts, and the like are constantly moving through the mind. This is a reality that just has to be accepted. In infused forms of prayer, God can "suspend the intellect"—draw the person into a silencing of thought and movement, external and internal. Teresa herself knew such experiences intimately. But unless and until God chooses to do so, we must be content with trying gently to maintain our awareness and our silent, loving gaze in the face of distractions—returning to the "representation" of Christ as we find our attention dissipating:

> If His Majesty has not begun to absorb us, I cannot understand how the mind can be stopped. There's no way of doing so without bringing about more harm than good, although there has been a lengthy controversy on this matter among some spiritual persons. For my part I must confess my lack of humility, but those in favor of stopping the mind have never

> given me a reason for submitting to what they say. One of them tried to convince me with a certain book by the saintly Friar Peter of Alcántara—for I believe he is a saint—to whom I would submit because I know that he knew. And we read it together, and he says the same thing I do; although not in my words. But it is clear in what he says that love must be already awakened. (IC 4.3.4)

Staying Faithful

One of the basic foundations of building any habit of prayer is accepting the fact that we will not always "feel" the divine presence. We may not have a felt experience of God's presence or of consolation in prayer. This does not mean that our prayer is not genuine or that we should give up on our prayer. The same is true of the practice of recollection. Teresa writes about her own experience of trying to practice recollection after receiving communion (she speaks in the third person): "Since she believed that this Lord truly entered her poor home, she freed herself from all exterior things when it was possible and entered to be [with] Him. She strove to recollect the senses so that all of them would take notice of so great a good, I mean that they would not impede the soul from recognizing it. . . . And even though she didn't feel devotion, faith told her that He was indeed there" (W 34.7). The prayer of recollection, like all prayer, is more fundamentally an act and an exercise of faith than of feeling or consolation.

Teresa insists that the building up of the practice of recollection generally takes time, patience, and resolve. It is difficult at first because we are accustomed to having our attention wandering about: "For so we sinners are: our soul and our thoughts are so accustomed to wandering about at their own pleasure—or grief, to put it better—that the poor soul doesn't understand itself. In order that it get to love remaining at home once again, a great deal of skill is necessary" (W 26.10). Addressing her nuns, she writes: "O sisters, those of you who cannot engage in much discursive reflection with the intellect or keep your mind from distraction, get used to this practice! Get used to it!" (W 26.2). In the *Life*, using the image of different ways of watering a garden, she teaches that, at first, prayer is like the hard work of drawing up water from a well: "Beginners in prayer, we can say, are those who draw water from the well. This involves a lot of work on their own part, as I have said. They must tire themselves in trying to recollect their senses. Since they are accustomed to being distracted, this recollection requires much effort. They need to get accustomed to caring nothing at all about seeing or hearing, to practicing the hours of prayer, and thus to solitude and withdrawal" (L 11.9).

It is only by such faithful effort that one can arrive at a habit of recollection in prayer and in daily living: "This is a manner of praying that the soul gets so quickly used to that it doesn't go astray, nor do the faculties become restless, as time will tell. I only ask that you try this method, even though it may mean some struggle; everything involves struggle before the habit is acquired. But I assure you that before long it will be a great consolation for you to know that you can find this holy Father, whom you are beseeching, within you without tiring yourself in seeking where He is" (W 29.6).

Nonetheless, Teresa offers us hope that consistent effort over six months to a year can lead to a solid practice:

> Since nothing is learned without a little effort, consider, sisters, for the love of God, as well employed the attention you

> give to this method of prayer. I know, if you try, that within a year, or perhaps half a year, you will acquire it, by the favor of God. See how little time it takes for a gain as great as is that of laying a good foundation. If then the Lord should desire to raise you to higher things He will discover in you the readiness, finding that you are close to Him. May it please His Majesty that we not consent to withdrawing from His presence. Amen. (W 29.8)

But it is fidelity of effort, not success, that is essential: "And if we cannot succeed in one year, we will succeed later. Let's not regret the time that is so well spent. Who's making us hurry? I am speaking of acquiring this habit and of striving to walk alongside this true Master" (W 26.2). Little by little, there will be progress in the prayer of recollection, because "there are greater and lesser degrees of recollection" (W 28.7).

From Acquired to Infused

Teresa records that, having taken up the practice of recollection after reading Osuna, she was rather soon granted the beginnings of true contemplation—even though, at that point, she lacked the resources to understand what she was experiencing. As she waited for several months for a visit to a local healer to cure a serious ailment, she records:

> I was almost nine months in this solitude. . . . At the end of this time that I mentioned there, the Lord, as I was saying, began to favor me by means of this path [of recollection]; so much so that He granted me the prayer of quiet. And sometimes I arrived at union, although I did not understand what the one was or the other, or how much they were to

> be prized—for I believe it would have done me great good to have understood this. True, this union lasted for so short a time that I do not know if it continued for the space of a Hail Mary. (L 4.7)

Her own experience taught her—confirmed by those she consulted—that the practice of re-collecting our attention by our own effort serves generally as a necessary preparation for the action of God in drawing us into quiet: "Those who by such a method can enclose themselves within this little heaven of our soul, where the Maker of heaven and earth is present, and grow accustomed to refusing to be where the exterior senses in their distraction have gone or look in that direction should believe they are following an excellent path and that they will not fail to drink water from the fount [i.e., of contemplation]; for they will journey far in a short time" (W 28.5; see also W 28.7).

But the introduction of the first movements of true contemplative prayer can be quite subtle—like a gentle whistling: "Once the great King, who is in the center dwelling place of this castle, sees their good will, He desires in His wonderful mercy to bring them back to Him. Like a good shepherd, with a whistle so gentle that even they themselves almost fail to hear it, He makes them recognize His voice and stops them from going so far astray so that they will return to their dwelling place. And this shepherd's whistle has such power that they abandon the exterior things in which they were estranged from Him and enter the castle" (IC 4.3.2).

Many people of prayer, she believes, enter into the fifth dwelling places where God introduces true contemplative prayer: "And although I have said 'some,' there are indeed only a few who fail to enter this dwelling place [i.e, the fifth dwelling places] of which I shall now speak. There are various degrees, and for that reason I say that most enter these places. But I believe that only a few will experience some of the things that I will say are in this room. Yet even if souls do no more than reach the door, God is being very merciful to them; although many are called few are chosen" (IC 5.1.2).

John of the Cross, too, noted that many people of faithful prayer receive the divine gift of contemplation without realizing it. Because they do not know the signs of the giving of this gift, rather than embracing it, they feel that they must continue to practice active forms of prayer such as discursive meditation even though they no longer satisfy. Sadly, in John's experience, there are too many spiritual directors who, due to ignorance, fail to assist people of prayer to listen for and embrace this gentle divine whistling, as St. Teresa calls it.[20]

Teresa is not always consistent in what she calls the first experience of contemplative prayer. Sometimes, it is the prayer of quiet: "This prayer is called [acquired] 'recollection,' because the soul collects its faculties together and enters within itself to be with its God. And its divine Master comes more quickly to teach it and give it the prayer of quiet than He would through any other method it might use" (W 28.4). But later, she refers to an infused form of the prayer of recollection in which it is God, rather than ourselves, who draws in the senses: "The first prayer I experienced that in my opinion was supernatural . . . is an *interior recollection* felt in the soul. For it appears that just as the soul has exterior senses it also has other interior senses through which it seems to want to

20. John of the Cross offers three signs that God is introducing the gift of contemplation and counsel on how to embrace it. See *Ascent of Mt. Carmel*, 2.13; also *Dark Night*, 1.9. *The Collected Works of St. John of the Cross*, 3rd. ed., trans. Kieran Kavanaugh and Otilio Rodriguez (Washington, D.C.: ICS Publications, 2017).

withdraw within, away from the outside noise. So, sometimes this recollection draws these exterior senses after itself, for it gives the soul the desire to close its eyes and not hear or see or understand anything other than that in which it is then occupied, which is communion with God in solitude" (ST 59.3, emphasis added; see also IC 4.3.1). In this latter schema, the infused prayer of recollection is a kind of transition or doorway to the contemplative prayer of quiet.

In any case, the practice of acquired recollection is usually the groundwork for receiving the gift of contemplation: "If you can, practice this recollection often during the day; if not, do so a few times. As you become accustomed to it you will experience the benefit, either sooner or later. *Once this recollection is given by the Lord*, you will not exchange it for any treasure" (W 29.7, emphasis added). Having urged her readers to be resolved in the practicing recollection, she offers this hope: "If then the Lord should desire to raise you to higher things He will discover in you the readiness, finding that you are close to Him" (W 29.8).

Conclusion

Although Teresa of Jesus did not generally teach methods of prayer, she did see the need for them. Christians of her time could find ample resources to guide them in finding a method of discursive meditation that would work for them. But Teresa saw a need for passing on a kind of method for a quieter, essentially wordless prayer that could set the stage for the reception from God of the gift of contemplation. In her teaching about acquired recollection, she offers her own "manner of prayer" to help her readers to grow accustomed to a form of prayer that does not involve thinking or imagining. Focused on the presence of Christ—simply gazing at the One who is always gazing at us with love—the prayer of acquired recollection can thereby serve as preparation for God's action in drawing us into a quiet receptivity and silent awareness of the divine presence that is always with us.

5

An Excursus: Acquired Recollection and Contemporary Contemplative Practice

The late Carmelite author Ernest Larkin concluded in a number of his publications that Teresa's acquired recollection was virtually equivalent to the contemporary practice of Centering Prayer (associated especially with Cistercian Thomas Keating) and Christian Meditation (associated with Benedictine John Main).[1] Both are prayer practices that seek a form of wordless, imageless prayer certainly similar to the acquired form of recollection that Teresa teaches. "Teresa's active recollection . . . can rightly be called centering prayer,"[2] Larkin writes. And, in the same work, he also

1. Carmelite Luis Jorge González, in his *Mindfulness y Santa Teresa: estar con Quien sabemos nos ama* (Mexico City: Ediciones Duruelo, 2017), views Teresa's teaching on acquired recollection as parallel to contemporary secular and Buddhist discussions of "mindfulness." See also Peter Tyler, *Christian Mindfulness: Theology and Practice* (London: SCM Press, 2018) and Tyler, "Oración Mental, Mindfulness, and Mental Prayer." Both González and Tyler write that "mindfulness" can also be understood as "heartfulness." Daniel de Pablo Maroto cites a few authors that speak of acquired recollection in relation to "Christianized yoga." *Teresa en oración*, 364n21.

2. Ernest E. Larkin, *Contemplative Prayer for Today: Christian Meditation* (Singapore: Medio Media, 2007), 15. See also Larkin, "St. Teresa of Avila and Centering Prayer," in *Carmelite Studies* 3: *Centenary of Saint Teresa*, ed. John Sullivan, 191–211 (Washington, D.C.: ICS Publications, 1982).

concludes: "Teresa also practiced and taught a silent prayer of recollection that is a counterpart of Christian Meditation"[3]—though he suggests (without explanation) that "there is a closer affinity between Centering Prayer and Teresa of Ávila and between Christian Meditation and John of the Cross."[4] And more broadly, Larkin affirms: "Centering Prayer is like a variant of the active recollection of St. Teresa of Ávila. The Carmelite tradition has a great affinity with these new forms of contemplative prayer."[5]

For those who are familiar with contemporary writings on Christian contemplative practice,[6] our discussion of Teresa's teaching on acquired recollection may already suggest that Larkin's conclusion seems, at least to a large degree, correct—at least at the level of practice. "Recollection"—as a gathering in of our attention—can rightly be seen as a form "centering." Without engaging in a broad and lengthy examination of the literature of contemporary contemplative practice, looking at the basic outlines of Centering Prayer and Christian Meditation may serve to clarify for modern readers what Teresa taught about acquired recollection as well as serve to highlight some distinctive elements of Teresa's viewpoint. To some degree, we will also be raising questions of these other practices in light of St. Teresa's teaching.

---

3. Larkin, *Contemplative Prayer*, 66.

4. Larkin, *Contemplative Prayer*, 16.

5. Ernest E. Larkin, "The Carmelite Tradition and Centering Prayer/Christian Meditation," in *Carmelite Prayer: A Tradition for the 21st Century*, ed. Keith J. Egan (Mahwah, N.J.: Paulist Press, 2003), 220.

6. In addition to the works of Centering Prayer and Christian Meditation which we will mention here, for a further example of works on contemplative practice, see the trilogy offered by Martin S. Laird, beginning with his *Into the Silent Land: A Guide to the Christian Practice of Contemplation* (Oxford: Oxford University Press, 2006).

Centering Prayer and Christian Meditation

Centering Prayer is largely associated with the Trappist Thomas Keating,[7] though his work has been expanded and moved in new directions by many followers and collaborators. Christian Meditation, as a particular form of contemplative practice, was taught by Benedictine John Main.[8] His work has been continued by his close collaborator Laurence Freeman. The basic structure, foundations, and underpinnings of the practices offered by Centering Prayer and Christian Meditation are largely similar. Both recommend the use and repetition of a word or phrase to enter into and sustain a period of quiet prayer and prayerful awareness or mindfulness. Both are grounded in the belief that God dwells within each person, and the practice is meant to help the person of prayer to disengage from the normal world of thought and external engagement in order to attend to the divine presence and action within. Both look to the *Conferences* of John Cassian and to the medieval classic *The Cloud of Unknowing* as foundational to their ideas—Centering Prayer perhaps more to *The Cloud* and Christian Meditation more to Cassian.[9] Both also

---

7. Keating's foundational work is *Open Heart, Open Mind: The Contemplative Dimension of the Gospel*, 20th anniversary edition (London: Bloomsbury Continuum, 2006). Keating viewed this work as a part of a trilogy with his *Invitation to Love: The Way of Christian Contemplation*, 20th anniversary edition (London: Bloomsbury, 2012); and *The Mystery of Christ: The Liturgy as Spiritual Experience* (Amity, N.Y.: Amity House, 1987).

8. Main's foundational work is *Word into Silence* (New York: Paulist Press, 1981), followed by a number of others which are collections of his conferences, brief articles, and letters.

9. Laurence Freeman pointed to the conclusion reached by eminent scholar of the Rule of Saint Benedict, Adalbert de Vogüé, that the Christian West embraced Cassian's general teachings on prayer while leaving aside his teaching on the repetition of a prayer phrase to sustain quiet prayer—which de Vogüé concludes is a major "lacuna." Laurence Freeman, "The Contemplative Oblate Today," *Vita Vitae* Benedictine Oblate Newsletter, 11 (January 2010): 3–4. See Adalbert de Vogüé, "From John Cassian to John Main: Reflections on Christian Meditation," *Monastic Studies* 15 (1984): 90–92.

note the connection with the Jesus Prayer of Eastern Christianity. At the same time, there are some differences between them, especially in their understanding of the role and use of the word (or "mantra," as Main calls it), but, for the most part, these need not concern us here. Keating finds a basic affinity of Centering Prayer with the "prayer of simplicity" articulated by traditional manuals of prayer (which often referred to Teresa's acquired recollection as their source).[10]

The basic practice of Centering Prayer and Christian Meditation are essentially the same. They recommend finding a comfortable but not overly cozy position for the time of prayer. For most people today, this would probably be seated in a chair that supports the back, allowing a person to sit without either distraction or the promotion of drowsiness. The person then takes up the silent repetition of a word or phrase that serves as a tool for arriving at and maintaining an inner attitude of quiet attention, "alert receptivity," or what other authors call "mindfulness." The goal is not to arrive at a completely blank mind (which is generally not possible) nor at a forced concentration but rather at a general, relaxed spirit of attentiveness. In Centering Prayer, the "sacred symbol" is usually a word of one or two syllables. It is not chosen for any particular significance in the word itself, and it is not itself the focus of any meditation on its meaning. Rather, it is a simple expression of consent to God's presence and action in one's life and prayer. The word is repeated until the person arrives at a general state of attentiveness. The word is taken up again when the mind begins to wander or distractions begin to take over. In Christian Meditation, on the other hand, the word is believed to actually carry the prayer. It is an expression of the prayer and is repeated throughout the time

10. Keating, *Open Mind*, 4.

of the practice—unless and until, as Teresa would phrase it, the person's consciousness is "absorbed" and thus unable to repeat it without effort. Both Keating and Main recommend two daily periods of prayer, each for at least twenty minutes. Over time, it is taught, the faithful practitioner is able to enter into deeper and more sustained periods of quiet receptivity—until, it is hoped, God brings about the inner quiet that is true contemplation (parallel to what Teresa would see as the transition from acquired to infused recollection).

Keating writes that, although the use of a "sacred word" is more common, practitioners might find it more useful to use their breathing or "an inward glance toward God dwelling within."[11] This possibility of using a "sacred glance" in Centering Prayer practice is expanded by David Frenette.[12] The term itself suggests that what is being recommended is not an exercise in actively imagining the face of Christ or God during the period of prayer but rather a silent gazing. It is this suggestion that seems parallel to St. Teresa's counsel to "represent" Christ—again, not imagining Christ nor really even visualizing him but rather attending to Christ's presence and hidden gaze. Interestingly, in explaining the contemplative prayer of quiet, Teresa does say that a gentle word can be useful in sustaining the experience (though one cannot cause the prayer or hold on to it): "At most, a gentle word from time to time is sufficient, as in the case of one who blows on a candle to enkindle it again when it begins to die out. But if the candle is burning, blowing on it will in my opinion serve no other purpose than to put it out. I say that the blowing should be gentle

---

11. Keating, *Open Mind*, 7.

12. David Frenette, *The Path of Centering Prayer: Deepening Your Experience of God* (Boulder, Colo.: Sounds True, 2012), 59–74.

lest the will be distracted by the intellect busying itself with many words" (W 31.7).

She goes on to note that distractions are possible here, too, even in true contemplation. Both Centering Prayer and Christian Meditation offer the same advice as St. Teresa in regard to the time of prayer: minimize distractions as much as possible in preparation for prayer but otherwise simply accept them and return to the sacred word or glance/gaze.

For both Keating and Main, deeper inner healing and transformation are the result of faithful practice of the prayer. Over time and with fidelity, by leaving aside the largely superficial concerns of daily life and entering into a silent being present to the God who dwells within, the practitioner enters, too, more deeply into self. This is itself a form of ascetical practice, as the person freely lets go of the concerns of everyday life and comes to rest in inner silence and poverty in the divine presence within. In the process, deep-seated fears, anxieties, and wounds come to be revealed and thus gradually set free—thus undoing the roots of sin itself, bringing about an inner liberation and transformation.[13] The time of prayer is not the place for thinking about or actively trying to resolve one's inner discoveries. Outside of prayer, reflection and sharing with others might be helpful. But the prayer itself, again over time, will have its own effect of releasing the negative energies of these inner realities. Contemplative practice thus serves to deconstruct the false self—built up by attachment to superficialities and sin—by "unloading the unconscious" of the emotional baggage that are its roots.

---

13. Teresa may be making a similar point in the sixth dwelling places of *The Interior Castle* by addressing the prolonged suffering brought about by being confronted with reality of one's own sinfulness. See IC 6.7.

Both Centering Prayer and Christian Meditation could, in Teresa's framework, be understood as forms of acquired recollection—which Teresa herself would likely not expect to be practiced in the exact manner that she describes in her writing. Keating, in fact, understands Centering Prayer to be preparation for the divine gift of contemplation, though he believes that contemplation is "a fundamental constituent of human nature and thus available to every human being."[14] Often, in his writing and that of his collaborators, there does not always seem to be a clear distinction between the mature practice and experience of Centering Prayer (our action) and true contemplation (divine action). For Teresa, the distinction is clear, though she notes that the movement from acquired to infused recollection can be subtle. John Main is less concerned for the distinction in practice, using the term *meditation* "synonymously with such terms as contemplation, contemplative prayer, meditative prayer, and so on."[15]

Teresa's Acquired Recollection as Distinct

Ernest Larkin's conclusion that the practice of acquired recollection as described by Teresa is essentially the same as contemporary contemplative practices like Centering Prayer and Christian Meditation seems largely to be correct—at least in regard to the practice itself and in its goal of arriving at quiet receptivity to the God who dwells within. Nonetheless, there are differences—at least in emphasis and development—and these are not insignificant.

14. Keating, *Open Mind*, 3.

15. Main, *Word into Silence*, 1.

Focus on Christ

Keating and Main are offering a form of Christian prayer, found in the tradition of the desert fathers (represented by John Cassian), in the Jesus Prayer of Eastern Christianity, in *The Cloud of Unknowing*, and in the writings of the Doctor of the Church St. Teresa of Ávila. But, once Keating begins to write about the practice itself, it is not always clear how Centering Prayer is distinctively *Christian* prayer—complicated by explicit interest (especially in some who have expanded on his work) in showing connections with non-Christian practices, whether Buddhist meditation or secular mindfulness. Keating does assert at one point that the focus of Centering Prayer "is to deepen our relationship with Jesus Christ, the Divine-Human Being, and through him with the Trinity."[16] But in his writings, it is not entirely clear how this is so. The monastic person of Cassian's time would have practiced the repetition of a sacred phrase as part of a life immersed in reading, memorizing, and studying the Scriptures. It is difficult to imagine how that monastic person's prayer would not be in some way Christ-focused. But, as regards Centering Prayer, one author notes that it is not really evident how *lectio divina* fits with the practice of Centering Prayer as really integral to it, leading some to suggest, unfairly, that it seems more "indebted to Asian religiosity."[17] One does not have to doubt the authentically Christian roots of Centering Prayer to wonder about the place of Christ in the practice itself.

John Main, on the other hand, is insistent that Christian Meditation fundamentally involves joining Christ's own prayer and thus entering into the life of the Trinity itself: "There is only

---

16. Keating, *Open Mind*, 41.

17. Kevin Mongrain, Review of *Centering Prayer and the Healing of the Unconscious* by Murchadh Ó Madagáin, *Spiritus* 9 (Fall 2009): 261.

one prayer, the stream of love between the Spirit of the risen Jesus and His Father in which we are incorporated. . . . The mantra is the focus of our joining ourselves to the Son's returning to the Father."[18] John Main's collaborator Laurence Freeman concludes that the only true Christian prayer is Christ's own prayer in which we are invited to participate through the practice of Christian Meditation.[19] This is a valuable insight into the nature of all Christian prayer—the fruit of our baptismal union with Christ.

The Christocentrism of Teresa's teaching on prayer is, however, more insistent and explicit. All Christian prayer involves intimate sharing with Christ the friend. Acquired recollection involves "representing Christ"—gazing silently at, beholding, resting in a silent awareness of the presence of Christ who, in his sacred humanity, knows us intimately and saved us in love. Recollection feeds a deeper sharing with the divine friend who we know loves us. In the prayer of recollection, the encounter with Christ becomes yet more intimate and immediate since it is moving, in a sense, from the exterior into the depths of the person where Christ dwells. It is now the silent sharing of very close friends, hidden even from the person's own consciousness. Acquired recollection is not a drawing away from Christ; rather, it is a drawing yet closer to him by withdrawing one's attention from the world around us. As John Main is suggesting, all Christian prayer—including acquired recollection—is intimately

18. Main, *Word into Silence*, 39. See also Main, *Moment of Christ: The Path of Meditation* (New York: Continuum, 1998), xi–xii; Main, *The Way of Unknowing: Expanding Spiritual Horizons Through Meditation* (Norwich, England: Canterbury Press, 2012), 33–34. Basil Pennington, also an early proponent of Centering Prayer, makes a similar statement in his "Centering Prayer," in *Finding Grace at the Center*, eds. Thomas Keating, M. Basil Pennington, and Thomas Clarke (Petersham, Mass.: St. Bede's Publications, 1978), 13.

19. Laurence Freeman, "The Monastic Tradition of Meditation," *Meditatio* (Newsletter of the World Community for Christian Meditation, Talks Series 2016 B: April–June 2016): 5.

tied to Christ and his relationship with the Father. Christ is the doorway, the bridge. Apparently against positions held by experts of her time, Teresa is insistent that focus on the humanity of Christ must not be abandoned, even in the highest stages of prayer—though she acknowledges that the person can stop being explicitly conscious of Christ during the time of prayer (L 22; IC 6.7.6).

What would Teresa make of drawing connections between acquired recollection and non-Christian and secular practices? First of all, the religious culture of her time would probably not have allowed her even to entertain the idea. But it does seem that Teresa's thinking is so thoroughly and consciously focused on Christ that she might not be able to engage the question. Christian faith and Christian prayer is Christ, and she probably could not think of it beyond that.

Stages of Growth in Prayer

As we have seen, in *The Way of Perfection*, Teresa lays out a traditional progression in prayer from simple vocal prayer, through meditation, to acquired recollection, and then (if God wills it) into true contemplative prayer. This idea of a general line of development in prayer was not an innovation on her part. It was a general expectation of the Christian spiritual tradition before and after her. In the *Life*, she had offered the four ways to water a garden—again, suggesting ongoing development and maturing. *The Interior Castle* is built on a symbol of progression. This was her own experience, and she was offering a general pattern to help guide her readers. At the same time, she was aware that everyone is different, and God decides how the divine action will be realized in our life and prayer. Even in the movement from dwelling place to dwelling place in *The Interior Castle*, she says there are many rooms in each dwelling—meaning that people will experience the spiritual journey in their own way (IC 1.2.12; Epil.3).

Books on prayer after Teresa picked up on her schema and often seemed to suggest that everyone must expect to follow the exact pattern that she had laid out in exactly the way that she taught it. But, beyond offering a sense of progression and general patterns of growth, this was not her intention. Contemporary writers on prayer rightly react negatively to the overly rigid schemas of movement in prayer. This seems reflected in books on contemporary contemplative practice that offer—even to beginners in prayer—a manner of prayer that Teresa and traditional authors would have considered more proper to more mature lives of prayer—after having developed habits of meditation, especially on the Word of God. Centering Prayer and Christian Meditation intentionally cast their net wide, offering their way of prayer to all. Other forms of prayer are encouraged, especially *lectio divina*. But perhaps it is noteworthy that Keating speaks of *lectio divina*, meditation on the Word of God, and participation in the liturgical life of the church as "supporting practices."[20]

Would Teresa of Jesus have been comfortable offering acquired recollection to all of her readers before they had already developed habits of regular prayer, reading of Scripture, and active participation in the sacraments? The answer to that speculative question might be found in returning to her fundamental definition of prayer as friendship. Prayer is always, in all of its stages, an intimate sharing with a friend who we know loves us. And it is fidelity over time to vocal prayer, to meditating on the Word, learning about the faith, and sharing the sacramental life of the church that brings us to know this divine friend more

20. Keating, *Intimacy* (chapter seven: "Supportive Practices"), 94–106.

deeply—again, over time. At least this is the way that human friendship grows. People whose relationship is just beginning do not usually spend quiet time together, able to share at a deep level without speaking and without a deeper knowledge of the other. Peter Feldmeier, in offering a largely sympathetic critique of Centering Prayer, makes a similar point, noting that from the practice of devotions and meditation "one learns not only about the Christ with whom one desires intimacy and the mysteries of the faith that one is meditating on, but most importantly one comes to know Christ himself. It is this Christ whose intimate graces one then can recognize in contemplation. Without a deep intimacy with God already established in meditational prayer, how would one recognize his very subtle presence in contemplation?"[21] This would seem to be Teresa's viewpoint as well.

At the time of Teresa, in Spain, there was a heretical movement—groups of people—called generally *alumbrados* (enlightened ones).[22] They practiced the prayer of recollection, taught to them at first by observant Franciscans who sincerely wanted to "democratize" contemplative prayer. (By speaking of a heretical movement here, I do *not* mean to imply that heresy is at work in contemporary contemplative practice—merely, instead, to point to a movement in history that might suggest caution in trying to advance in prayer without a firm faith background.) But sixteenth-century Spain was a time of very poor catechesis. Many of those who began to practice recollection lacked the knowledge of the faith to understand their spiritual experience in an authentically Christian and Catholic way. They

21. Peter Feldmeier, "The Centering Prayer Movement and the Christian Contemplative Tradition," *Spiritual Life* 49 (Winter 2003): 237.

22. For an overview of the *alumbrado* movement at the time of St. Teresa, see my *In Context: Teresa of Ávila, John of the Cross, and Their World* (Washington, D.C.: ICS Publications, 2020), 151–71.

began to view their individual, personal experience in prayer as the true and only arbiter of their understanding of God, of the divine will and ways, and of the right way of living in response to their own experience in prayer. For some, this included viewing the Bible as no longer necessary since they had private experiential knowledge of God. For some of these *alumbrados,* the prayer of recollection seemed to be a "shortcut" (*atajo*) to union with God—but the shortcut included bypassing the resources by which to authentically understand their prayer as genuinely *Christian* prayer. Mystical movements in every age have gone astray by failing to form and assess their experiences in light of firm pillars of faith—most especially the Word of God. How will people without a firm foundation in the Christian faith and without a history of a relationship with God in Jesus Christ understand their prayer experience and the God whom they believe that they are encountering?

Would Teresa of Jesus be comfortable in offering the prayer of recollection to a wide audience? To people of mature Christian faith, certainly the answer would be affirmative. To those who do not have a mature sense of the faith, who have no real prior habit of prayer, to those without spiritual guidance, she would probably suggest caution and patience. At the very least, the practice of recollection would necessarily be accompanied by insistence on study and prayer over the Scriptures, by growth in knowledge of the Christian faith, by sharing in the liturgical life of the Christian community, and—if at all possible—sound spiritual guidance and study of the spiritual tradition. Our human capacity for self-deception—leading us to conclude that what we are experiencing in prayer is the God of Jesus Christ when it might be an illusion, a comforting consequence of relaxation techniques, or a pathway to very mistaken ideas—is just too great. And growth in authentic relationship with the God who is revealed in Jesus

Christ is just too important—essential—for the Christian to jeopardize through seeking shortcuts to what has traditionally and reliably been understood over the centuries as a lifelong journey.

Three Essential Virtues

The Way of Perfection was written as a primer—an introduction—to contemplative prayer. But the first half of the book is devoted to three virtues that Teresa of Jesus believes are the necessary foundation for the reception of the gift of contemplation: a practical love for others, detachment, and humility. We will address these virtues in a later chapter, but here it is important to see that Teresa is insistent that, without a firm foundation in these three virtues—except by some rare divine intervention—it is impossible to receive the gift of contemplation. As she unfolds her teaching about the three virtues, she imagines her nuns complaining that they had asked her to write about contemplative prayer, not about virtues. But she responds that it would be pointless to explain contemplation without this essential preparation for it (W 16.3–5).

Works on Centering Prayer and Christian Meditation do mention—almost in passing, it seems—that how we live has an important bearing on our growth in prayer. Their emphasis, however, is not so much on our ongoing conversion as a foundation of prayer but rather on how transformation and self-knowledge are the fruit of prayer. Teresa experienced these fruits herself in abundance, and she promises such effects for those who faithfully practice prayer. But she remains emphatic that the prior work of conversion is simply essential.[23] She feels

23. I address these issues in my *The Way of Transformation: St. Teresa of Avila on the Foundation and Fruit of Prayer* (Washington, D.C.: ICS Publications, 2016).

that she cannot usefully write about contemplative prayer unless she devotes significant attention to the necessary preparation. Any effort to equate Teresa's prayer of acquired recollection with contemporary contemplative practice must attend to this fact. She begins to address recollection in chapter twenty-six of *The Way of Perfection*—after the discussion of the essential virtues—and a reader cannot be true to her thought without acknowledging and addressing the foundation that she establishes. For her, the practice of recollection requires this prior and concurrent preparation.

The Interior Castle presents the Christian life as a journey of prayer, deeper self-knowledge, and transformation. Again, Teresa does not intend to suggest that the path is set according to a predetermined mold or pattern for every person, but she is offering a general road map, based on her experience and learning. She places the prayer of acquired recollection in the fourth of seven dwelling places—in which the transition can occur between acquired and infused forms of prayer, beginning with the movement from acquired to infused recollection. But there are three dwelling places prior to these fourth dwelling places during which prayer has grown, one's friendship with Christ has matured and developed, and one's life has become more consistent with a deepening friendship and more profound intimate sharing with Christ. Just as, in the prayer of recollection, the person is withdrawing their attention from the regular activities of daily life and especially its "vanities," so the person is—and must be—increasingly disengaged from all that is not of God.[24]

One of the key images of *The Interior Castle* is the cocoon and the silkworm, introduced in the fifth dwelling places (IC

24. Daniel de Pablo Maroto, *Teresa en oración: historia, experiencia, doctrina* (Madrid: Editorial de Espiritualidad, 2004), 368–69.

5.2), in which the person enters more substantially into the prayer of contemplation. It is a symbol of the transformation experienced by the person blessed with true contemplation. The silkworm is an ugly, awkward-looking creature, but it weaves its cocoon and "dies" within it, to emerge as a beautiful white butterfly. (Teresa got her biology a bit wrong, because the silkworm technically becomes a moth rather than a butterfly.) Such is the transformation brought about by the contemplative union with Christ, who likewise died and rose. But Teresa notes that the silkworm must first weave its cocoon, which she says means ridding ourselves of "self-love and self-will, our attachments to any earthly thing, and by performing deeds of penance, prayer, mortification, obedience, and all of the other things you know" (IC 5.2.6). For the silkworm: without weaving the cocoon, the transformation cannot occur.

Teresa herself was advanced in the life of prayer when she wrote *The Way of Perfection*. *The Interior Castle* is her mature masterpiece, written after she had attained habitual union with God in the "spiritual marriage." But as she looks back on the path along which God has led her, she does not repudiate the traditional wisdom that, in some critical way, the ascetical life lays the groundwork for the contemplative, the purgative for the illuminative and unitive, the *praktikos* for the *theoria* (as the desert tradition taught).[25] Rather, she insists on it. Again, the Christian journey does not follow a set pattern. At its best, the traditional three ways of purgative, illuminative, and unitive (which has roots in the presentation of desert wisdom by Evagrius Ponticus) was not the manual for an assembly line for the spiritual life. But the necessity of the prior and concurrent work of conversion—human effort aided by grace—was deemed

25. Again, Feldmeier makes a similar point in "Centering Prayer Movement," 234–35.

essential, requiring more than passing mention in any discussion of the pursuit of contemplative prayer.[26] That deepening prayer would subsequently bear fruit in a yet more profound transformation and a deeper self-knowledge was no less viewed as the normal expectation of the mature life of prayer.

The expectation of a prior conversion is also viewed as essential to the specific sources from which contemporary contemplative practices draw their teaching. Cassian's discussion of prayer takes place in the context of his presentation of the wisdom of the desert tradition. The desert monks were in pursuit of purity of heart—that single-hearted openness and surrender to the divine will that prepared for true contemplation and for truly self-forgetful love. Prayer plays an important role in its attainment; but it also requires ascetical struggle. This is clear in Cassian's *Conferences* nine and ten, from which Centering Prayer claims some of its roots.[27] The Jesus Prayer of Eastern Christianity is built on the same desert foundation and thus on the same expectation of prior and concurrent moral effort in order to hope for contemplative fruit from the practice of repeating the divine name. The anonymous author of *The Cloud of Unknowing* makes clear in the book's prologue that it should only be read by those who are serious about their practice of the "active life" (i.e., of ascetical practice): "He will be one who is doing all that he can, and has been, presumably, for a long time, to fit himself for the contemplative life by the virtues and exercises of the

26. Feldmeier makes the same point ("Centering Prayer Movement," 228): "It is my belief that the classical tradition [upon which CP says it is based] is often glossed over and that the requisites, which the tradition insists upon as preceding contemplative prayer, are not taken seriously. I do not intend to disparage the movement but to raise the bar of discussion with concerns that I have never encountered yet think as important."

27. De Vogüé, while affirming Cassian's use of a repeated prayer phrase, also notes his insistence on the necessity of the prior ascetical practice. "From John Cassian to John Main," 94.

active life. Otherwise this book is not for him."[28] This is consistent with the fact that work is directed to a solitary hermit who, after long religious life and the practice of prayer, is ready to embrace a manner of prayer that can serve as a foundation for true contemplation.[29]

Keating writes that one of the major sources of his ideas is John of the Cross, particularly John's discussion of the purifying effects of prayer in the night of sense and spirit.[30] And, indeed, John of the Cross does see that a great deal of the work of our transformation comes as the fruit of grace made increasingly available through deepening prayer. But for John of the Cross, there are "passive" nights of sense and spirit (which Keating is addressing), but there are also "active" nights of sense and spirit (which Keating does not address). In the passive nights, God is the principal agent; while in the active nights, it is our graced effort that seems to predominate. In fact, John of the Cross lays out the Christian journey in what is essentially a two-volume work: *The Ascent of Mt. Carmel* and *The Dark Night*. And that journey consists essentially of both active and passive nights. One cannot be true to his thought without noting this fact. This is true as well of Keating's use of the example of St. Anthony of the Desert.[31] Anthony attained victory over the demons that plagued him and drew close to God through a life of deep and faithful prayer, but Anthony's story also includes accounts of his ascetical preparation in the desert life that complete the picture. This cannot be ignored while remaining true to the story.

---

28. *The Cloud of Unknowing*, ed. James Walsh, The Classics of Western Spirituality (New York: Paulist Press, 1981), 101–2.

29. Feldmeier, "Centering Prayer Movement," 232–33.

30. Keating, *Open Mind*, 150–52; *Invitation to Love*, chs. 11,12, 14, and 16.

31. Keating, *Invitation to Love*, chs. 10 and 13.

Keating concludes that "Transformation is completely God's work. We can't do anything to make it happen. We can only prevent it from happening."[32] At the moment or event of transformation, this may be true. But Rosemary Haughton showed decades ago that transformation almost always depends on the formation (conversion) that precedes it.[33] Without the stage set by the prior work of formation, the elements for the transformation would be lacking. Monastic persons, like the Trappists, who follow the Rule of St. Benedict make the vow of *conversatio morum*—a lifelong commitment to the graced work of ongoing conversion—embracing what Haughton calls a "formation community" that seeks to set the stage for a deeper graced transformation.

Ernest Larkin's claim that Teresa's acquired recollection is largely the equivalent of contemporary contemplative practice—in terms of "method" or "manner"—seems largely accurate. But she is offering the prayer of recollection to her readers with the understanding—as laid out insistently in *The Way of Perfection*—that the practice of recollection, with its hope of providing the gateway to true contemplation, requires three essential virtues (humility, detachment, and charity) that are the tools of the graced work of conversion. Without the larger picture, Teresa's teaching on prayer would be taken out of context. The same can be said for Cassian, the Jesus Prayer, and *The Cloud*. All of them offer a practice that should be reclaimed today, but lifting that teaching out of its foundational context—without explicitly explaining why the spiritual wisdom of centuries concerning prior ascetical preparation has

32. Keating, *Open Mind*, 66.

33. Rosemary Haughton, *The Transformation of Man: A Study of Conversion and Community* (Springfield, Ill.: Templegate, 1980).

become obsolete—seems untrue to the sources being cited. It may be that Keating and others mean to claim that, in fact, modern psychology, philosophy, and social sciences have shown that ascetical preparation is largely unnecessary. If so, it is a claim that would need a far broader theological analysis—as the following points may suggest.

Sin and Christ as Savior

Teresa of Jesus, especially in the *Life*, might be accused of an overemphasis on sin. Certainly she lived in a different time and religious culture, with a more acute awareness of human sinfulness. But, although she regularly refers to her own wretchedness ("*miserias*"—her miserable condition or sin), she is intentionally setting up a contrast with the overarching, undeserved mercy ("*misericordia*") of God. In *The Interior Castle*, she balances the recognition of the great beauty and dignity of the human person created in the image of God (IC 1.1) with the ugly reality of sin that mars that beauty (IC 1.2). In the end, her view of the human person is fundamentally balanced and positive, though she is keenly aware of the reality of sin in herself and in humanity in general.

It is the recognition of sin and its pervasiveness and power in human life that grounds the traditional sense of the need for conversion in the Christian life. We need purgation and ascetical struggle as a foundation for contemplative prayer, because sin is a wound and a power in us that prevents us from being open, receptive, and docile to the presence and inflow of God. And it is a recognition of sin and our unaided inability to free ourselves of it that likely helps to explain Teresa's focus on Christ in his humanity. If there is no sin, humanity doesn't need a savior. It would only need a teacher, a guide, or a model. But, for Teresa, Christ in his humanity is the accessible human face of God's merciful love and the divine friend who—precisely in his humanity—has saved us from the power of death and sin.

Neither Main nor Keating are trying to develop an entire systematic theology, nor are they completely inattentive to the reality of sin. But their tendency seems to be to view sin in almost exclusively psychological terms.[34] What has been traditionally understood as sin is understood as a "hindrance"[35] or as the "ripe fruit of the emotional programs for happiness."[36] The answer, then, is the need for a "divine psychotherapist."[37] But it is one's perspective on sin that importantly helps to form our sense of who Christ is, what he did for us, and what role he seeks to play in the Christian life. How we view sin plays an important part in how we understand the central Christian belief in the paschal mystery of the death and resurrection of Jesus.[38] An overly psychological view of sin—overcome as the fruit of the emotional healing brought about through prayer—seems consistent with a downplaying of the necessity of prior ascetical preparation and a strong sense of a necessary process of growth in prayer and relationship with Christ, friend and Savior.

For John Main, Christ seems especially to be the risen, almost cosmic Christ who now dwells fully within the life and love of the Triune God. Authentic prayer is always our participation

---

34. Ó Madagáin, in his sympathetic review of Centering Prayer, notes the problem of its discussion and overly psychological interpretation of sin, but he does not suggest how it might be resolved: *Centering Prayer and Healing*, 30–33, 282.

35. "The hindrances that we could describe as the seven deadly sins. . ." Laurence Freeman, Talks to the Monks of Gethsemane Abbey, *Meditatio* (Talks Series D 2005, October–December): 12.

36. Keating, *Invitation to Love*, 31.

37. Keating, *Intimacy with God*, 42; *Open Mind, 95; Invitation to Love*, 32–33.

38. Feldmeier, "Centering Prayer Movement," 238.

through Christ in the Trinitarian mutuality. This perspective is not foreign or contrary to Teresa's view, but, for her, Christ in his humanity and his redeeming work is the divine friend with whom we enter into the quiet intimate sharing of recollection. Like Main, Keating encourages meditation on the Scriptures and the practice of *lectio divina* alongside the practice of Centering Prayer. Taking up this recommendation would keep one in touch with the Jesus of the Synoptic Gospels. But, again, when it comes to speak of the practice of Centering Prayer itself, it is not clear what role Christ plays.

It is true that Teresa of Ávila knew nothing of modern psychology, though this is not to say that she did not possess a keen psychological sense and deep insight into our humanity. She could not have conceived of the fruit of prayer in explicitly psychological terms as a process of emotional and deep psychological healing. But she knew that deep prayer yielded deeper self-knowledge, including recognition of the roots of sin deep within us. Today, it can hardly be denied that our sin is often rooted in deep psychological wounds in need of healing. The desert tradition, represented by the writings of Evagrius Ponticus and John Cassian, spoke of afflictive thoughts that often become the root of our sins—which Keating seems to speak of as "afflictive emotions."[39] But the necessary response to sin is not just psychological, emotional healing. Sin is a matter of choices made, choices that form us into the persons that we are, and the fundamental directions we have taken in life. Psychological healing is critical to uncovering and loosening the deep roots of sin—necessary but not sufficient. Also necessary are the positive—sometimes difficult and habitual—choices that can undo and weaken the negative aspects of what we have

---

39. Keating, *Invitation to Love*, 23–30.

made ourselves to be. This is the point that Teresa is making when she speaks of the need for a habit of practical love of others, often expressed in simple other-directed acts at cost to self, as a virtue essential to the reception of contemplative graces. John of the Cross makes a similar point when he speaks of the *active* night of spirit in which we must claim the theological virtue of love, given to us by God in grace, in order to purify ourselves through selfless acts of love. We are vessels made for the inflow of God—whether we conceive that influx as from outside us or from deep within us. But we are vessels that have and will make choices that determine whether we are apt, ready, spacious, and ultimately empty to receive. Psychological insight and healing as the fruit of deep prayer, together with the graced work of conversion, are all necessary elements of preparing the human vessel to receive the special outpouring of divine life in true contemplative prayer.

Conclusion

A review of two major contemporary forms of contemplative practice has sought to clarify what Teresa of Jesus means when she speaks of what can be called acquired recollection. Understanding the kind of prayer envisioned by contemporary authors can help to clarify the "manner" of prayer that Teresa addresses in *The Way of Perfection*. As Ernest Larkin has concluded, the practices themselves seem essentially the same, seeking a receptive awareness of God who dwells in the deepest center of the human person. Teresa, too, understood the practice of acquired recollection as setting the stage for the reception of the yet deeper prayer of true contemplation. Such prayer will bear fruit in deeper knowledge of self, inner liberation, and growth in authentic Christian living.

But the larger picture of Teresa's teaching on recollection suggests some important areas of divergence with Centering Prayer and Christian Meditation. The primary purpose of presenting these differences has not been to suggest a foundational critique of these practices in themselves. By placing Teresa's teaching in dialogue with other practices, we have tried to clarify her distinct emphases but also to suggest some ways in which her teaching might serve as a challenge to present-day presentations of contemplative practice: As forms of Christian prayer for disciples of Christ, what is the place of Jesus Christ in contemplative practice? What is the place of traditional meditation on the Word of God and on the Christian mysteries, the life of personal devotion, and participation in the sacraments and in the life of church? Are such practices merely supportive of contemplative practice or are they essential to it? What is the place of ongoing conversion, the graced effort to overcome the roots of sin, and growth in virtue, not only as a fruit of prayer but as its necessary foundation? Anyone who claims similarities or support from the teaching of Teresa of Jesus's writings on prayer must confront such questions. She is a preeminent teacher of prayer in the long Christian tradition, not only for her explicit teaching on prayer itself, but also because she places prayer on a solid foundation and in a wider context. Her writings are true Christian classics for good reason, and any reflection on contemporary Christian prayer can benefit from careful dialogue with what she teaches.

6

Trials and Helps

Teresa of Jesus had profound mystical experiences and wrote high mystical doctrine, and yet her feet were firmly planted on earth. She was human, and she struggled to grow in prayer for many years. Most people who have tried to develop a habit of prayer over time can identify with Teresa's description of her own experience:

> And very often, for some years, I was more anxious that the hour I had determined to spend in prayer be over than I was to remain there, and more anxious to listen for the striking of the clock than to attend to other good things. And I don't know what heavy penance could have come to mind that frequently I would not have gladly undertaken rather than recollect myself in the practice of prayer. It is certain that so unbearable was the force used by the devil, or coming from my wretched habits, to prevent me from going to prayer, and so unbearable the sadness I felt on entering the oratory, that I had to muster up all my courage (and they say I have no small amount of that, and it is observed that God has given me more than women usually have, but I have made poor use of it) in order to force myself; and in the end the Lord helped me. After I had made this effort, I found myself left with greater quiet and delight than sometimes when I had the desire to pray. (L 8.7)

Teresa writes from her own experience of long and difficult efforts to grow in prayer. Although she is not usually writing for those beginning in prayer, she has practical counsel about both trials and helps to offer people at every stage of prayer. In the next chapter, we will look separately at the trial of feeling discouragement about our prayer and at its remedy: a "very determined determination" that challenges us to never give up on prayer.

Trials in Prayer

Distractions

Our minds, it seems, are always busy. Perhaps this fact is no more obvious to us than when we sit down for quiet prayer. Like Teresa, we may find that a book can help us to stay attentive and focused. But when we try just to remain quiet and still, attentive to the divine presence, it can seem like our minds never stop, pulling us out of our inner silence and quiet awareness. Sometimes our thoughts keep returning to some important business, but often it seems that what is passing through our minds is nothing more than nonsensical jibber-jabber, random thoughts and memories that seem to have no connection whatsoever to our earlier activities, immediate plans, and certainly not to our prayer. We know that sometimes we are the cause of our own distractions: we rush into prayer from our regular activities without taking time to settle down, to take some deep breaths, and perhaps to take up a prayer word or gaze at a holy image. Sometimes our life in general is too busy and our attention too regularly dissipated. But often enough, we can be afflicted with distractions even after our best efforts.

Distractions were part of Teresa's experience in the years that she faithfully struggled with her prayer. She consulted widely to try to understand and to find a way to overcome her own distractions in prayer—only to discover that, unless and until God absorbs or suspends our consciousness in very deep prayer, distractions are a fact of life that must be accepted even in a mature life of prayer. In a letter of counsel to a priest, she repeats what a confessor had explained to her: "In regard to being distracted during the recitation of the divine office, although I am perhaps much at fault, I like to think it is due to a weakness of the head. And you should think the same, for the Lord knows well that when we pray we would like to pray very well. Today I confessed this to Padre Maestro Fray Domingo, and he told me not to pay attention to it, and I beg of you the same, for I consider it an incurable evil" (Ltr 409.2).

The best response to distractions, Teresa came to understand, is just to endure them and keep going: "If they come, as they do, from one of the many miseries inherited through the sin of Adam, let us be patient and endure them for the love of God" (IC 4.1.11). Distractions are not necessarily a sign of "bad" prayer and certainly not a reason to give up on prayer:

> These miseries will not afflict or assail everyone as much as they did me for many years because of my wretchedness. . . . And since the experience was something so painful for me, I think perhaps that it will be so for you too. And I so often speak of it here and there that I might sometime succeed in explaining to you that it is an unavoidable thing and should not be a disturbance or affliction for you but that we must let the millclapper [the mind] go clacking on, and must continue grinding our flour and not fail to work with the will and the intellect. (IC 4.1.13)

"Good" prayer is not necessarily prayer without distractions: "Don't think the matter lies in thinking of nothing else, and that if you become a little distracted all is lost" (IC 4.1.7).

Carmelite author Vilma Seelaus notes that distractions can be a window into a deeper self-knowledge, so highly valued by Teresa.[1] When engaged in some form of active prayer, it can be helpful to pause and ponder our passing thoughts as they may reveal our real desires, deeper attachments, or areas for conversion. But in general—and certainly when we are trying to develop a habit of quiet recollection—during the time of prayer, the best response is not to engage or dwell on our distractions but rather to accept their nearly inevitable presence and let them pass. But later, outside the time of prayer, our distractions can give us insight into ourselves. Proponents of Centering Prayer in particular note that a regular time of quiet awareness can release deeply held inner emotions that must simply be accepted in the time of prayer but can sometimes be profitably considered and even discussed outside of prayer.

For a time, the presence of distractions during her practice of quiet prayer made Teresa doubt that her prayer was genuine. How could she be authentically in deep prayer if she found her mind going in different directions? Ultimately, she came to understand that there is a distinction between what she calls the "mind" (or "imagination") and the "intellect": "A little more than four years ago I came to understand through experience that the mind (or imagination, to put it more clearly) is not the intellect. I asked a learned man and he told me that this was so; which brought me no small consolation" (IC 4.1.8).[2] Essentially,

---

1. Vilma Seelaus, *Distractions in Prayer: Blessing or Curse? St. Teresa of Avila's Teachings in* The Interior Castle (Staten Island, N.Y.: St. Paul's, 2005), 37–40.

2. Teresa is not seeking scholastic precision in her use of the terms *intellect, mind, imagination,* and *memory*. In fact, her use of these words in the course of her writings is not entirely consistent.

she is saying that there can be a part of ourselves that is genuinely resting deeply in the presence of God even while our imagination is spitting out random memories, thoughts, images, and even emotions:

> Just as we cannot stop the movement of the heavens, but they proceed in rapid motion, so neither can we stop our mind; and then the faculties of the soul go with it, and we think we are lost and have wasted the time spent before God. But the soul is perhaps completely joined with Him in the dwelling places very close to the center while the mind is on the outskirts of the castle suffering from a thousand wild and poisonous beasts, and meriting by this suffering. As a result we should not be disturbed; nor should we abandon prayer, which is what the devil wants us to do. (IC 4.1.9)

In another place, Teresa speaks of the memory—from which the imagination draws its images and thus our distractions in prayer. Sometimes, both imagination and memory must simply be left to carry on their activities even in the time of quiet prayer: "The only remedy I have found, after having tired myself out for many years, is the one I mentioned in speaking of the prayer of quiet: to pay no more attention to the memory than one would to a madman—leave it go its way, for only God can stop it" (L 17.7).

It is significant that Teresa addresses this issue in the fourth dwelling places of *The Interior Castle*—that is, when she is addressing the transition from active recollection and the beginnings of true contemplative prayer. It is important to note that true recollection, acquired or infused, can coincide with the presence of distractions. (This point is emphasized in contemporary discussions of contemplative practice.) In later, deeper places of prayer, God may choose to "suspend the intellect"—that is, absorb the person's consciousness for a time during prayer—but we must not try to turn off our thinking or make the mind a blank, as if we could. The time may come when God suspends the intellect, but we must not try to make it happen: "the intellect ceases to work because God suspends it, as I shall explain afterward if I know how and He gives me His help to do so. Taking it upon oneself to stop and suspend thought is what I mean should not be done" (L 12.5; see also IC 4.3.7).

Dryness

Anyone who has tried to practice prayer for any length of time knows the experience of dryness or aridity in prayer. Teresa of Jesus was no exception, and because of her own experience of aridity, she has a good deal of counsel to offer about how to respond. It is normal to want good feelings, the felt presence of God, or consolations in our times of prayer. And such things, especially as we are beginning and forming a habit of prayer, can be a real blessing. But we learn very quickly that we cannot depend on having such good feelings in prayer. If our decision to keep praying depended on feeling good in prayer, no one would be faithful to prayer—except perhaps in an occasional or sporadic way. Prayer is time and attention given to our divine friend, whatever our personal experience of any particular period of prayer: "But this little bit of time that we resolve to give Him. . . . let us be wholly determined never to take it back from Him, neither because of trials on this account, nor because of contradictions, nor because of dryness. *I should consider the time of prayer as not belonging to me and think that He can ask it of me in justice when I do not want to give it wholly to Him*" (W 23.2, emphasis added).

To engage in prayer in order to receive or with the expectation of receiving consolations in prayer is "mercenary": "Prize being able to help God carry the cross and don't be clinging to delights, for it is the trait of mercenary soldiers to want their daily pay at once. Serve without charge, as the grandees do the king" (Ltr 449.4).

As we have seen, in the *Life*, Teresa uses the image of the four ways of watering a garden to describe growth in prayer. The first way, she writes, is like watering a garden by manually drawing water from a well and carrying the water by bucket. Beginners in prayer must simply expect that it will take work. Dryness is to be expected. In itself, it is no reason to give up on prayer. Rather, one should remember that one is praying as a service to God and as a demonstration of love.

> But what will they do here who see that after many days there is nothing but dryness, distaste, vapidness, and very little desire to come to draw water? So little is the desire to do this that if they don't recall that doing so serves and gives pleasure to the Lord of the garden, and if they aren't careful to preserve the merits acquired in this service (and even what they hope to gain from the tedious work of often letting the pail down into the well and pulling it back up without any water), they will abandon everything. It will frequently happen to them that they will even be unable to lift their arms for this work and unable to get a good thought. This discursive work with the intellect is what is meant by fetching water from the well.
>
> These labors take their toll. Being myself one who endured them for many years (for when I got a drop of water from this sacred well I thought God was granting me a favor), I know that they are extraordinary. It seems to me more courage is necessary for them than for many other labors of this world. But I have seen clearly that God does not leave one, even in his life, without a large reward; because it is certainly

> true that one of those hours in which the Lord afterward bestowed on me a taste of Himself repaid, it seems to me, all the anguish I suffered in persevering for a long time in prayer. (L 11.10–11)

The "reward" for remaining faithful to dry prayer, while not consciously experienced during the time of prayer, will be manifest later, whether in prayer or in one's broader life.

Beginning a regular habit of prayer with the expectation of regular consolations in prayer is to begin on a very shaky foundation: "Souls shouldn't be thinking about consolations at this beginning stage. It would be a very poor way to start building so precious and great an edifice. If the foundation is on sand, the whole building will fall to the ground" (IC 2.1.7). To begin prayer with the expectation of consolations sets a person up for the abandonment of prayer: "For there are many who begin, yet they never reach the end. I believe this is due mainly to a failure to embrace the cross from the beginning; thinking they are doing nothing, they become afflicted" (L 11.15).

Those who can remain faithful to prayer even in times of aridity have already advanced in the authentic life of prayer:

> It should be carefully noted—and I say this because I know it through experience—that that the soul that begins to walk along this path of mental prayer with determination and that can succeed in paying little attention to whether this delight and tenderness is lacking or whether the Lord gives it (or to whether it has much consolation or no consolation) has traveled a great part of the way. However much it stumbles, it should not fear that it will turn back, because the building has been started on a solid foundation. This is true because the love of God does not consist in tears or in this delight and tenderness, which for the greater part we desire and find

> consolation in; but it consists in serving with justice and fortitude of soul and in humility. (L 11.13)

As Teresa writes to one of her nuns: "As for the dryness, it seems to me that the Lord is now treating you as one who is strong. He wants to try you in order to know the love you have for him, whether it is present in dryness as well as in spiritual delights. Take it as a very great favor from God. Don't let it cause you any grief, for perfection does not consist in delight but in the virtues. When you least expect, devotion will return" (Ltr 351.2). Aridity in prayer, then, can be a sign of our firm commitment to give our time and attention to God, no matter how we experience it. And fidelity even in dry prayer strengthens a habit of prayer.

By praying faithfully through the dryness, the person is being invited, in some small way, to carry the cross with Christ and demonstrating that he or she does not come to prayer for some merely superficial feeling or passing benefit: "It is an important matter for beginners in prayer to start off by becoming detached from every kind of satisfaction and to enter the path solely with the determination to help Christ carry the cross like good cavaliers, who desire to serve their king at no salary since their salary is certain" (L 15.11). Just as Jesus was denied consolations on his cross, so too must we not abandon him by turning from prayer because it fails to give us consolations: We must "not allow ourselves to be seekers of spiritual consolations. Thus, embracing the cross, come what may, is an important thing. This Lord was deprived of every consolation; they left Him alone in His trials. Let us not abandon Him" (L 22.10; see also IC 2.1.7). Following the image of prayer as different ways of watering a garden, Teresa writes:

> But, as I am saying, what will the gardener do here? He will rejoice and be consoled and consider it the greatest favor to be able to work in the garden of so great an Emperor! Since

> he knows that this pleases the Lord and his intention must be not to please himself but to please the Lord, he gives the Lord much praise. For the Master has confidence in the gardener because He sees that without any pay he is so very careful about what he was told to do. This gardener helps Christ carry the cross and reflects that the Lord lived with it all during His life. He doesn't desire the Lord's kingdom here below or ever abandon prayer. And so he is determined, even though this dryness may last for his whole life, not to let Christ fall with the cross. The time will come when the Lord will repay him all at once. He doesn't fear that the labor is being wasted. He is serving a good Master whose eyes are upon him. (L 11.10)

The experience of arid prayer can be an encounter with the Cross of Jesus, and our effort to pray nonetheless can be an instrument of our deeper surrender to God's will in our lives.

Fidelity to prayer in the face of dryness can promote a true poverty of spirit in which one accepts the will of God: "I fear that it [the soul] will never attain true poverty of spirit, which means being at rest in labors and dryness and not seeking consolation or comfort in prayer—for earthly consolation has already been abandoned—but seeking consolation in trials for love of Him who always lived in the midst of them" (L 22.11). Further, the calm acceptance of aridity in prayer can teach us humility:

> I am of the opinion that to some in the beginning and to others afterward the Lord often desires to give these torments and the many other temptations that occur in order to try His lovers and know whether they will be able to drink the chalice and help Him carry the cross before He lays great treasures within them. I believe His Majesty desires to bring us along this way for our own good so that we may understand well

> what little we amount to. The favors that come afterward are of such great worth that He desires first that before He gives them to us we see by experience our own worthlessness so that what happened to Lucifer will not happen to us. (L 10.11)

Poverty of spirit and humility are essential characteristics of the mature Christian life, and they can be learned and practiced in fidelity to prayer in the face of aridity.

Referring to the image of prayer as drawing water from a well, Teresa teaches that, if during the time of prayer, it feels that there is refreshing water to be drawn from the well, then so be it. But if the well seems dry, that experience of prayer must simply be accepted:

> So I return to the advice—and even if I repeat it many times this doesn't matter—that it is very important that no one be distressed or afflicted over dryness or noisy and distracting thoughts. If people wish to gain freedom of spirit and not be always troubled, let them begin by not being frightened by the cross, and they will see how the Lord also helps them carry it and they will gain satisfaction and profit from everything. For, clearly, if the well is dry, we cannot put water into it. True, we must not become neglectful; when there is water we should draw it out because then the Lord desires to multiply the virtues by this means. (L 11.17)

We must not seek consolations—good feelings in prayer—as an end, nor view them as essential to our prayer, "measure" our prayer by their presence or absence, nor complain to God about aridity in prayer. Teresa believes strongly that expecting consolation in prayer—as if God owed us a reward for our effort—shows a lack of humility: "Oh, humility, humility! I don't know what kind of temptation I'm undergoing in this matter that I cannot help but think that anyone who makes such an issue of this dryness is a little lacking in humility" (IC 3.1.7). Fidelity to dry prayer—the prayer that God seems to want for us at any particular time—can help us to grow in that deeper spirit of humility which is necessary to be open to receive the gift of contemplation: "Well, I say that it is dangerous to count the number of years in which you have practiced prayer; even though humility may be present, I think there can remain a kind of feeling that you deserve something for the service. I don't mean that you don't gain merit and that you will not be well paid. But I consider it certain that spiritual persons who think that they deserve these delights of spirit for the many years they have practiced prayer will not ascend to the summit of the spiritual life" (L 39.15).

Teresa has strong words for people who should know better:

> But when I see servants of God, men of prominence, learning, and high intelligence make so much fuss because God doesn't give them devotion, it annoys me to hear them. I do not mean that they shouldn't accept it if God gives it, and esteem it, because then His Majesty sees that this is appropriate. But when they don't have devotion, they shouldn't weary themselves. They should understand that since His Majesty doesn't give it, it isn't necessary; and they should be masters of themselves. They should believe that their desire for consolation is a fault. I have experienced and seen this. They should believe it denotes imperfection together with a lack of freedom of spirit and the courage to accomplish something. (L 11.14)

In the end, the best prayer is the prayer that God chooses to give—whatever our experience of it: "I would not want any other prayer than that which makes the virtues grow in me. If it should be accompanied by great temptations, dryness, and trials leaving me with greater humility, I would consider it good prayer. That prayer is the best prayer that pleases God the most. It shouldn't be thought that he who suffers isn't praying, for he is offering this to God. And often he is praying much more than the one who is breaking his head in solitude, thinking that if he has squeezed out some tears he is thereby praying" (Ltr 136.5).

In sum, Teresa tells us that distractions and dryness in prayer should not concern us. They are largely out of our control. They are not an obstacle or an impediment to growth in prayer. In fact, when accepted as what seems to be the divine will for our prayer during a particular period, they can serve to purify our prayer of seeking after superficial rewards in our prayer. They can teach us humility, to embrace the cross, and to grow in an authentic poverty of spirit. Thus, rather than hindering our prayer, they can be a tool for the deepening and maturing of our prayer: "It should be carefully noted—and I say this because I know it through experience—that the soul that begins to walk along this path of mental prayer with determination and that can succeed in paying little attention to whether this delight and tenderness is lacking or whether the Lord gives it (or to whether it has much consolation or no consolation) has traveled a great part of the way" (L 11.13).

Still, as prayer develops, infused prayer can bring a deeper experience that is somewhat akin to consolations. Describing the transition from acquired to infused prayer in the fourth dwelling places of *The Interior Castle*, Teresa makes a distinction between consolations (*contentos*) and spiritual delights (*gustos*) (IC 4.1). Consolations (what we have been addressing in the paragraphs above) are not unlike the pleasurable experiences that we can have in life outside of prayer: satisfactions, warmth, joy, pleasure. Their origin is largely human, though "God in the end does have a hand in them" (IC 4.1.4). They are transient; they come and go. These can be good in themselves; they can keep us faithful to prayer and entice us to move forward; but they remain superficial and not to be expected nor understood as at all necessary. The spiritual delights, on the other hand, are infused by God. They are experienced by inner, spiritual senses, though they can be experienced in our external senses as kind of an overflow from deeper encounter with God. Their principal effect is a kind of inner expansion—an expansion of the heart—to receive the deeper intimate sharing with the divine friend.

Busyness

Perhaps it is easy to imagine that St. Teresa was a solitary mystic who spent her whole life in quiet contemplation in a tranquil, cloistered monastery. But her life and her letters reveal otherwise. She was a busy woman—certainly making time for her prayer, as she could, but also founding and overseeing monasteries of her reform, traveling between those communities on bad roads in uncomfortable means of transport, and maintaining a very large correspondence with many people. She was a contemplative nun, but this did not mean that she did not have frequent and important dealings with ecclesiastical authorities, donors, people of commerce, and friars and nuns. She knew what it meant to be busy. And she heard from the prioresses of Discalced monasteries as well as from others about their seeming endless activities. If we might sometimes complain about feeling too busy to pray or about the difficulty of finding time to pray, Teresa would be most sympathetic.

Teresa recognized that there can be times or periods of our lives when the authentic demands of our life and ministry, works of obedience (for religious, consecrated persons), and the requirements of loving attention to others can legitimately demand our time—even time that we had planned or hoped to devote to prayer. In *The Book of Her Foundations*, Teresa offers a narrative of the busy and sometimes complicated work of establishing the monasteries of her reform. It is perhaps fitting that, in the course of that narrative, in the fifth chapter, she should offer counsel about prayer to unavoidably busy people:

> There was a person to whom I spoke a few days ago who for about fifteen years was kept so busy through obedience with work in occupations and government that in all those years he didn't remember having had one day for himself, although he tried the best he could to keep a pure conscience and have some periods each day for prayer. His soul in its inclination is one of the most obedient I have seen, and so he communicates this spirit of obedience to all those with whom he deals. The Lord has repaid him well; for he has found that he has, without knowing how, that same precious and desirable liberty of spirit that the perfect have. In it, they find all the happiness that could be wanted in this life, for in desiring nothing they possess all. Nothing on earth do they fear or desire, neither do trials disturb them, nor do consolations move them. In sum, nothing can take away their peace because these souls depend only on God. . . . This is not the only person, for I have known others of the same sort, whom I had not seen for some, or many, years. In asking them about how they had spent these years, I learned that the years were all spent in the fulfillment of the duties of obedience and charity. On the other hand, I saw such improvement in spiritual things that I was amazed. Well, come now, my daughters, don't be sad when obedience draws you to involvement in exterior matters. Know that if it is in the kitchen, the Lord walks among the pots and pans helping you both interiorly and exteriorly. (F 5.7–8)

Sometimes, when unavoidably busy in the work required of our state in life, we must adjust our prayer time and expectations ("adjust," not eliminate)—confident, Teresa assures us, that our progress in prayer will not necessarily be impeded.

What is ultimately important is not the amount of time spent in prayer and solitude but rather conformity with what God wills for us: "And let souls believe me that it is not the length of time spent in prayer that benefits one; when the time is spent as well in good works, it is a help in preparing the soul for the enkindling of love. The soul may thereby be better prepared in a very short time than through many hours of reflection" (F 5.17). God has called each of us to our vocations in life, with their legitimate demands on our time. Attending to those duties, it seemed to Teresa, was simply doing God's will, and this, in itself, would bring the deeper growth in relationship with God than one might have hoped to gain from time spent in prayer: "Observe, sisters, whether leaving the pleasure of solitude is not well repaid. I tell you that it is not because of a lack of solitude that you will fail to dispose yourselves to reach this true union that was mentioned, that is, to make your will one with God's. This is the union that I desire and would want for all of you, and not some absorptions, however delightful they may be, that have been given the name 'union'" (F 5.13).

Teresa advises her readers not to be upset or worried about legitimate busyness, but she urges us to be self-critical about whether or not the activity is really necessary: "Note that I am always presupposing that these things are done out of obedience or charity. For if these latter are not factors, I always repeat that solitude is better, and even that we must desire it. We must desire solitude even when involved in the things I'm speaking of; indeed, this desire is continually present in souls that truly love God" (F 5.15). While recognizing that important tasks must sometimes draw us away from prayer, Teresa cautions against making it a habit (See Ltr 217).

Grounded in a definition of prayer that involves "taking time frequently to be alone with him who we know loves us," Teresa presupposed that our overarching concern is deepening our relationship with our divine friend, whether in prayer or in the activity that flows from our vocation in life. She also presupposed that we are always pursuing a deeper self-knowledge, which necessarily includes the ability to be self-critical about our motives and thus of the real "need" to choose activity over prayer. Teresa recommends finding a spiritual director who is discerning—that is, who can help us to discern God's will and the Spirit's movements in our lives. Spiritual friends and guides can assist us in discerning if busyness that keeps us from prayer is really a surrender to God's will for us at particular times in our lives or if, on the other hand, we are being moved by other needs or motives.

Helps to Prayer

Ever the good teacher, Teresa of Jesus offers her readers ideas, drawn from her own experience, for practices that can help them to remain faithful to and focused in prayer. Ultimately, individuals must find what works for them during different periods of their own prayer journey, but she suggests the use of books, images, and nature, as well as the support and guidance offered by a praying community, spiritual friends, and a spiritual director.

The Value of Having a Book

Teresa of Jesus, from her childhood, was an avid reader. As her own spiritual life deepened, together with wide consultation with theologians, she depended on books to help her to gain a vocabulary and categories to understand her experience. Her reading gave her access to the spiritual wisdom of the past, keeping her interpretation of her own experience from passing beyond the pale of sound Christian doctrine. In her own monasteries of the Carmelite reform, she wanted the nuns to be literate and to have access to good books (C 8). Her preference for reading the gospels (whether directly or through the many books of the time that excerpted or summarized gospel texts) is further evidence of her central focus on Christ: "I have always been fond of the words of the Gospels [that have come from that most sacred mouth in the way they were said] and found more recollection in them than in very cleverly written books. I especially had no desire to read these books if the author was not well approved" (W 21.3).

But beyond gaining intellectual insights, reading helped her to fend off distractions and deal with times of dryness as she tried to remain faithful to her prayer. Finding herself unable to engage in traditional discursive meditation, she reports that, for many years, she depended on having a book in order at least to begin her period of prayer. Reading often became an easier path to arriving at a spirit of recollection:

> Now it seems to me that it was the Lord's providence that I not find anyone to instruct me, for, on account of my being unable as I say to reflect discursively, it would have been impossible, I think, to have persevered for the eighteen years I suffered this trial, and in that great dryness. *In all those years, except for the time after Communion, I never dared to begin prayer without a book.* For my soul was as fearful of being without it during prayer as it would have been should it have had to battle with a lot of people. *With this recourse, which was like a partner or a shield by which to*

> *sustain the blows of many thoughts, I went about consoled.* For the dryness was not usually felt, but it was always felt when I was without a book. Then my soul was thrown into confusion and my thoughts ran wild. *With a book I began to collect them, and my soul was drawn to recollection. And many times just opening the book was enough*; at other times I read a little, and at others a great deal, according to the favor the Lord granted me" (L 4.9, emphasis added; see also W 17.3; 26.10)

Reading a book, by promoting attentiveness and focus, can serve as a doorway to wordless, imageless prayer.

Reading is important, but it is not a replacement for personal engagement and communion with Christ. A book can be a useful tool and help to prayer, but it is not a replacement for the act and relationship that is prayer—nor for the deeper knowledge that comes, not from books alone, but from communion with Christ. When the Inquisition had banned almost all vernacular books on contemplative prayer, Christ promised Teresa that he would himself be the true book:

> The Lord said to me: "Don't be sad, for I shall give you a living book." I was unable to understand why this was said to me, since I had not yet experienced any visions. Afterward, within only a few days, I understood very clearly, because I received so much to think about and such recollection in the presence of what I saw, and the Lord showed so much love for me by teaching me in many ways, that I had very little or almost no need for books. His Majesty had become the true book in which I saw the truths. (L 26.5)

A good book can lead us into deep prayer, but it cannot become a substitute for the intimate sharing of prayer.

A Walk in Nature

Like many people, Teresa often it found it helpful to her prayer to attend to nature: "It helped me also to look at fields, or water, or flowers. In these things I found a remembrance of the Creator" (L 9.5). For many of us, sitting or walking quietly in nature can bring calm and focus. As Teresa says, it can be a pathway to rest quietly and attentively in the Creator of the natural beauty that is a reflection of the Divine.

An Image of Christ

There is good reason that many people of faith possess and wear images of Christ and that Christian art throughout the centuries has been used to raise the hearts and minds of people of prayer to God. St. Teresa, too, found such art helpful to her own prayer and recommended its use to others. Of herself, she says that she had trouble using the imagination in prayer: "This was the reason I liked images so much" (L 9.6). She writes, as she explains the prayer of recollection, that an image of Christ can help to draw a person into a spirit of quiet: "What you can do as a help in this matter is try to carry about an image or painting of this Lord that is to your liking, not so as to carry it about on your heart and never look at it but so as to speak often with Him; for He will inspire you with what to say. Since you speak with other persons, why must words fail you more when you speak with God?" (W 26.9).

For Teresa, Christ is the true friend. Since we cannot see him in the flesh, an image can draw our attention to him. Still, the image of Christ is meant to draw us into an encounter with him which is deeper than our imagination. Such images are a tool to arrive at "representing" Christ which, as we have seen, involves being attentive and open to the divine presence without depending on any particular image. A painting, a holy card, or an icon is meant to be a doorway to a deeper communion with Christ. Speaking specifically of post-Communion prayer, she writes:

> If you have to pray to Him by looking at His picture, it would seem to me foolish. You would be leaving the Person Himself in order to look at a picture of Him. Wouldn't it be silly if a person we love very much and of whom we have a portrait came to see us and we stopped speaking with him so as to carry on a conversation with the portrait? Do you want to know when it is very good to have a picture of Christ and when it is a thing in which I find much delight? When He himself is absent, or when by means of a great dryness He wants to make us feel He is absent. It is then a wonderful comfort to see an image of One whom we have so much reason to love. (W 34.11)

Like a good book, an image of Christ can help to lead us into prayer, but it remains merely an instrument or a doorway.

Supportive Friends and Community

Teresa of Jesus wrote especially for her own nuns and at the direction of her confessors (all of whom were themselves professed religious). Therefore, even as she focuses her attention on personal prayer and on each Christian's personal friendship with Christ, she is presuming a life of common prayer and the support of a praying community. Growth in faith and in prayer is helped by the example and support of friends and communities of faith and prayer:

> I would counsel those who practice prayer to seek, at least in the beginning, friendship and association with other persons

> having the same interest. This is something most important even though the association may be only to help one another with prayers. The more of these prayers there are, the greater the gain. Since friends are sought out for conversations and human attachments, even though these latter may not be good, so as to relax and better enjoy telling about vain pleasures, I don't know why it is not permitted that persons beginning truly to love and to serve God talk with some others about their joys and trials, which all who practice prayer undergo. . . . I believe that they who discuss these joys and trials for the sake of this friendship with God will benefit themselves and those who hear them, and they will come away instructed; even without understanding how, they will have instructed their friends. (L 7.20; see also L 23.4)

Spiritual friendship is important and useful, not only in the beginning. Especially as one's prayer deepens, it can be helpful to speak with people whose own prayer is more mature: "It's a wonderful thing for a person to talk to those who speak about this interior castle, to draw near not only to those seen to be in these rooms where he is but to those known to have entered the ones closer to the center. Conversation with these latter will be a great help to him, and he can converse so much with them that they will bring him to where they are." (IC 2.1.6)[3] Our personal friendship with Christ is not individualistic or closed. We are on a journey together and must often count on the support and help of others.

3. Elsewhere, Teresa cautions against allowing the nuns to speak too freely with one another about their prayer (Ltr 6.3). Perhaps she feared unhelpful comparisons or posturing.

Spiritual Direction

Teresa encourages people of prayer to seek out a good spiritual director to provide guidance, support, and sometimes cautions about the life of prayer and Christian living. She herself reports that she was both helped and hindered by the different directors that she had sought out in her own life. Her own experience led her to recommend that potential directors should be learned, experienced, and discerning—that is, who knew the wisdom of the spiritual tradition and Scriptures, who were mature in their own spiritual life, and who could help the person discern the Spirit's movements at the particular moments in the person's life (L 13.16).[4]

Teresa reports that she felt the lack of a good spiritual director especially as she tried to grow in more stable and deeper prayer. The gift of a book on the prayer of recollection was extremely helpful to her, but she believed that lack of a reliable spiritual guide hindered her from putting into practice the book's lessons:[5]

> I was very happy with this book and resolved to follow that path with all my strength. Since the Lord had already given me the gift of tears and I enjoyed reading, I began to take time out for solitude, to confess frequently, and to follow that path, taking the book for my master. For during the twenty years after this period of which I am speaking, I did not find a

4. For a lengthier study of Teresa's advice about spiritual direction, see my *Learned, Experienced, and Discerning: St. Teresa of Avila and St. John of the Cross on Spiritual Direction* (Collegeville, Minn.: Liturgical Press, 2020).

5. In sixteenth-century Spain, only priests would give regular spiritual counsel. For cloistered nuns, what we would today call spiritual direction would have occurred most often when a priest came to hear the nuns' confession, but the direction would generally be provided outside of the sacrament. Teresa therefore typically refers to directors as "confessors." Reflecting her desire for "learned" guides, she also refers to them as (spiritual) "masters."

> master, I mean a confessor, who understood me, even though I looked for one. This hurt me so much that I often turned back and was even completely lost, for a master would have helped me flee from the occasions of offending God. (L 4.7; see also L 6.4, 7.20)

Because of her own early struggles to grow in prayer, Teresa urges that her nuns have access to reliable spiritual guides: "It would benefit them greatly to be given good confessors. If in those monasteries to which the discalced nuns are sent you do not provide help of this kind, I fear for the fruitfulness of the effort. Oppressing them with exterior practices and not providing someone to help them interiorly would be like burdening them with a heavy trial. I had this problem at the Incarnation until the discalced friars came" (Ltr 174.2).

The journey of prayer is aided by having an experienced guide who is familiar with the ways of the Holy Spirit, with Scripture, and with the Christian tradition and thus able to help us to avoid pitfalls, stay on course, and overcome obstacles.

Solitude

"Taking time frequently to be alone with Him who we know loves us"—this is an essential phrase in Teresa's concise foundational definition of prayer (L 8.5). For Teresa, solitude is a necessary element in growth in prayer. Friendship grows when friends can pursue their "intimate sharing" in moments and periods of being alone together. When the soul reaches the most interior room of the interior castle of the soul, she says: "So in this temple of God, in this His dwelling place, He alone and the soul rejoice together in the deepest silence" (IC 7.3.11). Though solitude seeks withdrawal from external engagements, it promotes encounter and communion with the divine companion. Solitude promotes receptivity and serves communion. Speaking of the prayer of recollection, Teresa writes: "Then, daughters, since you are alone, strive to find a companion. Well what better companion than the Master Himself who taught you this prayer? Represent the Lord Himself as close to you and behold how lovingly and humbly He is teaching you. Believe me, you should remain with so good a friend as long as you can" (W 26.1).

Although she herself had an extroverted and gregarious personality, Teresa was insistent on the need for time alone, and she sought it out and embraced it: "All my longing is to be alone. And even though sometimes I do not pray or read, solitude consoles me" (ST 1.6). She reminds her readers that the gospels show us that Jesus himself sought out solitude for prayer and taught his disciples to go into their inner room to pray in secret (W 24.4 [Mt 6:6]). She notes that silence and solitude were characteristic of the lives of many saints (L 13.7).

Her nuns, thought Teresa, should generally work separately when possible, in order to preserve silence and promote the solitude necessary for the contemplative life: "The nuns should be excused from having a common workroom, for although having one is a laudable custom, silence is better observed when each nun is by herself; and *to get used to solitude is a great help for prayer*. Since prayer must be the foundation of this house, it is necessary that we strive to dedicate ourselves to what most helps us in prayer" (W 4.9, emphasis added). Beginners in prayer, she writes, must grow accustomed to being alone: "They need to get accustomed to caring nothing at all about seeing or hearing, to practicing the hours of prayer, and thus to solitude and withdrawal" (L 11.9).

Exterior solitude serves an inner withdrawal in which one can be present to Christ. But it is the interior withdrawal that is essential. Teresa's encouragement of a spirit of recollection, even in the midst of daily activities, makes this evident. Sometimes the inner receptivity and communion with Christ must coincide with external activity. At other times, we must be ready to embrace the activity required of us, even if it takes away from our opportunity for solitary prayer. She recognizes the inevitable tension between good works and time alone with God:

> I always repeat that solitude is better, and even that we must desire it. We must desire solitude even when involved in the things I'm speaking of [i.e., good works demanded by charity and obedience]; indeed, this desire is continually present in souls that truly love God. As for my saying that leaving solitude is a gain, I say this because doing so makes us realize who we are and the degree of virtue we have. For people who are always recollected in solitude, however holy in their own opinion they may be, don't know whether they are patient or humble, nor do they have the means of knowing this. (F 5.15)

What is ultimately important for Teresa is conformity to God's loving will. Prayer serves this goal, but practical love for others manifests it. The busy person must strive to find what solitary time is available, confident that the length of time is not the essential element of time alone with God: "It's necessary to be on one's guard and careful in the performance of good works by having frequent interior recourse to God, even though these works are done in obedience and charity. And let souls believe me that it is not the length of time spent in prayer that benefits one; when the time is spent as well in good works, it is a help in preparing the soul for the enkindling of love" (F 5.17). Still, sometimes solitude is not possible, but the sustained longing for it can itself promote growth in friendship with Christ. She writes to a busy prioress:

> I am sorry about the great trial you have had, my daughter, and still must endure with so many business affairs and such important ones, for I know what it is. But I don't think you would feel any better if you had the quiet you speak of, but worse. Of this I am very certain, for I know your temperament and I accept the fact that you will have to suffer trials because in one way or another you must become a saint; and *this desire you have for solitude is better than having the solitude.* (Ltr 63, emphasis added)

We must not give up on trying to find times and places for solitude nor on promoting an inner spirit of recollection even in the midst of necessary activity, but, as always, Teresa insists on conformity to the divine will for us as mediated by the legitimate demands made on us.

Eucharist

Teresa presumed that her readers participated in the daily Eucharist. She herself received Communion frequently when this was not a usual practice in the church at the time (L 19.12), and she taught that her nuns should receive Communion regularly and frequently (C 5). She often felt a deep desire to receive Communion (L 39.22; 30.14; SS 2.23), and she reports that many of her extraordinary experiences occurred during or after receiving Communion.[6] She entered into the transforming union or "spiritual marriage" upon receiving Communion (ST 31).

---

6. ST 1.23; 6.1; 12.6; 13.1; 39.1; 42.1; 44.1; 50.1; 52.1; L 16.2; 20.5; 28.8; 32.11; 33.12,13; 34.19; 38.19; 39.22–23; 40.5; F 28.15; 29.6; 31.49; and IC 7.2.1.

For Teresa, receiving Communion during Mass kept her focused on the humanity of Christ, which was so essential to her faith and her prayer (L 22.4). And it provided a privileged invitation and opportunity to practice the prayer of recollection and to promote a spirit of loving attention. In the context of a kind of extended commentary on the Our Father, reflecting on the phrase "Give us this day our daily bread" (W 34–35), Teresa invites the reader to take the opportunity after receiving Communion to enter into oneself and rest in Christ's special presence. She writes of herself (using the third person):

> But I know that for many years, when she received Communion, this person, though she was not very perfect, strove to strengthen her faith so that in receiving her Lord it was as if, with her bodily eyes, she saw Him enter her house. Since she believed that this Lord truly entered her poor home, she freed herself from all exterior things when it was possible and entered to be Him. She strove to recollect the senses so that all of them would take notice of so great a good, I mean that they would not impede the soul from recognizing it. (W 34.7)

A quiet time of prayer after receiving Communion can become a fruitful opening to deeper prayer.

Believing firmly in the Real Presence of Christ, she urged a loving attention to Christ, which is not the same as imagining him present: "Receiving Communion is not like picturing with the imagination, as when we reflect upon the Lord on the cross or in other episodes of the Passion, when we picture within ourselves how things happened to Him in the past. In Communion the event is happening now, and it is entirely true" (W 34.8). Rather than trying to picture Christ with our imagination, we should strive to behold with a spiritual vision: "But after having received the Lord, since you have the Person Himself present, strive to close the eyes of the body and open those of the soul and look into your own heart. For I tell you, and tell you again, and would like to tell you many times that you should acquire the habit of doing this every time you receive Communion" (W 34.12).

Since it was not the practice at the time to receive Communion every day, she urged her nuns to take the opportunity nonetheless to enter into a spiritual communion with Christ through the prayer of recollection: "When you do not receive Communion, daughters, but hear Mass, you can make a spiritual communion. Spiritual communion is highly beneficial; through it you can recollect yourselves in the same way after Mass, for the love of this Lord is thereby deeply impressed on the soul. If we prepare ourselves to receive Him, He never fails to give in many ways which we do not understand" (W 35.1).

Teresa of Jesus does not present to us an entire theology or even a spirituality of the Eucharist, but it is obvious that the Mass was an essential element of her spirituality and of her growth in prayer. Eucharistic participation fed her friendship with Christ especially in his sacred humanity. The time after Communion served as a special time for the practice of recollection and thus promoting the spirit and prayer of recollection at other times and circumstances.

Conclusion

Throughout her writings, Teresa of Jesus presents an honest description of her prayer—not only the special graces and experiences but also the struggles and difficulties. And it is from her own journey that she offers her readers invaluable counsel about the obstacles to growth in prayer as well as helps to overcome these difficulties. We have left for the next chapter a look at her teaching and advice about discouragement about our prayer, the temptation to give up, and the strong and persistent resolve to grow in prayer that must characterize anyone who is sincere about developing a life of prayer.

7

Discouragement and Determination

In describing Teresa's own journey of prayer in the first chapter, we noted that she struggled for a time with discouragement about her prayer. She felt unworthy of prayer. For about a year and a half, she even gave up personal prayer (though her participation in the substantial common, liturgical prayer of the nuns would have continued). She looked back on that period of discouragement as a temptation of the devil to draw her away from prayer. But her own experience of rising up from discouragement with a determined spirit and with trust in God's help serves as the foundation for the counsel that she has to offer her readers.

Prayer Requires Our Effort

The invitation and the ability to pray comes from God. Teresa's definition of prayer reminds us that prayer is "taking time frequently to be alone with Him who we know loves us," and it is this remembrance of God's prior, constant, and gratuitous love that can serve as a continual motivation to pray. And yet, although God is always calling and aiding us, we can find it very difficult to make the effort and remain faithful to it, especially through the kinds of trials that we reviewed in the last chapter—distractions, dryness, and busyness. Even beyond these trials specific to the time of prayer, there are our sins and our lack of virtue that draw us away from spending our time and energy in prayer. This is simply the sad human condition after the Fall—even for people who want to embrace the divine life. Teresa's counsel to us is simply to accept and remember the fact that growth in prayer necessarily involves consistent work, whether we feel like it or not.

Teresa believed that one of the reasons that God was able to give her growth in prayer was her own willingness to remain faithful in her effort: "For the Lord endured so much with me only because I desired and strove to have some place and time in order that He might be with me. And this I often did without eagerness but through my own great struggles or through the strength the Lord Himself gave me" (L 8.8). Beginners in prayer, most especially, must be ready for the effort required to grow in a habit of prayer: "Beginners in prayer, we can say, are those who draw water from the well. This involves a lot of work on their own part, as I have said. They must tire themselves in trying to recollect their senses. Since they are accustomed to being distracted, this recollection requires much effort. They need to get accustomed to caring nothing at all about seeing or hearing, to practicing the hours of prayer, and thus to solitude and withdrawal—and to thinking on their past life" (L 11.9).

Further, when Teresa explains the more mature prayer of recollection, she notes that this, too, requires effort and even struggle with the contrary forces within us: "For in the little amount of time we take to force ourselves to be close to this Lord, He will understand us as if through sign language. . . . I only ask that you try this method, even though it may mean some struggle; everything involves struggle before the habit is acquired" (W 29.6; see also W 26.8).

Don't Let Falls Hold You Back

We saw earlier that Teresa herself gave up the practice of prayer because she felt that the lack of congruence between her prayer and her manner of living made her unworthy of prayer. But she came to see that her way of thinking had been misguided and even a temptation of the devil. No one should give up prayer because they have fallen into sin. Rather, such times are when the person most needs prayer! And it is this opening to God that will allow God to bring about in us a deeper conversion: "If you should at times fall don't become discouraged and stop striving to advance. For even from this fall God will draw out good" (IC 2.1.9). Elsewhere, she writes:

> I say that no one who has begun to practice prayer should become discouraged by saying: "If I return to evil, matters will become worse should I continue the practice of prayer." I believe matters become worse if one abandons prayer and doesn't amend one's evil ways. *But if people don't abandon it, they may believe that prayer will bring them to the harbor of light.* The devil carried out a great assault upon me in this matter. Since I was wretched, I spent so long a time in thinking it was a lack of humility to practice prayer that, as I have already said, I abandoned it for a year and a half—at least for a year; I don't remember well about the half. And doing this was no more, nor could it have been, than putting myself right in hell without the need of devils to urge me on. Oh, God help me, what great blindness! *And how right the devil is to direct his attacks so that the soul give up prayer! The traitor knows that he has lost the soul that practices prayer perseveringly and that all the falls he helps it to take assist it afterward, through the goodness of God, to make a great leap*

> *forward in the Lord's service*. No wonder he's so concerned! (L 19.4 emphasis added)

In her own life, Teresa had found that returning immediately to prayer after a fall helped her not to fall again:

> After I had begun to live in such havoc, and without practicing prayer, and since I saw that he [her father] thought I was living as usual, I could not bear to let him be deceived. For thinking it was the more humble thing to do, I had gone a year and more without prayer. And this, as I shall say afterward, was the greatest temptation I had, because on account of this I was heading just about straight to perdition. *For when I practiced prayer, I offended God one day but then others I turned to recollection and withdraw more from the occasions.* (L 7.11 emphasis added)

On the other hand, giving up on prayer only made it worse: "For the love of God let all those who practice prayer observe this. Let them know that during the time in which I was without prayer my life was much worse" (L 19.11). Closing the door to the encounter with God in prayer only makes it even more likely to fall again and again:

> If through weakness and wickedness and a miserable nature they should fall, as I did, let them keep ever in mind the good they have lost and be suspicious and walk with the fear—for they are right in doing so—that *if they don't return to prayer, they will go from bad to worse*. What I call a true fall is abhorrence of the path by which one gained so much good; and to these souls I am speaking. For I am not saying that they should never offend God or fall into sin, although it would be right for anyone who has begun to receive these favors to

> be very much on guard against sinning; but we are miserable creatures. *What I advise strongly is not to abandon prayer*, for in prayer people will understand what they are doing and win repentance from the Lord and fortitude to lift themselves up. And you must believe that *if you give up prayer, you are, in my opinion, courting danger*. I don't know if I understand what I'm saying because, as I said, I'm judging by myself. (L 15.3 emphasis added)

Once begun, the slide into sin can be steep and rapid, but it is prayer than can ensure the openness to God's merciful power to pull us out of our descent.

Teresa is trying to convince her readers that prayer is precisely the space in which the mercy of God can be manifest and can bring us to embrace divine grace more deeply and humbly:[1]

> I have recounted all this at length, as I already mentioned, so that the mercy of God and my ingratitude might be seen; also, in order that one might understand the great good God does for a soul that willingly disposes itself for the practice of prayer, even though it is not disposed as is necessary. I recount this also that one may understand how if the soul perseveres in prayer, in the midst of the sins, temptations, and failures of a thousand kinds that the devil places in its path, in the end, I hold as certain, the Lord will draw it forth to the harbor of salvation as—now it seems—He did for me. (L 8.4)

She pleads with her readers to learn from her experience and never abandon prayer because of having fallen into sin:

---

1. Sancho Fermín, *Orar con Santa Teresa de Jesús*, 49.

> I can speak of what I have experience of. It is that in spite of any wrong they who practice prayer do, *they must not abandon prayer since it is the means by which they can remedy the situation; and to remedy it without prayer would be much more difficult.* May the devil not tempt them, the way he did me, to give up prayer out of humility. May those persons believe that God's words cannot fail. For if we are truly repentant and resolve not to offend God, He will return to the former friendship and bestow the favors He previously did, and sometimes more if the repentance merits it. *Whoever has not begun the practice of prayer, I beg for the love of the Lord not to go without so great a good.* (L 8.5, emphasis added)

Our sins and failures should direct us all the more to prayer rather than tempt us to discouragement. Our divine friend remains faithful even if we, for a time, do not.

A False Humility

The virtue of humility, for Teresa of Jesus, is important in the Christian life, and it is utterly essential for the reception of true contemplation. Without it, the person cannot be truly open and receptive to the divine inflow of contemplative prayer. For her, humility means to "walk in truth"—that is, to know the truth of what we are and what we are not before God. We are created in the image of God and precious to our divine friend. But we are, at the same time, sinners always in need of God's mercy. True humility requires an ever vigilant and self-critical self-knowledge.

But, as much as Teresa values true humility, she warns against a false humility that believes that we can be unworthy to pray or that God would not welcome our prayer when we have fallen into sin. Reflecting on giving up prayer earlier in her life, she laments:

> This was the most terrible trick the devil could play on me, under the guise of humility: that seeing myself so corrupted I began to fear the practice of prayer. It seemed to me that, since in being wicked I was among the worst it was better to go the way of the many, to recite what I was obliged to vocally and not to practice mental prayer and so much intimacy with God, for I merited to be with the devils. And it seemed to me that I was deceiving people since exteriorly I kept up such good appearances (L 7.1).

For Teresa, authentic humility should lead us to—rather than away from—prayer. The truth of our sinfulness should not be allowed to eclipse the prior truth that God is always merciful and loving.

She associates such false humility with the tricks of the devil who wants to tempt us away from prayer: "I believe the devil harms people who practice prayer and prevents them from advancing by causing them to misunderstand humility. He makes it appear to us that it's pride to have great desires and want to imitate the saints and long to be martyrs. Then he tells us or causes us to think that since we are sinners the deeds of the saints are for our admiration, not our imitation" (L 13.4).

In this, the devil is very sly, but people of faith must not be fooled. God's goodness and love as well as the divine commitment to our friendship is greater than the devil and greater than our sin. God is always calling us back to relationship and thus to prayer: "But when, as I have said, it falls, it should be extremely careful for the love of the Lord not to be tricked into giving up prayer, as I was by the devil through false humility—as I have already said and would like to say many times. *It should trust in the goodness of God, which is greater than all the evils we are capable of. And He doesn't remember our ingratitude when we, although knowing about it, desire to return to His friendship*" (L 19.15, emphasis added).

Even though one's life is not yet fully in coherence with prayer, prayer is still an opening to God's love and assistance. It will be the avenue to bring about change as we open ourselves to the good news that God is the friend who always loves. It makes no sense to Teresa why anyone would abandon prayer and the help that comes from it:

> For if those who do not serve Him but offend Him derive so much good from prayer and find it so necessary—and no one can truly discover any harm that prayer can do, the greatest harm being not to practice it—why do those who serve God and desire to serve Him abandon it? I, indeed, cannot understand why, unless it is that they want to undergo the trials of life with greater trial and close the door on God so that He may not make them happy. I certainly pity those who serve the Lord at their own cost, because for those who practice prayer the Lord Himself pays the cost since through their little labor He gives them delight so that with the help of this delight they might suffer the trials. (L 8.8)

Even if we are tempted to feel that we are unworthy of prayer, we must be patient and hopeful; and we must strive to maintain fidelity to prayer, even when we find ourselves suffering—for now—the lack of full congruence between our life and our prayer. In the end, prayer is not simply for the perfect but rather the path by which God can draw us into deeper communion.[2] One of the reasons, says Teresa, that she wrote the *Life* was to serve as a lesson to others never to give in to discouragement: "That one ought not to grow discouraged is one of the reasons that encouraged me—being what I am—to obey and write an account of my wretched life and of the favors the Lord granted me without my serving Him but rather offending Him. I should certainly like to have a great deal of authority in this matter so that I might be believed. I beseech the Lord to give it" (L 19.4).

Hope—this is really the message of St. Teresa in the face of our failures and sin. Hope places its expectations on God and what God can do. Giving into a spirit of discouragement and abandoning prayer are the contrary of hope. As Teresa looks back on her own journey, she believes that it was hope that sustained her—even though, for a time, she had held the misguided expectation that somehow God would first make her perfect as the means of growing in prayer:[3]

> How it was able to go on amazes me. I did so by means of hope because I never thought (insofar as I now recall, for this must have happened twenty-one years ago) I would cease being determined to return to prayer—but I was waiting to be very purified of sin. Oh, how wrong was the direction in which I was going with this hope! The devil would have kept me hoping until judgment day and then have led me into hell. (L 19.11)

---

2. Maximiliano Herráiz García, *La oración, historia de amistad*, 6th ed. (Madrid: Editorial de Espiritualidad, 2003), 65–66.

3. Herráiz, *La oración*, 64–65.

God is good, and the divine help is sure, if—with God's help—we just remain faithful to our prayer, never losing hope.

Determination and Perseverance[4]

In *The Interior Castle*, Teresa describes the journey of prayer as it progresses from its beginnings until it attains, if God wills it, the transforming union of the soul and God. In the first of the seven dwelling places of *The Interior Castle*, Teresa addresses the importance and the manner of entering into the castle of the soul. It is so important simply to enter, because the sad truth is that too many people live outside their own castles—that is, they are dissipated by concerns for superficial things rather than attending to their relationship with God who dwells intimately deep within them. But, having entered the castle, the challenge becomes staying the course: perseverance. The description of the second dwelling places of *The Interior Castle*—unlike the other six—has only one chapter, and it is devoted to the foundational importance of persevering in prayer. She entitles it: "Discusses the importance of perseverance if one is to reach the final dwelling places. . . ."

We have seen that the journey of prayer is often burdened with distractions and dryness. Life can be so busy that it is difficult to find time for prayer and to prudently balance attention to our legitimate responsibilities with the time that prayer requires. Sometimes, we face environments that are not really supportive of our prayer, or we lack the help of spiritual directors and other spiritual friends. Unlike Teresa

4. For a lengthier discussion of Teresa's teaching on determination, see my *The Way of Transformation: Saint Teresa of Avila on the Foundation and Fruit of Prayer* (Washington, D.C.: ICS Publications, 2016), 133–52.

and her nuns, we may lack the structure and foundation of a rhythm of communal prayer. And, perhaps most importantly, despite our sincere intentions, we are sinners, often pulled in different directions in our life and decisions—sometimes tempted to sin but often just drawn to superficialities as Teresa was early in her religious life. More deeply still, true communion with God in prayer requires a profound spirit of surrender on our part. But there is an obscure part of ourselves that forcefully, if often subtly, resists such surrender. The fact is that maintaining and growing in a life of prayer—despite God's constant offer of grace—is often simply difficult.[5] It requires consistent effort over time even, and perhaps most especially, when we are busy, distracted, or discouraged. No wonder that Teresa places such emphasis on the need for perseverance—or what Teresa more frequently and emphatically calls a "very determined determination" (*muy determinada determinación*).

In *The Way of Perfection*, which is focused on teaching her nuns about prayer, determination is a frequent and insistent topic. Chapter twenty-one is titled: "Tells how important it is to begin the practice of prayer with great determination and not to pay attention to obstacles set up by the devil." She writes elsewhere: "These first acts of determination are very important" (L 13.3). And, having begun the journey of prayer, she insists on the need for a continued resolute determination, entitling the twenty-third chapter: "Treats of how important it is for one who has begun the path of prayer not to turn back and speaks once more of the great value that lies in beginning with determination." She is emphatic in writing about it:

5. Herráiz, *La oración*, 138.

> Now returning to those who want to journey on this road [of deepening prayer] and continue until they reach the end, which is to drink from this water of life. I say that how they are to begin is very important—in fact, all important. They must have a great and very resolute determination to persevere *[una grande y muy determinada determinación]* until reaching the end, come what may, happen what may, whatever work is involved, whatever criticism arises, whether they arrive or whether they die on the road, or even if they don't have courage for the trials that are met, or if the whole world collapses. (W 21.2)

Speaking of consolations in prayer as a kind of refreshing water to help us on the journey, Teresa urges her nuns to remain determined even if they find their prayer lacking in consolations:

> So, sisters, do not fear that you will die of thirst on this road. Never is the lack of consoling water such that it cannot be endured. Since this is so, take my advice and do not stop on the road but, like the strong, fight even to death in the search, for you are not here for any other reason than to fight. You must always proceed with this determination to die rather than fail to reach the end of the journey. If even though you so proceed, the Lord should lead you in such a way that you are left with some thirst in this life, in the life that lasts forever He will give you to drink in great plenty and you will have no fear of being without water. May it please the Lord that we ourselves do not fail, amen. (W 20.2)

The devil, she says, is deterred by a spirit of determination in the person of prayer: "If the devil sees that it has the strong determination to lose its life and repose and all that he offers it rather than return to the first room, he will abandon it much more quickly" (IC 2.1.6). In fact, she believes that the devil is "extremely afraid of determined souls" (W 23.4). And such determination is precisely what God desires (L 11.15).

Hope in God, we have seen, is the true foundation of resisting discouragement and the temptation of abandoning prayer. In the same way, our determination is not solely a matter of strong human resolve and discipline. God is its source: "Indeed a great mercy does He bestow on anyone to whom He gives the grace and courage to resolve [*determinarse*] to strive for this great good with every ounce of energy. For God does not deny Himself to anyone who perseveres. Little by little He will measure out the courage sufficient to attain this victory" (L 11.4). This is evident, says Teresa, in the example of the martyrs: "I see clearly that the martyrs did nothing of themselves in suffering torments, for the soul well knows that fortitude comes from another" (L 16.4).

Our determination in prayer is made possible by God, and it is sustained by remembering that our prayer is an intimate sharing with the God who we know loves us. When Teresa begins a long section of the *Life* devoted to prayer, she writes: "Well, let us speak now of those who are beginning to be servants of love. This doesn't seem to me to mean anything else than to follow resolutely [*determinarnos a seguir*] by means of this path of prayer Him who has loved us so much" (L 11.1). The key is to remember that everything worthwhile is found in seeking Jesus with a firm determination: "What helps is that the soul embrace the good Jesus our Lord with determination, for since in Him everything is found, in Him everything is forgotten" (W 9.5).

Move Forward, Aim High

Determination is not simply the resolve to remain stationary or not to give up. For Teresa, it is the firm resolve to keep moving and to aim high. In the fifth dwelling places of *The Interior Castle*, she writes: "Let this, in sum, be the conclusion: that we strive always to advance. And if we don't advance, let us walk with great fear. Without doubt the devil wants to cause some lapse, for it is not possible that after having come so far, one will fail to grow. Love is never idle, and a failure to grow would be a very bad sign. A soul that has tried to be the betrothed of God Himself, that is now intimate with His Majesty, and has reached the boundaries that were mentioned, must not go to sleep" (IC 5.4.10).

It is another kind of false humility to aim too low in the life of prayer. We must be realistic about our current practice and place of prayer, and we must be prudent about not trying to move too fast—beyond what the Spirit is calling and enabling us to do and be at the moment. But the spirit of determination is fed by the firm aspiration to grow into the deepest possible relationship with God:

> Have great confidence, for it is necessary not to hold back one's desires, but to believe in God that if we try we shall little by little, even though it may not be soon, reach the state the saints did with His help. For if they had never determined to desire and seek this state little by little in practice they would never have mounted so high. His Majesty wants this determination, and He is a friend of courageous souls if they walk in humility and without trusting in self. I have not seen any cowardly soul or any of these who under the pretext of humility remain along the bottom of this path who do not take many

> years to advance as far as these courageous ones do in a few. I marvel at how important it is to be courageous in striving for great things along this path. (L 13.2)

Aim high in the spiritual life, urges Teresa, even while we must remain firmly grounded in humility, prudence, and ongoing discernment about where and how God is directing our prayer.

Teresa's own spirit of determination and trust in the help of God is beautifully expressed when she writes:

> Your will, Lord, be done in me in every way and manner that You, my Lord, want. If you want it to be done with trials, strengthen me and let them come; if with persecutions, illnesses, dishonors, and a lack of life's necessities, here I am; I will not turn away, my Father, nor is it right that I turn my back on You. Since Your Son gave You this will of mine in the name of all, there's no reason for any lack on my part. But grant me the favor of Your kingdom that I may do Your will, since He asked for this kingdom for me, and use me as You would Your own possession, in conformity with Your will. (W 32.10)

8

Prayer and Personal Transformation

Teresa of Jesus is a great teacher of prayer, but her focus is not on the *act* of prayer or even the "how to" of prayer. She is concerned with a *life* of prayer and with the formation of the *person* who prays—not simply with people who "practice" prayer but rather with true people of prayer.[1] Without this more fundamental perspective on a life of prayer, the act of prayer always remains limited or held back from further growth. Prayer must be understood in the context of a person's whole life. And if a person does not have a commitment to be transformed by grace and by one's own personal effort, the desire to grow in prayer is doomed from the beginning.

Teresa learned from personal experience the importance and necessity of holding together the life of prayer and the graced work of ongoing transformation. As we have seen, in the years before her mature conversion, she felt heavily the inconsistency between her manner of life and the graces that God had already begun to give her in prayer. In her case, she had not been engaged in dire moral evil, but she felt that she was spending too much time and energy on superficial pursuits and concerns.

1. Maximiliano Herráiz Garcia, *La oración, historia de amistad*, 6th ed. (Madrid: Editorial de Espiritualidad, 2003), 123–26.

This seemed inconsistent with and not conducive to the deeper prayer to which she felt called, leaving her feeling discouraged and tempted to give up on serious prayer all together. Having passed through this period of struggle and discouragement in her own life, Teresa came to insist on the importance of seeking a proper coherence between life and prayer. Consistent with the Christian spiritual tradition before and after her, Teresa insists that the work of personal conversion and transformation must accompany the graced effort to grow in prayer. Prayer grows on a foundation of transformation, and a more complete transformation blossoms as a fruit of deepening prayer.

If prayer is the intimate sharing of friends, then, as Teresa insists, our wills and our lives must be brought more fully in line with that of our divine friend. The mutuality of friendship and its ongoing growth requires a growing conformity between the person of prayer and Christ. Otherwise, our friendship in prayer cannot grow (L 8.5). Prayer will never mature and deepen without a commitment to be transformed in and by Christ.[2] Prayer, understood as friendship with Christ, is impossible without a commitment to a real conversion of life, because one will not be the kind of person who is capable of growing into the deeper and more intimate sharing of contemplation and union. The same Christ who draws and welcomes us in prayer also teaches us how we are to live. Authentic sharing with him requires that we grow increasingly conformed to him and to his teaching in our daily living outside the times of prayer. At the same time, it is precisely by deepening our communion with him in prayer that we are formed and learn by a kind of loving intuition to act and to be in conformity with his life and teaching.

2. Herráiz, *La oración*, 27–28.

For Teresa, a key image of the transformation necessary to grow in prayer is that of the silkworm and the cocoon (IC 5.2). Just as the silkworm builds up the cocoon in which (according to Teresa's understanding) it would die, we must work to grow in the authentic Christian life—overcoming sin, growing in virtue, engaging in ascetical practices, overcoming selfishness and self-centeredness, going to confession, reading good books, listening to good preaching as well as by praying and meditating. The ugly little silkworm then enters its cocoon and mysteriously—in a hidden process—"dies" and is transformed into a beautiful little butterfly (actually, technically, it is a moth). The image of the silkworm, building its cocoon, and the resulting butterfly symbolizes the transformation that must precede, accompany, and flow out from deepening prayer and union. In a shift in the use of the image of the cocoon, Teresa invites us to understand the cocoon to be Christ himself—we die in and with him, die to our old self, and are transformed into Christ.

The Three Essential Virtues

Teresa addresses the necessary relationship between growing in prayer and the graced work of the transformation of our lives in all of her major works. In the *Life*, it is addressed especially through the description of her own struggles to arrive at a consistency between prayer and living. In *The Interior Castle*, the more active phase of this relationship is discussed rather briefly in the first through the third dwelling places. The person on the path of prayer must leave aside the sinful, the superficial, and all that enslaves us in order to receive the gift of infused forms of prayer. But it is in *The Way of Perfection*, which Teresa intended as a kind of fundamental text on contemplative prayer, that she gives more focused attention to the graced work of transformation. There, she devotes the first half of this textbook on deep prayer to three essential virtues (love, humility, and detachment) that provide the necessary foundation to receive and grow in infused prayer. She writes that unless her readers understand and are committed to growing in these three virtues, there is no need to address contemplative prayer since it would be virtually impossible to attain.

Teresa recognizes that her readers may wonder why she is devoting so much attention to these virtues, and so she explains:

> It is about prayer that you asked me to say something, and I beg you that in recompense for what I am going to say you eagerly do what I have said up until now, and read it often. Before I say anything about interior matters, that is, about prayer, I shall mention some things that are necessary for those who seek to follow the way of prayer; so necessary that even if these persons are not very contemplative, they can be far advanced in the service of the Lord if they possess these things. And if they do not possess them, it is impossible for them to be very contemplative. And if they think they are, they are being highly deceived. . . . I shall enlarge on only three things, which are from our own constitutions, for it is very important that we understand how much the practice of these three things helps us to possess inwardly and outwardly the peace our Lord recommended so highly to us. The first of these is love for one another; the second is detachment from all created things; the third is true humility, which, even though I speak of it last, is the main practice and embraces all the others. (W 4.3–4)

Teresa insists that it would be pointless for her to teach about contemplative prayer without first addressing the necessary conversion that must precede and accompany growth in prayer.

A practical love expressed in action, detachment, and humility are the necessary ascetical tools for arriving at the openness and emptiness to receive the inflow of God in contemplation. Reception of the divine gift of contemplation and union requires of us an increasing capacity for self-donation, because they involve a true mutuality with God. We must be free of our egocentrism and our enslavements to things that are less than or not conformable to God. We must be receptive to God becoming the principal agent of our lives, as occurs in divine union. Growth in virtues is the necessary preparation for this self-giving, freedom from self, and openness to receive. Later in *The Way of Perfection*, after Teresa has already been addressing contemplative prayer, she looks back (in a text that we reviewed earlier in a different context) on what she had already written:

> Because everything I have advised you about in this book is directed toward the complete gift of ourselves to the Creator, the surrender of our wills to His, and detachment from creatures . . . For we are preparing ourselves that we may quickly reach the end of our journey and drink the living water from the fount we mentioned. Unless we give our wills entirely to the Lord so that in everything pertaining to us He might do what conforms with His will, we will never be allowed to drink from this fount. Drinking from it is perfect contemplation, that which you told me to write about. (W 32.9)

For Teresa, there is no direct and easy route to contemplation—except by God's occasional direct intervention, for reasons known to God alone—that does not pass through ongoing conversion of our lives.

In the present chapter, our focus is the broad interrelationship that Teresa believes must exist between growth in prayer and personal transformation. In this context, there is no need to offer an extended review of her teaching on each of the three necessary virtues,[3] but a brief comment on each of the three may be useful.

The *virtue of love* is essential because selfless love and service often run so contrary to our sin-caused self-focus and selfishness. For that reason, chosen acts of service for others are a necessary tool for undermining and weakening the hold of our tendency to egocentrism. Love lived out in service, in patience, and in forgiveness in our everyday lives carves out a space for God and conforms our wills to God's loving will. Practical love for others thereby prepares us for deeper communion and sharing. Growing in a "disinterested" love—a more self-forgetful loving expressed in practice—prepares us to make the free gift of self in response to the divine self-giving in contemplation and union.

In the same way, *detachment* from things is essential because it liberates us from our enslavement to what is less than God—whether that involves material possessions or consolations in prayer (L 11.3). We cannot be open to embrace God if we are clinging to what is less than God. She challenges her readers: "Do you think it is possible for a person who really loves God to love vanities? No, indeed, he cannot; nor can he love riches, or worldly things, or delights, or honors, or strife, or envy" (W 40.3). The more that we grow in faith and in our friendship with Christ, the more we know that we are already abundantly rich in him: "For how can people benefit and share their gifts lavishly if they do not understand that they are rich?" (L 10.6). The more that we "embrace the good Jesus our Lord," the more we realize that "in Him everything is found, in Him everything is forgotten" (W 9.5). Or, as the famous bookmark of St. Teresa

3. For an extended discussion of the topic of this chapter and for examination of Teresa's teaching on each of the three essential virtues, see my *The Way of Transformation: Saint Teresa of Avila on the Foundation and Fruit of Prayer* (Washington, D.C.: ICS Publications, 2016).

concludes: "Whoever has God lacks nothing. God alone is enough." This is the motto of a detached person.

Humility frees us from the need to aggrandize, defend, or promote ourselves. For Teresa, humility means walking in the truth about ourselves—both that we are created in the image of God and thus precious and that we are creatures and sinners. Self-knowledge is a critical factor at every stage of prayer: "Along this path of prayer, self knowledge and the thought of one's sins is the bread with which all palates must be fed no matter how delicate they may be; they cannot be sustained without this bread" (L 13.15). Humility is the foundation for any real growth in the Christian life: "Since this edifice is built entirely on humility, the closer one comes to God the more progress there must be in this virtue; and if there is no progress in humility, everything is going to be ruined" (L 12.4; see also IC 7.4.8). And more specifically of the essential relationship between prayer and humility, she teaches: "What I have come to understand is that this whole groundwork of prayer is based on humility and that the more a soul lowers itself in prayer the more God raises it up" (L 22.11). Love, prayer, and humility are all intimately linked: "For love is the genuine fruit of prayer when prayer is rooted in humility" (L 10.5). A critical sign of the lack of humility is the idea that one deserves consolations or advance in prayer (IC 3.1.7; 4.2.9).

Although Teresa does not speak of a "very determined determination" as one of the essential virtues, she is insistent that those three virtues, the graced effort at transformation, and the life of prayer must be pursued with just such resolve and perseverance. We saw in the previous chapter that determination is a consistent message of *The Way of Perfection* as necessary to growth in prayer. It functions as a kind of fourth essential virtue. (For St. Thomas Aquinas, perseverance is indeed a distinct virtue.)

Later, in *The Way of Perfection*, Teresa reasons that explaining these virtues before any teaching about deeper prayer is like doing the necessary setup before a game of chess: "Don't think that what I have said so far is all I have to say, for I am just setting up the game, as they say. You asked me to mention something about the foundation for prayer. Even though God did not lead me by means of this foundation, for I still don't have these virtues, I know of no other. Now realize that anyone who doesn't know how to set up the pieces for a game of chess won't know how to play well" (W 16.1).

And, again, she cautions her nuns that they will never receive the gift of true contemplation without growing in these necessary virtues:

> Therefore, daughters, if you desire that I tell you about the way that leads to contemplation, you will have to bear with me if I enlarge a little on some other matters even though they may not seem to you so important; for in my opinion they are. And if you don't want to hear about them or to put them into practice, stay with your mental prayer for your whole life, for I assure you and all persons who aim after true contemplation (though I could be mistaken since I am judging by myself for whom it took twenty years) that you will not thereby reach it. (W 16.5)

It is apparent that Teresa suspects that her first readers—perhaps like many readers today—might naively hope to arrive at contemplation without walking the sometimes arduous path of personal conversion.

Though not at equal length, Teresa's insistence on building a strong foundation in a life of virtues is not lacking in *The Interior Castle*, where she writes: "Yet few of us dispose ourselves that the Lord may communicate it ["the precious pearl of contemplation"] to us. In exterior matters we are proceeding well so that we will reach what is necessary; but in the practice of the virtues that are necessary for arriving at this point we need very, very much and cannot be careless in either small things or great" (IC 5.1.2). In the seventh dwelling places, she writes: "I repeat, it is necessary that your foundation consist of more than prayer and contemplation. If you do not strive for the virtues and practice them, you will always be dwarfs. And, please God, it will be only a matter of not growing, for you already know that whoever does not increase decreases" (IC 7.4.9).

For Teresa, as for the long tradition before and after her, the virtues are a kind of thermometer or measure of prayer. We can speak of the virtues as the foundation of prayer; but we can equally understand them as a fruit of prayer. The ongoing transformation of our lives prepares us for communion with God even as intimate sharing with Christ forms us for living in ways more conformed to him and to the divine will. In the end, we can say that growth in virtue precedes prayer, flows from it, and accompanies it.

Prayer Itself Is Transformative

The graced effort to overcome sin and grow in virtue is a necessary foundation for growth in prayer, but, at the same time, prayer is transformative of the person who prays. This is a thread that runs through all of Teresa's major works, and Teresa offers herself as evidence of this claim:[4]

> I have recounted all this at length, as I already mentioned, so that the mercy of God and my ingratitude might be seen;

4. Herráiz, *La oración*, 69–70.

> also, in order that one might understand the great good God does for a soul that willingly disposes itself for the practice of prayer, even though it is not disposed as is necessary. I recount this also that one may understand how if the soul perseveres in prayer, in the midst of the sins, temptations, and failures of a thousand kinds that the devil places in its path, in the end, I hold as certain, the Lord will draw it forth to the harbor of salvation as—now it seems—He did for me (L 8.4)

Later, in the *Life*, after she describes her mature conversion, Teresa writes:

> I now want to return to where I left off about my life, for I think I delayed more than I should have so that what follows would be better understood. This is another, new book from here on—I mean another, new life. The life dealt with up to this point was mine; the one I lived from the point where I began to explain these things about prayer is the one God lived in me—according to the way it appears to me—because I think it would have been impossible in so short a time to get rid of so many bad habits and deeds. May the Lord be praised who freed me from myself. (L 23.1)

Teresa credits the origin of her "new life" after her conversion and more regular reception of infused gifts of prayer to the action of God living and at work within her.

During prayer—in encounter and deepening communion with God—God works a transformation in the person. The deeper the intimacy with our divine friend, the more that we are transformed by it. Not only growth in virtue, but a new life slowly emerges from the dialogue and mutuality of friendship with Christ. The praying person comes increasingly to live and act as a true friend of God. Even as we strive, with divine help, to grow in love, detachment, and humility, our sharing with Christ in prayer transforms us more and more into Christ who is loving, free, and humble. And, even more fundamentally, prayer enables us to become more surrendered to the divine will. As Teresa writes to her brother Lorenzo: "God is granting you a great favor by your being able to bear so well the lack of prayer, for this is a sign that you are resigned to his will. This I believe is the greatest good that prayer brings about" (Ltr 185.7). Over time, prayer unseats whatever is false within us, built up by attachments to superficialities and by sin and its resulting constant self-focus: "The first effect is a forgetfulness of self, for truly the soul, seemingly, no longer is" (IC 7.3.2).

From the very beginning and throughout the process of our prayer-enabled transformation, we do our part, but God is the principal agent:

> These are the things we can do of ourselves, with the understanding that we do so by the help of God, for without this help as is already known we cannot have so much as a good thought. These things make up the beginning of fetching water from the well, and please God that it may be found. At least we are doing our part, for we are already drawing it out and doing what we can to water these flowers. God is so good that when for reasons His Majesty knows—perhaps for our greater benefit—the well is dry and we, like good gardeners, do what lies in our power, He sustains the garden without water and makes the virtues grow. Here by "water" I am referring to tears and when there are no tears to interior tenderness and feelings of devotion. (L 11.9)

God's action and our effort (or really, our active cooperation with the divine action) effect our transformation—though increasingly it becomes our task to get out of the way of God's working in and through us.

Teresa attests that she would want no prayer that did not lead to a greater transformation of her life and growth in virtues: "I would not want any other prayer than that which makes the virtues grow in me. If it should be accompanied by great temptations, dryness, and trials leaving me with greater humility, I would consider it good prayer. That prayer is the best prayer that pleases God the most" (Ltr 136.5).

Transformation Is the Measure of Prayer

Precisely because authentic prayer changes us, transformation in living is the measure of true prayer and of the authenticity of any extraordinary phenomena in prayer. Teresa writes in *The Interior Castle*: "But it is in the effects and deeds following afterward that one discerns the true value of prayer; there is no better crucible for testing prayer" (IC 4.2.8). She writes to Friar Jerome Gratian advising about another friar: "Tell him that he should now be content with his prayer. . . . The best effects are those confirmed by works and that the desires for the honor of God become apparent in an authentic solicitude for it and that the intellect and memory be occupied in how best to please him and show him the love one has for him" (Ltr 136.4).

In the end, it is not mystical experiences that give evidence of true holiness. Rather, it is the presence of virtues and goodness in living. Teresa writes: "A prioress should not think that since a sister has experiences like these she is better than the others. The Lord leads each one as He sees is necessary. This path is a preparation for becoming a very good servant of God, provided that one cooperate. But sometimes God leads the weakest along this path. And so there is nothing in it to approve or condemn. One should consider the virtues and who it is who serves our Lord with greater mortification, humility, and purity of conscience; this is the one who will be the holiest" (IC 6.8.10).

Speaking of herself in the third person, Teresa attests that, although some special experience might seem to her to have come from God, she remained focused on seeking growth in virtue rather than any particular spiritual experience:

> She never did anything based on what she understood in prayer. Rather, if her confessor told her to do the contrary, she did it immediately, and always informed them about everything. She never believed so decidedly that an experience was from God that, no matter how much they told her it was, she would swear to the fact; although by reason of the effects and great favors that were granted her in some matters, the experience may have seemed to her to be from the good spirit. But she always desired virtues, and this desire she urged upon her nuns, saying that the most humble and mortified would be the most spiritual. (ST 58.11)

We have seen elsewhere that Teresa says that the union that she always ultimately and fundamentally desired was the union of her will with that of God. In a similar way, in the text above, she adds that we must strive for virtue in a fundamental way. The presence of virtues in us will prepare the foundation for growth in prayer but also serve as an indication of the authenticity and growth of our prayer.

Love in Prayer, Love in Action

For Teresa, prayer itself can be apostolic—that is, its fruits impact not only the person who prays but can extend to others.[5] She sees prayer on behalf of the church, of priests, and of "learned men" as one of the founding reasons for her reform. Even more fundamentally, by being "good friends" with a God who seems to have so few, the nuns could be a prayerful force in and for the church (see W 1.2; 3.1–2, 5). "Your prayer," she tells her nuns, "must be for the benefit of souls" (W 20.3). As Teresa's own prayer matured and deepened, she felt a greater longing that her prayer would benefit others. And she hoped that, although cloistered, her nuns would always "dedicate themselves to the good of souls and the increase of His Church" (F 1.6).

For Teresa, to pray is to be committed to love, because prayer is an intimate sharing with the Divine Love: "Well, let us speak now of those who are beginning to be servants of love. This doesn't seem to me to mean anything else than to follow resolutely by means of this path of prayer Him who has loved us so much" (L 11.1). Prayer, she teaches, is an expression of love. As much as she urges her readers to pursue the life of prayer with great determination and discipline, she recognizes that the more urgent demand of love at any particular moment may not be spending time in quiet prayer but rather service of others and, in religious life, the demands of obedience and obligation. In such a case, when we are able to return to prayer, we will find it blessed by our loving service: "Prayer is an exercise of love, and it would be incorrect to think that if there is no time for solitude there is no prayer

5. Herráiz, *La oración*, 182–85.

at all. With a little care great blessings can come when because of our labors the Lord takes from us the time we had set for prayer" (L 7.12). Love is the foundation of all, "for love alone is what gives value to all things; and a kind of love so great that nothing hinders it is the one thing necessary" (Sol 5.2). Teresa counsels her brother Lorenzo not to worry about time spent away from prayer to lend practical help to his children: "Make no mistake about this, for time well spent, like looking after your children's property, does not hurt prayer. God often gives more in a short moment than in a long time. His works are not measured by time" (Ltr 172.10).

Teresa's teaching manifests a deep intuition into the unity of love of God and neighbor. True charity—the divine gift of love—draws the person into God's own loving. Love of neighbor is not an afterthought, a mere external command, or a requirement deduced from loving a God who is love. True charity means participation in God's loving, and God loves everything and everyone that God has created. We cannot love God, we cannot participate in divine loving, we cannot be conformed with God's will or enter into union with God, unless and to the degree that we love our neighbor. For Teresa, love of God must be the heart and source of renewal for love of neighbor. She writes: "If we practice love of neighbor with great perfection, we will have done everything. I believe that, since our nature is bad, we will not reach perfection in the love of neighbor if that love doesn't rise from love of God as its root" (IC 5.3.9). All of this explains why practical love of neighbor is the measure of our love for God: "We cannot know whether or not we love God, although there are strong indications for recognizing that we do love Him; but we can know whether we love our neighbor. And be certain that the more advanced you see you are in love for your neighbor the more advanced you will be in the love of God, for the love His Majesty has for us is so great that to repay us for our love of neighbor He will in a thousand ways increase the love we have for Him. I cannot doubt this" (IC 5.3.8).

And it is for this reason that what matters is not the greatness of the work but rather the love with which it is done:

> In sum, sisters, what I conclude with is that we shouldn't build castles in the air. The Lord doesn't look so much at the greatness of our works as at the love with which they are done. And if we do what we can, His Majesty will enable us each day to do more and more, provided that we do not quickly tire. But during the little while this life lasts—and perhaps it will last a shorter time than each one thinks—let us offer the Lord interiorly and exteriorly the sacrifice we can. His Majesty will join it with that which He offered on the cross to the Father for us. Thus even though our works are small they will have the value our love for Him would have merited had they been great. (IC 7.4.15)

Love of neighbor is the measure of our love for God, and it is the measure of the authenticity and depth of our prayer.

A Love Expressed in Works

Writing especially for her nuns and for others who wish to pursue the life of deep prayer, Teresa may have felt a special need to emphasize the fundamental importance of good works. The God who is our true friend in Christ and with whom we seek union is a God of love. Being conformed to the divine will and entering in deepening communion with this God, are necessarily expressed in active works of love: "Works are what the Lord wants! He desires that if you see a sister who is sick to whom you can bring some relief, you have compassion on her and not worry about losing this devotion; and that if she is suffering pain, you also feel it; and that, if necessary, you fast so that she might eat—not so much for her sake as because you know it is your Lord's desire. This is true union with His will" (IC 5.3.11).

She would reiterate this central importance of good works when she teaches about the chief demand of those who reach the spiritual marriage (IC 7.4.6).

An Unavoidable Tension

Prayer is an exercise in love of God. But we live our love for God, not only in prayer, but necessarily in our daily interactions with others and in carrying out the work that comes with our God-given vocations in life. It seems almost inevitable that for most of us, we will experience a tension between love expressed in prayer and love expressed in actions and the regular responsibilities of our lives. Teresa herself experienced this tension as she desired time to be frequently alone with the divine friend and, at the same time, she needed to carry on the work of leading a reform and making foundations in response to God's direction.

The Book of Her Foundations chronicles Teresa's often busy and sometimes challenging work of making foundations of her reform. Perhaps it is appropriate and to be expected that—while describing the travels, headaches, negotiations, and the rest—she would devote a chapter to the apparent tension between quiet prayer and the work that needs to get done during time that otherwise might be devoted to prayer. Her letters and other writings show us that this was a tension that she frequently experienced in her own life. And as devoted as she was to the life of prayer, she knew that sometimes God's will draws us away from the delight of quiet prayer, and we should respond generously without complaint or regret. Our progress in prayer is linked with progress in our love expressed in generous giving of our time. Writing about the occasional need to leave aside a time of prayer, she writes:

> The soul loses its delight and counts the loss as gain, for it doesn't think about its own satisfaction but rather about how it can best do the Lord's will, and this it does through obedience. It would be a distressing thing if God were clearly telling us to go after something that matters to Him and we would not want to do so but want to remain looking at Him because that is more pleasing to us. What an amusing kind of progress in the love of God it is, to tie His hands by thinking that He cannot help us except by one path! (F 5.5)

We progress in our love of God in prayer but also in love expressed in action and obedience in the works that God seems to will at any particular moment. We may experience this as a tension, but it is really one love.

Works done for the love of God and out of obedience to what our vocations demand of us can serve to enkindle the love that is at the heart of all prayer: "And let souls believe me that it is not the length of time spent in prayer that benefits one; when the time is spent as well in good works, it is a help in preparing the soul for the enkindling of love. The soul may thereby be better prepared in a very short time than through many hours of reflection" (F 5.17). Teresa is not promoting the misguided idea that "my work is my prayer"—as if our work can simply replace time for prayer—but it is true that we can love God by doing our work and in the midst of our working. The prayer that arises from our hearts during our work, brief but sincere, can then have power to bring growth in prayer: "Moreover, the true lover loves everywhere and is always thinking of the Beloved! It would be a thing hard to bear if we were able to pray only when off in some corner. I do realize that prayer in the midst of occupations cannot last many hours; but, O my Lord, what power over You a sigh of sorrow has that comes from the depths of our hearts on seeing that it isn't enough that we are in this exile but that we are not even given the chance to be alone enjoying You" (F 5.16).

While we may experience an unavoidable tension between our activities and prayer, if love grounds both the activity and the prayer, nothing is lost. In fact, a great deal can be gained even in a busy life.

Martha and Mary

The gospel story of the two sisters Martha and Mary (Luke 10:38–42), the first sister busy with the work of hospitality and the second sitting raptly at the feet of Jesus, introduces a seeming tension that has traditionally been understood as a tension between action and contemplation. It is a story to which Teresa often refers in her writings, and she follows the traditional understanding of Martha as representative of the apostolic life and Mary as a model of the contemplative life. But Teresa does not interpret the story to mean that the contemplative life is higher or better than the apostolic life. Rather, she notes that the two are sisters who must work together and walk hand-in-hand in the life of each individual: "The active and the contemplative lives are joined. The faculties all serve the Lord together: the will is occupied in its work and contemplation without knowing how; the other two faculties serve in the work of Martha. Thus Martha and Mary walk together" (W 31.5). In the final chapter of the final dwelling places in *The Interior Castle*, Teresa writes: "Believe me, Martha and Mary must join together in order to show hospitality to the Lord and have Him always present and not host Him badly by failing to give Him something to eat. How would Mary, always seated at His feet, provide Him with food if her sister did not help her? His food is that in every way possible we draw souls that they may be saved and praise Him always" (IC 7.4.12). Both Martha and Mary loved Jesus. In the same way, our prayer and work can be expressions of love, mutually feeding one another.

St. Thomas Aquinas taught that "love is the form of the virtues." Love for God and neighbor must shape, direct, and empower the growth of all of our virtues. And it is the same love that is expressed in and promotes our intimate sharing with the One who we know loves us. True prayer bears fruit in love—in all of the many forms that love can take in our daily lives. Both prayer and action, then, are central to the work of our transformation in love. We must be transformed by and in love—in and through both prayer and in action.

9

The Gift of Contemplation

Receiving the gift of infused recollection is only the first step in a journey that goes deeper into quiet prayer and into more profound union with God. The experience of the presence of the divine friend in the first introduction of true contemplation opens into yet deeper encounters of presence and union. What Teresa describes as stages of growth in prayer are the deepening intimacy of sharing with God in Christ. One passes from infused recollection to the prayer of quiet and the sleep of the faculties, and then prayer passes beyond the most intimate of encounters and communion into what she describes as stages of union with God—from brief and transitory experiences of union into the spiritual betrothal and finally the abiding spiritual marriage or transforming union. Some of her descriptions are at times difficult to follow, reflecting the deepening of her own experience and the difficulty in attempting to describe and explain it. She found, as many mystical writers report, the more profound the experience, the more difficult it is to find words and images to express it.

We have already noted that, in the *Life*, Teresa used the image of the four ways of watering a garden to describe growth in prayer—the first way represents active forms of prayer while the next three are describing infused prayer. The person of prayer becomes less the active agent of prayer and increasingly the willing and open recipient. In *The Way of Perfection*, she uses the image of a mother nursing her infant: in the prayer of recollection, the baby suckles; in the prayer of quiet, the mother puts the milk in the infant's mouth, and it has only to swallow; and in the prayer of union, without the child knowing how, the milk is placed within it without even so much as the action of swallowing:

> The soul is like an infant that still nurses when at its mother's breast, and the mother without her babe's effort to suckle puts the milk in its mouth in order to give it delight. So it is here; for without effort of the intellect the will is loving, and the Lord desires that the will, without thinking about the matter, understand that it is with Him and that it does no more than swallow the milk His Majesty places in its mouth, and enjoy that sweetness. For the will knows that it is the Lord who is granting that favor. And the will rejoices in its enjoyment. It doesn't desire to understand how it enjoys the favor or what it enjoys; but it forgets itself during that time, for the One who is near it will not forget to observe what is fitting for it. If the will goes out to fight with the intellect so as to give a share of the experience, by drawing the intellect after itself, it cannot do so at all; it will be forced to let the milk fall from its mouth and lose that divine nourishment.
>
> This is the way this prayer of quiet is different from that prayer in which the entire soul is united with God, for then the soul doesn't even go through the process of swallowing this divine food. Without its understanding how, the Lord places the milk within it. In this prayer of quiet it seems that He wants it to work a little, although so gently that it almost doesn't feel its effort. (W 31.9–10; see also SS 4.4)

Normally, the journey of deepening prayer requires years of practice, determination, and fidelity, but God remains always free: "Often the contemplation the Lord doesn't give to one in twenty years he gives to another in one" (L 34.11).

More Than One Possible Path

Although Teresa describes stages in the growth of prayer leading to union, as we noted earlier, she is not suggesting that everyone's experience will be exactly the same. Although the appearance of a direct linear progression seems most prominent in the journey through the seven dwelling places in *The Interior Castle*, it is clear nonetheless that she is not suggesting that others will experience it in the same way:

> You mustn't think of these dwelling places in such a way that each one would follow in file after the other; but turn your eyes toward the center, which is the room or royal chamber where the King stays, and think of how a palmetto has many leaves surrounding and covering the tasty part that can be eaten. So here, surrounding this center room are many other rooms; and the same holds true for those above. The things of the soul must always be considered as plentiful, spacious, and large; to do so is not an exaggeration. The soul is capable of much more than we can imagine, and the sun that is in this royal chamber shines in all parts. It is very important for any soul that practices prayer, whether little or much, not to hold itself back and stay in one corner. Let it walk through these dwelling places which are up above, down below, and to the sides, since God has given it such great dignity. (IC 1.2.8)

God has created each soul individually and uniquely in the divine image with an infinite capacity to receive the superabundant and ineffable presence of God. While Teresa is laying out a general path in order to provide some clarity for those who are advancing on the way, she knows that God leads each person in a distinctive way. And this fact should be the cause for delight.

Even within her framework of these seven dwelling places, she says that there are many rooms, signifying the many possible individual experiences: "Thus I say that you should think not in terms of just a few rooms but in terms of a million" (IC 1.2.12). She concludes *The Interior Castle* with a similar statement: "Although no more than seven dwelling places were discussed, in each of these there are many others, below and above and to the sides, with lovely gardens and fountains and labyrinths, such delightful things that you would want to be dissolved in praises of the great God who created the soul in His own image and likeness" (IC Epil.3).

We Must Be Truly Disposed

Whatever path God chooses for each of us to walk, there is no hope—except by a special divine intervention—of growing in truly contemplative prayer and union with God unless we are willing to dispose ourselves for it: "For myself I hold that there are many to whom our Lord God gives this test, but few who prepare themselves for the enjoyment of the favor of contemplation. When the Lord grants it and we do not fail on our part, I hold as certain that He never ceases to give until we reach a very high degree. When we do not give ourselves to His Majesty with the determination with which He gives Himself to us, He does a good deal by leaving us in mental prayer and visiting us from time to time like servants in His vineyard" (W 16.9). Addressing the nuns of her reform, she reminds them that they must be both rightly disposed and ready for the hard work of growing in the virtues that make true contemplation possible:

> So I say now that all of us who wear this holy habit of Carmel are called to prayer and contemplation. This call explains our origin; we are the descendants of men who felt this call, of those holy fathers on Mount Carmel who in such great solitude and contempt for the world sought this treasure, this precious pearl of contemplation that we are speaking about. Yet few of us dispose ourselves that the Lord may communicate it to us. In exterior matters we are proceeding well so that we will reach what is necessary; but in the practice of the virtues that are necessary for arriving at this point we need very, very much and cannot be careless in either small things or great. (IC 5.1.2)

If we hope to receive contemplative gifts—whether we are called to a formally contemplative state of life or not—we must be committed to do what we can to dispose ourselves to receive.

The reception of the gift of contemplation and of union requires us to be properly prepared to the degree that it is in our power, but even more fundamentally it requires a spirit of complete self-giving. God wishes to pour out the divine life in us and draw us into union, but we must be willing to do the same. The intimate sharing of friendship must be mutual: "But reflect, daughters, that He doesn't want you to hold on to anything, so that you will be able to enjoy the favors we are speaking of. Whether you have little or much, He wants everything for Himself; and in conformity with what you know you have given you will receive greater or lesser favors. There is no better proof for recognizing whether our prayer has reached union or not" (IC 5.1.3).

Infused Recollection

(L 14–15; IC 4.3.1; ST 59.3–4)

The fourth dwelling places of *The Interior Castle* describe the transition from acquired to infused prayer. The first experience of this gifted prayer often comes when one is practicing a more active form of wordless, imageless prayer—a gentle and often subtle transition from acquired into infused recollection: "I sometimes experienced, . . . although briefly, the beginning of what I will now speak about. It used to happen, when I represented Christ within me in order to place myself in His presence, or even while reading, that a feeling of the presence of God would come upon me unexpectedly so that I could in no way doubt He was within me or I totally immersed in Him" (L 10.1; see also ST 59.25). Instead of recollecting one's own consciousness, it is as if the Lord gently whistles and draws the person within: "Like a good shepherd, with a whistle so gentle that even they themselves almost fail to hear it, He makes them recognize His voice and stops them from going so far astray so that they will return to their dwelling place. And this shepherd's whistle has such power that they abandon the exterior things in which they were estranged from Him and enter the castle" (IC 4.3.2).

In one of the *Spiritual Testimonies* devoted to grades or steps of infused prayer, Teresa describes this first experience of infused or supernatural prayer:

> The first prayer I experienced that in my opinion was supernatural (a term I use for what cannot be acquired by effort or diligence, however much one tries, although one can dispose oneself for it which would help a great deal) is an interior recollection felt in the soul. For it appears that just as the soul has exterior senses it also has other interior senses through which

> it seems to want to withdraw within, away from the outside noise. So, sometimes this recollection draws these exterior senses after itself, for it gives the soul the desire to close its eyes and not hear or see or understand anything other than that in which it is then occupied, which is communion with God in solitude. In this state none of the senses or faculties are lost, for all are left intact. But they are left that way so that the soul may be occupied in God. And this explanation will be easy to understand for anyone to whom the Lord has granted this prayer; and for those to whom He has not, there will be need at least for many words and comparisons.
>
> A very pleasing *interior quiet* and *peace* sometimes flow from this recollection, so that it doesn't seem to the soul it is lacking anything. Even speaking tires it, I mean reciting vocal prayer and meditating. All it wants is to love. This quiet lasts a short while, and even a longer while. (ST 59.3–4; see also IC 4.3.1–2)

The divine friend is gently drawing the person into a deeper intimacy so that he or she can rest quietly with God without their own effort.

Infused recollection is experienced as being drawn inward by God: "But one noticeably senses a gentle drawing inward, as anyone who goes through this will observe, for I don't know how to make it clearer. It seems to me I have read where it was compared to a hedgehog curling up or a turtle drawing into a shell. (The one who wrote this example must have understood the experience well.) But these creatures draw inward whenever they want. In the case of this recollection, it doesn't come when we want it but when God wants to grant us the favor" (IC 4.3.3).

Being a transitional form of prayer, infused recollection is a kind of first step into true contemplative prayer, further disposing one to the prayer of quiet: "The prayer of recollection is much less intense than the prayer of spiritual delight [i.e., prayer of quiet] from God that I mentioned. But it is the beginning through which one goes to the other." (IC 4.3.8). Meanwhile, when during times in which God does not give infused recollection, it is best not to give up on more active forms of prayer (IC 4.3.8).

Prayer of Quiet

(L 14–15; W 30–31; IC 4.2.2–3; ST 59.4; SS 4)

With God's gift, the prayer of infused recollection passes into the prayer of quiet—though Teresa does not always clearly distinguish them. In the first of her major works, she speaks of them together as the second way of watering the garden (L 14–15): "this quietude and recollection" and "this first recollection and quiet" (L 15.1). In her mature work, *The Interior Castle*, she distinguishes them, but after she begins to speak of the prayer of quiet she then goes back to discuss the prayer of recollection as a kind of prayer that precedes it (IC 4.3.1). This apparent confusion or lack of clarity may reflect a maturing of her own experience and of her ability to explain it as well as the often subtle developments in the gentle movements of God. As we have seen, the prayer of recollection is a kind of portal or transition to inner quiet.

In *The Interior Castle*, Teresa distinguishes between "consolations" (*contentos*) and "spiritual delights" (*gustos*)—the latter she equates with the prayer of quiet. Consolations, as we commonly use the term, involve feelings of presence, peace, joy, and even passion that come as a result of our efforts in prayer and devotion. They can be a great blessings and encouragement in growing in a discipline and habit of prayer, but they are also transient and sometimes quite superficial. Spiritual delights, however, as Teresa understands them, flow from God's presence and action within us and produce a deeper peace, inner quiet, and sweetness. They can flow out into the body and into felt experience rather than coming as a result of our effort. She writes:

> [God] produces this delight with the greatest peace and quiet and sweetness in the very interior part of ourselves. I don't know from where or how, nor is that happiness and delight experienced, as are earthly consolations, in the heart. I mean there is no similarity at the beginning, for afterward the delight fills everything; this water overflows through all the dwelling places and faculties until reaching the body. This is why I said that it begins in God and ends in ourselves. For, certainly, as anyone who may have experienced it will see, the whole exterior man enjoys this spiritual delight and sweetness. I was now thinking, while writing this, that the verse mentioned above, *Dilatasti cor meum*, says the heart was expanded. I don't think the experience is something, as I say, that rises from the heart, but from another part still more interior, as from something deep. I think this must be the center of the soul. (IC 4.2.4–5)[1]

Consolations (*contentos*) are not substantially different in experience from other good feelings that we can experience in our daily lives, but spiritual delights (*gustos*) emerge from the depths and from the quiet presence and action of God.

---

1. Kieran Kavanaugh explains the difference between consolation and delights in St. Teresa of Avila, *The Interior Castle: Study Edition*, 2nd ed., trans/ed. Kieran Kavanaugh (Washington, D.C.: ICS Publications, 2020), 103–9.

Teresa believes that many people arrive at this stage of prayer, writing: "I have greatly enlarged upon this dwelling place because it is the one which more souls enter" (IC 4.3.15). Sadly, however, fewer move beyond it—though she feels certain that God, having been able to give this great gift of prayer, wants to give more if we are also disposed receive it: "There are many, many souls who reach it [the prayer of quiet] but few that pass beyond; and I don't know whose fault it is. Most surely God does not fail, for once His Majesty has granted a soul the favor of reaching this stage, I don't believe He will fail to grant it many more favors unless through its own fault" (L 15.2). She continues: "This little spark is the sign or the pledge God gives to this soul that He now chooses it for great things if it will prepare itself to receive them" (L 15.5). If we do not stand in the way, receiving the prayer of quiet is a reason to hope for far more: "A soul to whom God gives such pledges has a sign that He wants to give it a great deal; if not impeded through its own fault, it will advance very far" (W 31.11).

Description and Explanation

Teresa describes the experience of the prayer of quiet in terms of inner tranquility or silence and sweetness in which the whole person is touched from within his or her depths:

> In the interior of the soul a sweetness is felt so great that the soul feels clearly the nearness of its Lord. This experience is not merely one of devotion moving a person to shed many tears—which give satisfaction—either by thinking of the Passion of the Lord or of our sins. In this prayer of which I speak, that I call "quiet" because of the calm caused in all the faculties (for it seems the person has them well under

> control—although sometimes the experience is not like this, because the soul is not so absorbed in this sweetness), it seems that the whole man interiorly and exteriorly is comforted. It's as though there were poured into the marrow of one's bones a sweet ointment with a powerful fragrance. If we were suddenly to enter a place where this fragrance was strong and not from one thing but from many, and we did not know what it was or where it came from except that it permeated everything, we would have some idea of this most sweet love of our God. He enters the soul and does so with wonderful sweetness. He pleases and makes it happy, and it cannot understand how or from where that blessing enters. It would not want to lose that good; it would not want to stir or speak or even look lest the blessing go away. (SS 4.2)

The length of her descriptions may reflect the fact that she assumes that so many people can reach this stage of prayer:

> This prayer is something supernatural, something we cannot procure through our own efforts. In it the soul enters into peace or, better, the Lord puts it at peace by His presence . . . so that all the faculties are calmed. The soul understands in another way, very foreign to the way it understands through the exterior senses, that it is now close to its God and that not much more would be required for it to become one with Him in union. . . . The state resembles an interior and exterior swoon; for the exterior man (or so that you will understand me better, I mean the body [for some simpleton will come along who won't know what "interior" and "exterior" means]) doesn't want any activity. But like one who has almost reached the end of his journey he wants to rest so as to be better able to continue; in this rest his strength for the journey is doubled.

> A person feels the greatest delight in his body and a great satisfaction in his soul. He feels so happy merely with being close to the fount that he is satisfied even without drinking. It doesn't seem there is anything else for him to desire. (W 31.2–3)

With the experience of the prayer of quiet, the person is certain of the presence of God: "In no way is it able to believe at that time that God is not with it" (L 15.15).

But, beyond her *descriptions*, Teresa *explains* the experience of the prayer of quiet as an absorption or "capturing" of the will with a quieting of the intellect and imagination but without being absorbed along with the will. The person's only activity in prayer is to consent to being "imprisoned" by love:

> In this prayer the faculties are gathered within so as to enjoy that satisfaction with greater delight. But they are not lost, nor do they sleep. Only the will is occupied in such a way that, without knowing how, it becomes captive; it merely consents to God allowing Him to imprison it as one who well knows how to be the captive of its lover. O Jesus and my Lord! How valuable is Your love to us here! It holds our love so bound that it doesn't allow it the freedom during that time to love anything else but You. (L 14.2)

In other words, there is a profound sense of encounter with God, of the divine presence in love, and of being drawn to rest in that love, even while the person remains conscious and, to some degree, aware of one's surroundings. The full absorption of the consciousness is characteristic of the later prayer of union. She explains:

> The faculties are still; they wouldn't want to be busy; everything else seems to hinder them from loving. But they are not completely lost; they can think of who it is they are near, for

> two of them are free. The will is the one that is captive here. If there is some sorrow that can be experienced while in this state, that sorrow comes from a realization that the will must return to the state of being free. The intellect wouldn't want to understand more than one thing; nor would the memory want to be occupied with anything else. Persons in this prayer see that only this one thing is necessary, and everything else disturbs them. They don't want the body to move because it seems they would thereby lose that peace; thus they don't dare stir. It pains them to speak; in their saying "Our Father" just once a whole hour passes. (W 31.3)

Although the intellect and imagination may begin to pull at the will while in the prayer of quiet, it cannot be budged. In fact, it tends to draw the others back into the quiet: "I have already mentioned that in this first recollection and quiet the soul's faculties do not cease functioning. But the soul is so satisfied with God that as long as the recollection lasts, the quiet and calm are not lost since the will is united with God even though the two faculties are distracted; in fact, little by little the will brings the intellect and the memory back to recollection" (L 15.1).

Distractions—the product of an active intellect and memory/imagination—can still be present in the prayer of quiet, but because the quiet flows from the divine presence and gift, even the distractions may sometimes be gently pulled into the restful quiet.

In *The Interior Castle*, Teresa tries to clarify the experience of the prayer of quiet by distinguishing it from a sometimes sincerely mistaken counterfeit. Sometimes, she warns, people with a "weak constitution" can try too hard—too much time in prayer and excessive penance and fasting. The result can be a "dreamy state" (IC 5.1.4–5) in which the person experiences "some consolation interiorly and a languishing and weakness exteriorly," mistaking it for the action of God in drawing a person into a quiet resting in the divine presence. Instead, Teresa concludes, the person has been "carried away in foolishness" (IC 4.3.11).[2] Her recommendation is strikingly direct and practical: more sleep, less penance, and less time spent in prayer.

The Necessary Response

The reception of the prayer of quiet requires great humility, docility, and openness. It is received by the truly humble as Teresa explains:

> First, because the initial thing necessary for such favors is to love God without self-interest. Second, because there is a slight lack of humility in thinking that for our miserable services something so great can be obtained. Third, because the authentic preparation for these favors on the part of those of us who, after all, have offended Him is the desire to suffer and imitate the Lord rather than to have spiritual delights. Fourth, because His Majesty is not obliged to give them to us as He is to give us glory if we keep His commandments. . . . The fifth reason is that we would be laboring in vain; for since this water must not be drawn through aqueducts as was the previous water, we are little helped by tiring ourselves if the spring doesn't want to produce it. I mean that no matter how much we meditate or how much we try to squeeze something out and have tears, this water doesn't come in such a way. It is

2. Kavanaugh notes that Teresa is playing on two similar Spanish words: *arrobamiento* (rapture—what the mistaken person thinks that he or she is experiencing) and *abobamiento* (foolishness—what the person's own effort had led to): Teresa of Avila, *The Interior Castle: Study Edition*, 118n13.

> given only to whom God wills to give it and often when the soul is least thinking of it. (IC 4.2.8–9)

Teresa is warning against a subtle temptation to think that someone who has begun to experience infused contemplative prayer will be able progress simply by their own effort or as the "natural" progression of their prayer. Contemplative prayer always remains a gift to be received rather than an experience to be produced or expected as a reward.

During the prayer of quiet, the person must gently resist the efforts of the conscious mind to think thoughts and to intervene in order to understand, explain, or even, during the time of prayer, to give thanks for the gift:

> What the soul must do during these times of quiet amounts to no more than proceeding gently and noiselessly. What I call noise is running about with the intellect looking for many words and reflections so as to give thanks for this gift and piling up one's sins and faults in order to see that the gift is unmerited. Everything is motion here; the intellect is representing, and the memory hurrying about. For certainly these faculties tire me out from time to time; and although I have a poor memory, I cannot subdue it. The will calmly and wisely must understand that one does not deal well with God by force and that our efforts are like the careless use of large pieces of wood which smother this little spark. (L 15.6)

The appropriate response to the reception of the gift of the prayer of quiet is resting and gazing—not the composition of prayers, the contrite confession of sins, nor the making of good resolutions. For its part, the will must not pay any more attention to the intellect than it would to a madman (W 31.8).

Elsewhere, she says the same of the memory (L 17.7). In this prayer, we must accept the continued workings of the imagination and memory as "little moths at night, bothersome and annoying" (L 17.6).

Still, the silent repetition of a word can sometimes help to sustain and prolong the prayer of quiet just as a very gentle breath can sometime rekindle a candle that is about to extinguish itself:

> It is good to find more solitude so as to make room for the Lord and allow His Majesty to work as though with something belonging to Him. At most, a gentle word from time to time is sufficient, as in the case of one who blows on a candle to enkindle it again when it begins to die out. But if the candle is burning, blowing on it will in my opinion serve no other purpose than to put it out. I say that the blowing should be gentle lest the will be distracted by the intellect busying itself with many words. (W 31.7)

As we have seen, contemporary contemplative practices recommend the use of a prayer word to draw a person's consciousness into a spirit of tranquil prayer—and to draw the person's attention back when distractions have interfered. Here, Teresa is addressing infused contemplative prayer that is not produced or maintained by our effort; still, a prayer word of some sort "from time to time" may help to gently prolong the experience of quiet resting in God.

Despite the presence from time to time of the prayer of quiet, it is not necessarily the time to give up completely on more active forms of prayer. Beginning a period of vocal prayer or active mental prayer, it would become apparent to the person when she or he is being invited to rest instead in contemplative quiet: "Finally, at this stage one doesn't have to renounce completely discursive mental prayer or the use of some words, or even vocal prayers if there should be the desire or ability; if the quiet is great, it is difficult to speak without a good deal of effort" (L 15.9).

Fruits of the Prayer of Quiet

Teresa almost always follows a description of an experience of the deepening levels of prayer with an indication of the fruits of that prayer. She identifies many particular benefits that flow from the prayer of quiet:[3]

1. It brings a sense of "satisfaction and peace bestowed on the soul, along with great contentment and calm and a very gentle delight in the faculties" (L 15.1; see also W 31).
2. It brings growth in virtue since it is a deeper experience of God who, she says, is true Virtue and the source of all virtues (L 14.5; IC 4.3.9).
3. It promotes greater detachment from earthly things since they are now seen more clearly from the perspective of an experience of the true and lasting treasure (L 14.5; see also SS 4.3).
4. It offers a deeper insight into the faith, even without formal study: "And, in fact, it has happened to me that while in this quietude, and understanding hardly anything of the Latin prayers, especially of the psalter, I have not only understood how to render the Latin verse in the vernacular but have gone beyond to rejoicing in the meaning of the verse" (L 15.8).

3. Daniel de Pablo Maroto, *Teresa en oración: historia, experiencia, doctrina* (Madrid: Editorial de Espiritualidad, 2004), 376.

5. It brings growth in humility, a deeper self-knowledge, a sense of awe before God, a greater desire for solitude, and commitment to love God without self-interest:

> There are other signs as well which I shall now mention. When the prayer comes from God's spirit, there is no need to go dredging up things in order to derive some humility and shame because the Lord Himself gives this prayer in a manner very different from that which we gain through our nice little reasonings. For such humility is nothing in comparison with the true humility the Lord with His light here teaches and which causes an embarrassment that undoes one. It is well known that God gives a knowledge that makes us realize we have no good of ourselves; and the greater the favors, the greater is this knowledge. He bestows a strong desire to advance in prayer and not abandon it no matter what trial may come upon one. The soul offers itself up in all things. It feels sure, while still being humble and fearing, that it will be saved. He casts out from it all servile fear and grants a more mature trusting fear. It is aware of the beginning of a love of God that has much less self-interest. It desires periods of solitude in order to enjoy that good more. (L 15.14)

The blessing of the gift of deepening contemplative prayer yields yet more gifts and fruits even while it further promotes a spirit of humility and wonder.

Sleep of the Faculties

(L 16–17; ST 59.5)

As infused recollection was a kind of transition between acquired recollection and the prayer of quiet, the sleep of the faculties seems to be a kind of passage from quiet to the forms of union. In *Spiritual Testimonies*, Teresa provides a brief description of the sleep of the faculties:

> From this prayer [of quiet] there usually proceeds what is called a *sleep of the faculties*, for they are neither absorbed nor so suspended that the prayer can be called a rapture. Although this prayer is not complete union, the soul sometimes, and even often, understands that the will alone is united, and this is known very clearly; I mean it is clear in the soul's opinion. The will is completely occupied in God, and it sees it lacks the power to be engaged in any other work. The other two faculties are free for business and works of service of God. In sum, Martha and Mary walk together. I asked Father Francis [St. Francis Borgia, S.J.] if this experience could be deceiving because it puzzled me, and he told me that the experience is a frequent one. (ST 59.5; see also L 16.1)

But the description given above does not provide much clarity for distinguishing the sleep of the faculties from the prayer of quiet.

Again, there seems to be a development in Teresa's thought. In the *Life*, the sleep of the faculties is the third degree of prayer or the third way of watering the garden (L 16–17). She does the same in one of her *Spiritual Testimonies* (ST 59.5), though seeming to distinguish it less clearly from the prayer of quiet. The sleep of the faculties is not mentioned at all in the later *The Way of Perfection*. In *The Interior Castle*, it is mentioned only briefly and then as a form of the prayer of quiet, speaking of "a spiritual sleep (which is a prayer a little more intense than the prayer of quiet)" (IC 4.3.11). Later in the same work, she refers to them together: "a person may be very absorbed in the prayer of quiet and spiritual sleep" (IC 6.3.10). In *The Book of Her Foundations*, she writes: "But frequently it happens that there begins a kind of prayer of quiet, something that resembles spiritual sleep" (F 6.1). In the end, it is not clear if Teresa viewed the sleep of the faculties as an intensification of the prayer of quiet or as an introduction of union. But the fact that it is largely absent from her later works suggests that, as her own experience and understanding matured, she came to the conclusion that it was not a distinct stage or grade of prayer.[4]

The sleep of the faculties brings joy and delight: "This prayer is a glorious foolishness, a heavenly madness where the true wisdom is learned; and it is for the soul a most delightful way of enjoying" (L 16.1; see also L 16.3, 4; L 17.1). And it brings growth in virtue and in a humility that makes it yet more clear that the person did almost nothing except give consent to God's favor (L 17.3).

The introduction of true contemplative prayer is a great gift, and it represents a far more intimate sharing with the divine friend—a more profound exchange without words or images. But God has more in store for those who respond to the divine invitation and dispose themselves to receive. As and when God wills, and as the person is docile and open, communion opens into true union between the human person and God in the very center of the soul.

4. Maroto, *Teresa en oración*, 377n7.

10

Deepening Union

In this life, the deepest form of human friendship is the mutuality and one-flesh union of husband and wife. In *The Interior Castle*, as Teresa speaks of the introduction of the union of the human person with God, she transitions to the use of marital images. The deepening of union, she says, is like the movement from courtship to betrothal and finally to marriage itself. The intimate sharing of prayer becomes the profound sharing of the depths of the human person with God.

Prayer of Union

(L 18–19; W 32–33; IC 5; SS 4.4; ST 59.6)

The previous stages of contemplative prayer involved progressively more profound encounters, sharing, and communion with God. The person of prayer has become awakened more deeply to the presence of Love in the person's inmost center. The intimate sharing of friends has entered a new depth of relationship and exchange, without words, images, or thoughts. But what Teresa begins to describe in the fifth dwelling places of *The Interior Castle* is something yet deeper: union with God—brief and passing at first but growing in intensity and duration. This can only occur by divine gift, most often only in a person who has become conformed to God's will in life and docile to the divine movements and seductive whisperings deep within. Only then can the person be drawn into union. Without conformity in living and without humility and docility to receive, the person could not be disposed for true union with God.

Explanations and Descriptions

Teresa does not really attempt to define divine union in any theological depth, nor does she try to explain how it works. Since it is all God's doing, much remains ineffable mystery. She writes rather simply: "What union is we already know since it means that two separate things become one" (L 18.3). In the prayer of union, she says that God is "joined and united with the essence of the soul" (IC 5.1.5) and that "He wants to enter the center of the soul without going through any door" (IC 5.1.13). In the *Life*, she writes:

> Now let us come to what the soul experiences here interiorly. Let those who know how speak of it since it cannot be understood—much less put into words! After having received Communion and been in this very prayer I'm writing about, I was thinking when I wanted to write something on it of what the soul did during that time. The Lord spoke these words to me: "It detaches itself from everything, daughter, so as to abide more in me. It is no longer the soul that lives but I. Since it cannot comprehend what it understands, there is an understanding by not understanding." Whoever may have experienced this prayer will know something about it; since what happens is so obscure, it can't be explained more clearly. I can only say that the soul appears to be joined to God, and there remains such certitude about this union that the soul cannot help believing in the truth of it. In this prayer

> all the faculties fail and they are so suspended that in no way, as I said, does one think they are working. (L 18.14)

Mostly, she simply describes the experience of union as best she can. In the same chapter of the *Life*, she continues:

> While the soul is seeking God in this way, it feels with the most marvelous and gentlest delight that everything is almost fading away through a kind of swoon in which breathing and all the bodily energies gradually fail. This experience comes about in such a way that one cannot even stir the hands without a lot of effort. The eyes close without one's wanting them to close; or if these persons keep them open, they see hardly anything—nor do they read or succeed in pronouncing a letter, nor can they hardly even guess what the letter is. They see the letter; but since the intellect gives no help, they don't know how to read it even though they may desire to do so. They hear but don't understand what they hear. Thus they receive no benefit from the senses—unless it be that these latter do not take away their pleasure, since doing so would cause harm. In vain do they try to speak because they don't succeed in forming a word, nor if they do succeed is there the strength left to be able to pronounce it. (L 18.10)

In the earlier prayer of quiet, the person experienced the will absorbed in a loving rest while the intellect and memory/imagination—though sometimes gently called into the quiet—remain free to roam in the form of distractions. As the quiet deepened, a kind of spiritual "sleep" might come upon a person in which the will, intellect, and memory are all at rest. But in the experience of union, as Teresa is describing it, all of these faculties are truly absorbed by God—one's entire consciousness has been grasped by God. Teresa's own experience of this gift of deepening union is described most clearly and in greatest detail in the fifth, sixth, and seventh dwelling places of *The Interior Castle*. Especially in the sixth dwelling places, her descriptions of her own personal experience include amazing details of her mystical experiences.

Spiritual Courtship

(IC 5)

It is in the fifth dwelling places of *The Interior Castle* that Teresa takes up the image of marriage to describe deepening union with God. The fifth dwelling places are like the period of courtship in which the two parties come together on occasion to converse and to get to know each other intimately on the path to marriage. The experience of union here is brief and, though real, passing. Many people of faithful and mature prayer, Teresa believed, enter the fifth dwelling places and thus into the prayer of union at least from time to time, as God wills and as they remain disposed. But, she notes, there are differing degrees and experiences of union—though any experience of it is a great gift for any who receive it: "And although I have said 'some,' there are indeed only a few who fail to enter this dwelling place of which I shall now speak. There are various degrees, and for that reason I say that most enter these places. But I believe that only a few will experience some of the things that I will say are in this room. Yet even if souls do no more than reach the door, God is being very merciful to them; although many are called few are chosen" (IC 5.1.2). The prayer of union remains always as an unmerited divine gift, and any experience of it is beyond any person's deserving.

In the previous stages of contemplative prayer, as we have seen, Teresa had described an increasing "absorption" or "capturing" of the will and, to different degrees, the intellect and memory/imagination. This is to say that, in the previous stages, while there could be random thoughts and images passing through one's consciousness, a deep part of the self was captivated and held by the awareness of divine presence and love. But, in the prayer of union—at least in the often brief periods in which it is given by God and before the transforming union of the spiritual marriage—all of the faculties are absorbed. When God draws the person into union, normal consciousness—at least for the most part—simply ceases for as long as the union lasts. Even when it passes, the sense of being absorbed can linger in all of the faculties for several hours—that is, in the depths of one's consciousness—as the person remains in deep prayer (L 18.13). The experience is relatively brief but intense:

> The longest space of time, in my opinion, in which the soul remains in this suspension of all the faculties is very short; should it remain suspended for a half hour, this would be a very long time. I don't think I ever experienced this suspension for so long. It is true that since there is no sensory consciousness one finds it hard to know what is happening. But I am saying that in an occurrence of this prayer only a short time passes without one of the faculties returning to itself. It is the will that holds high the banner; the other two faculties quickly go back to being a bother. Since the will remains quiet, the others are again suspended for a little while—then return again to life. (L 18.12; see also IC 5.1.9)

These brief experiences of union begin to accustom the person to a new depth of relationship and life in and with God.

Images and Analogies

In order to describe and explain the experience of union to her readers, Teresa tries using a variety of often homey images and analogies. In the *Life*, as her prayer was still deepening, the prayer of union is described as the fourth and final way of watering the garden. In this first of her major works, she had not yet arrived herself at the transforming union, nor did she have the fuller understanding of union, its manifestation, and deepening that would be apparent in the clearer description of the progression that she lays out in *The Interior Castle*.[1]

Sleep is another image. Teresa writes that in the prayer of union, in a way, it is as if the faculties of will, intellect, memory, and imagination have fallen asleep. But she realizes that sleep may not be an entirely apt analogy:

> Don't think this union is some kind of dreamy state like the one I mentioned before. I say "dreamy state" because it only seems that the soul is asleep; for neither does it really think it is asleep nor does it feel awake. There is no need here to use any technique to suspend the mind since all the faculties are asleep in this state—and truly asleep—to the things of the world and to ourselves. As a matter of fact, during the time that the union lasts the soul is left as though without its senses, for it has no power to think even if it wants to. In loving, if it does love, it doesn't understand how or what it is it loves or what it would want. In sum, it is like one who in every respect has died to the world so as to live more completely in God. Thus the death is a delightful one, an uprooting from the soul of all the operations it can have while being

1. Daniel de Pablo Maroto, *Teresa en oración: historia, experiencia, doctrina* (Madrid: Editorial de Espiritualidad, 2004), 380n8.

> in the body. The death is a delightful one because in truth it seems that in order to dwell more perfectly in God the soul is so separated from the body that I don't even know if it has life enough to breathe. . . . Nonetheless, its whole intellect would want to be occupied in understanding something of what is felt. And since the soul does not have the energy to attain to this, it is so stunned that, even if consciousness is not completely lost, neither a hand nor a foot stirs, as we say here below when a person is in such a swoon that we think he is dead. (IC 5.1.4)

Although Teresa begins with the image of sleep to describe the prayer of union, she decides that a temporary "delightful death"—during the time of prayer—better describes the nearly complete absorption of normal consciousness during the time of union.

As we have seen, in the fifth dwelling places of *The Interior Castle*, Teresa begins to use the courtship and matrimonial images that will be important in her description of subsequent stages of union. The intimate sharing of friends will become the more deeply intimate marital union of husband and wife. In the fifth dwelling places, the passing experiences of union with God are like "visits" between man and woman in order to become more intimately acquainted. The betrothal and marriage will come later:

> It seems to me that the prayer of union does not yet reach the stage of spiritual betrothal. Here below when two people are to be engaged, there is a discussion about whether they are alike, whether they love each other, and whether they might meet together so as to become more satisfied with each other. So, too, in the case of this union with God, the agreement has been made, and this soul is well informed about the goodness

> of her Spouse and determined to do His will in everything and in as many ways as she sees might make Him happy. . . . But being who He is, the Spouse from that meeting alone leaves her more worthy for the joining of hands, as they say. The soul is left so much in love that it does for its part all it can to avoid disturbing this divine betrothal. But if it is careless about placing its affection in something other than Him, it loses everything. And the loss is as great as the favors He was granting her, and cannot be exaggerated. (IC 5.4.4)

The experience of union in these fifth dwelling places is, in some way, like the visits of man and woman in courtship, but, entering into even passing union with the divine bridegroom necessarily empowers change in the person, "making her more worthy" of their sharing.

In her *Meditation on the Songs of Songs*, Teresa begins a description of the experience of union with the image of marriage, but she passes into that of a nursing mother and her infant, which we have seen elsewhere in her writings:

> But when this most wealthy Bridegroom desires to enrich and favor the soul more, He changes it into Himself to such a point that, just as a person is caused to swoon from great pleasure and happiness, it seems to the soul it is left suspended in those divine arms, leaning on that sacred side and those divine breasts. It doesn't know how to do anything more than rejoice, sustained by the divine milk with which its Spouse is nourishing it and making it better so that He might favor it, and it might merit more each day.
>
> When it awakens from that sleep and that heavenly inebriation, it remains as though stupefied and dazed and with a holy madness. . . . While it was in that intoxication, the soul thought it had no farther to ascend. But when it saw

> itself in a higher degree and completely drenched in the countless grandeurs of God, and sustained in this way, it makes a delicate comparison and says: *Your breasts are better than wine.* An infant doesn't understand how it grows nor does it know how it gets its milk, for without its sucking or doing anything, often the milk is put into its mouth. Likewise, here, the soul is completely ignorant. It knows neither how nor from where that great blessing came to it, nor can it understand. It knows that the blessing is the greatest that can be tasted in life, even if all the delights and pleasures of the world were joined together. It sees that it is nourished and made better and doesn't know when it deserved this. It is instructed in great truths without seeing the Master who teaches it; fortified in virtues and favored by One who knows it well and can do these things for it. It doesn't know what to compare His grace to, unless to the great love a mother has for her child in nourishing and caressing it. (SS 4.4; see also W 31.9)

By using the image of marital love together with that of the tender intimacy of a baby nursing from a mother's breast, Teresa has provided powerfully evocative images of the tender, loving intimacy of divine union.

Union in Prayer and Union with the Divine Will

Teresa addresses the prayer of union in the fifth dwelling places of *The Interior Castle*. Nonetheless, in the third chapter of those dwelling places, she believes that it is important to make clear that the truly important union with God is the union of our will with the divine will. It is true that the prayer of union is a very great gift and blessing. It is the fruit of a will already greatly conformed to God in living and of a history of surrendering to God in prayer. And, as would be expected, union with God in prayer brings with it an even greater disposition to pursue complete conformity and union with God's will in our manner of living. But it is the union with the divine will in life—not the prayer of union itself—that must be the true goal in this life. Teresa assures her readers that this has always been her fundamental goal: "This union with God's will is the union I have desired all my life; it is the union I ask the Lord for always and the one that is clearest and safest" (IC 5.3.5). And it should be the true goal for the communities of her reform: "Here in our religious life the Lord asks of us only two things: love of His Majesty and love of our neighbor. These are what we must work for. By observing them with perfection, we do His will and so will be united with Him" (IC 5.3.7).

Teresa titles the third chapter of the fifth dwelling places: "Tells about another kind of union the soul can reach with God's help and of how important love of neighbor is for this union." Here, she makes clear that it is the union of our wills with the divine will that ultimately matters, and without the union of wills, we cannot hope to arrive at the "delightful" union in deep prayer. She writes:

> Since so much gain comes from entering this place, it will be good to avoid giving the impression that those to whom the Lord doesn't give things that are so supernatural are left without hope. True union can very well be reached, with God's help, if we make the effort to obtain it by keeping our wills fixed only on that which is God's will. Oh, how many of us there are who will say we do this, and it will seem to us that we don't want anything else and that we would die for this truth, as I believe I have said! Well I tell you, and I will often

> repeat it, that if what you say is true you will have obtained this favor from the Lord, and you needn't care at all about the other delightful union that was mentioned. That which is most valuable in the delightful union is that it proceeds from this union of which I'm now speaking; and one cannot arrive at the delightful union if the union coming from being resigned to God's will is not very certain. (IC 5.3.3)

The prayer of union, for Teresa, is a sublime blessing to those who receive it. Nonetheless, though less sublime and more humble and ordinary in experience, it is the conformity of our will to God's that ultimately matters.

Effects

The prayer of union bears an abundance of fruit in the life of the person of prayer—for self and in a firmer desire to offer loving benefit to others. One of these fruits is a certitude of the divine presence. One may have sensed, even profoundly, God's presence in various moments and stages of prayer, but the prayer of union in which God effects a union in the very center of the person's depths, results in a far more solid certainty:

> God so places Himself in the interior of that soul that when it returns to itself it can in no way doubt that it was in God and God was in it. This truth remains with it so firmly that even though years go by without God's granting that favor again, the soul can neither forget nor doubt that it was in God and God was in it. This certitude is what matters now, for I shall speak of the effects of this prayer afterward. Now, you will ask me, how did the soul see this truth or understand if it didn't see or understand anything?

> I don't say that it then saw the truth but that afterward it sees the truth clearly, not because of a vision but because of a certitude remaining in the soul that only God can place there. (IC 5.1.9–10)

Elsewhere, she writes: "I can only say that the soul appears to be joined to God, and there remains such certitude about this union that the soul cannot help believing in the truth of it" (L 18.14). Likewise, later, she affirms the same: "God so places Himself in the interior of that soul that when it returns to itself it can in no way doubt that it was in God and God was in it" (IC 5.1.9).

A second effect is a deeper understanding of God that is not based on study or ordinary reflection. Following again the image of courtship, Teresa says that, through the union experienced during the time of prayer, God wishes the person to come to a more profound, noncognitive knowledge of who God is, so that the person may be better prepared for yet deeper intimacy: "As a result He grants this mercy, for He desired her to know Him more and that they might meet together, as they say, and be united. We can say that union is like this, for it passes in a very short time. In it there no longer takes place the exchanging of gifts, but the soul sees secretly who this Spouse is that she is going to accept. Through the work of the senses and the faculties she couldn't in any way or in a thousand years understand what she understands here in the shortest time" (IC 5.4.4). The experience of union brings a loving knowledge of God not gained by study but rather by the intimate, loving union itself. The person knows God from having been in union with the divine.

Other effects include a new ardor and resolve, a deeper detachment from things that are now even more clearly seen as less than God, and most especially a greater humility as one realizes the awesome gift that one has received:

> Such prayer is the source of heroic promises, of resolutions, and of ardent desires; it is the beginning of contempt for the world because of a clear perception of the world's vanity. The soul is much more improved and in a higher state than it was after the previous degrees of prayer. Its humility is deeper because it sees plainly that through no diligence of its own did it receive that very generous and magnificent gift and that it played no role in obtaining or experiencing it. Since there is no hidden cobweb in a room where much sun enters, the soul sees clearly that it is most unworthy; it sees its misery. Vainglory goes off so far that it doesn't seem possible for the soul to have any. (L 19.2)

The authenticity of any prayer is known by the fruit it bears; and this is profoundly true of any experience of union with God.

The prayer of union brings a greater desire to share its benefits with others, not only in material ways but in the desire for others to share in its spiritual treasure: "This progress in virtue remains for some time with the soul. It can now, with clear understanding that the fruits are not its own, begin to distribute them since it has no need of them. It starts to show signs of a soul that guards heavenly treasures and has the desire to share them with others, and it beseeches God that it may not be the only rich one. It begins to be of benefit to its neighbors almost without knowing it or doing anything of itself" (L 19.3).

But the benefit to others is provided not only by intentional actions to do so but by the simple radiating of the impact of sharing so intimately in union with God: "I hold that it is God's desire that a favor so great not be given in vain; if a person doesn't herself benefit, the favor will benefit others. For since the soul is left with these desires and virtues that were mentioned, it always brings profit to other souls during the time that it continues to live virtuously; and they catch fire from its fire" (IC 5.3.1). It might seem that the prayer of union is so profoundly personal and interpersonal with God that it would be entirely private, but Teresa says that it reveals and promotes our sense of relationship and responsibility for others.

Spiritual Betrothal

(L 20–21; IC 6; SS 6; ST 59.7–17)

In the sixth dwelling places of *The Interior Castle*, Teresa discusses the progression of prayer into a deeper union with God, often accompanied by extraordinary experiences such as raptures, locutions, and visions. The quiet absorption of simple union in the fifth dwelling places passes into ecstatic prayer in the sixth—prayer that is sometimes delightful, other times painful, and often both at once. It is the longest section of *The Interior Castle*. Teresa herself had suffered greatly from doubt and confusion during this period, sometimes caused by her confessors who failed to understand these deep and authentic experiences of prayer. She hoped to help others who entered this stage but might lack other books or experienced spiritual guides to counsel and reassure them.

When Teresa had written the *Life* about twelve years earlier, she was herself in a long period of this ecstatic prayer with the many extraordinary manifestations she describes. This was her experience from when she was about forty-three to fifty-seven years old. She describes this stage of prayer in the *Life* as the third and fourth ways of watering the garden (L 16–21, 23–40).

At the time, she had thought that this was the very height of prayer. By the time she wrote *The Interior Castle*, however, she had entered what she called the seventh dwelling places. Her discussion in this later work, then, expresses her more mature experience and thus a better ability to organize and explain what she herself confesses is so often difficult to explain in ordinary words and concepts.[2]

Continuing with the courtship metaphor that she began in the fifth dwelling places, Teresa describes the spiritual betrothal which occurs in these sixth dwelling places. It is a deeper, more abiding experience of union—though yet short of the spiritual marriage of the seventh. It was brought on, in her experience, by a rapture: "And thus you will see what His Majesty does to conclude this betrothal, which I understand comes about when He gives the soul raptures that draw it out of its senses" (IC 6.4.2). What Teresa variously calls raptures, ecstasies, and flights of the spirit are precisely a reflection as well as external manifestations of this deeper union. As she understands it, according to the categories of the time, the human faculties of intellect, will, and memory are not yet ready for or fully accommodated to the deep inflow and communion with God. The union effected deep within the center of the soul overflows into the faculties and the body, producing these unusual, amazing and, at first, frightening effects. They prepare for the transforming union yet to come and will cease when it occurs.[3]

We must recall as we read her descriptions that Teresa has already told us that there are an immense number of rooms

2. Kavanaugh's commentary on the sixth dwelling places is particularly helpful in understanding what Teresa is trying to describe and explain. See St. Teresa of Avila, *The Interior Castle: Study Edition*, 2nd ed., ed. Kieran Kavanaugh, trans. Kieran Kavanaugh and Otilio Rodriguez (Washington, D.C.; ICS Publications, 2020), 191–356.

3. Teresa of Avila, *The Interior Castle: Study Edition*, 254.

in each dwelling and many authentic paths that might be walked—that is, not everyone will experience what she experienced in the way that it unfolded in her journey of prayer. She did not believe that any such experiences or phenomena were necessary for attaining the transforming union to come. Today we can see that our experience of personal encounter and communion with God—and certainly our naming and understanding of it—can be different in different cultures and times.[4] At the same time, Teresa clearly believes that others may find that they have similar experiences, and she is hopeful that her descriptions will be of help in this otherwise uncharted territory. In fact, her presentation of these experiences is virtually unmatched in the entire Christian mystical tradition in their detail, length, and ordering.

It might seem that Teresa or other mystics who have shared some of her experiences would thereafter be living in a kind of alternate universe of utter transcendence, beyond worldly activities and concerns, but, as we see in Teresa's own life, nothing could be farther from the truth. Through the many years that she lived in sixth dwelling places and into seventh, Teresa continued the work of founding and overseeing monasteries of her reform, negotiating with donors and ecclesiastical officials, addressing the controversies between the Discalced and Calced Carmelites, and writing countless letters of both profound spiritual advice and mundane practicalities. For Teresa, prayer and life were never separated. She was a woman of the deepest spiritual experience as well as a person with two feet firmly on the ground, living to the full the life that God had given her and embracing both its ordinary joys and its challenges.[5]

---

4. Maroto, *Teresa en oración*, 386.

5. Maroto, *Teresa en oración*, 386–87.

The Extraordinary Experiences

When people pass through the sixth dwelling places, as Teresa experienced and described it, extraordinary experiences are frequent and unavoidable—they come upon the person, sometimes unexpected and even unwanted. Speaking of raptures, she writes that they "are very common and there is no means to avoid them even though they may take place in public. Hence, persecutions and criticism" (IC 6.6.1). Again, her most systematic and mature discussion of these experiences appear in *The Interior Castle*, though she describes them more than defines them. Teresa addresses locutions (words that are heard deep within the person, independent of the use of one's normal hearing: IC 6.3), raptures, ecstasies, transports, and flights of the spirit—which are roughly the same, all of them involving some experience of being pulled out of normal consciousness (IC 6.4–5)—and visions (IC 6.8–9). They are special gifts of God that bear great fruit in the person, but they are not to be sought directly. Teresa warns of the danger of being deceived in at least some of these experiences—whether deceived by the devil or self-deceived, especially in persons who are just overly emotional, who are suffering physical manifestations of trying too hard, or confusing an intense (but ultimately superficial) consolation for these deeper infused gifts (IC 6.6).

In the *Life*, Teresa describes the difference between the simple union that she describes in the fifth dwelling places and the deeper experiences of union that overflows into the faculties and senses in the sixth:

> I should like to know how to explain, with God's help, the difference there is between union and rapture, or, as they call it, elevation or flight of the spirit, or transport, which are all the

> same. I mean that these latter terms, though different, refer to the same thing; it is also called ecstasy. The advantage rapture has over union is great. The rapture produces much stronger effects and causes many other phenomena. Union seems the same at the beginning, in the middle, and at the end; and it takes place in the interior of the soul. But since these other phenomena are of a higher degree, they produce their effect both interiorly and exteriorly. (L 20.1)

Teresa is aware that these phenomena are ultimately peripheral to the deeper union occurring in the deepest center of the soul, drawing the person closer to the transforming union of the final dwelling places.

Her description of a rapture will enable us to understand something of what she means in speaking of these types of phenomena:

> In a rapture, believe me, God carries off for Himself the entire soul, and, as to someone who is His own and His spouse, He begins showing it some little part of the kingdom that it has gained by being espoused to Him. However small that part of His kingdom may be, everything that there is in this great God is magnificent. And He doesn't want any hindrance from anyone, neither from the faculties nor from the senses, but he immediately commands the doors of all these dwelling places to be closed; and only that door to His dwelling place remains open so that we can enter. (IC 6.4.9)

A little later in the same text, she writes:

> For in desiring to carry off this soul, He takes away the breath so that, even though the other senses sometimes last a little longer, a person cannot speak at all; although at other times

> everything is taken away at once, and the hands and the body grow cold so that the person doesn't seem to have any life; nor sometimes is it known whether he is breathing. This situation lasts but a short while, I mean in its intensity; for when this extreme suspension lets up a little, it seems that the body returns to itself somewhat and is nourished so as to die again and give more life to the soul. Nevertheless so extreme an ecstasy doesn't last long. (IC 6.4.13; see also L 20.3, 18)

The experience of union in the sixth dwelling places can sometimes carry away the normal consciousness more completely and more dramatically than in the fifth dwelling places and overflow into manifestations in the body.

In the *Life*, Teresa does not really distinguish raptures, ecstasies, transports, and flights of spirit. The title of the fourth chapter of the sixth dwelling places of *The Interior Castle* suggests the same posture: "Treats of when God suspends the soul in prayer with rapture or ecstasy or transport, which are all the same in my opinion." Especially in the *Spiritual Testimonies* (ST 59.7–11), she does provide some distinctions among them based on differences in the way that they are experienced. But all of them are simply more exterior (but sublime) manifestations of the deeper union within. She writes, for example: "The difference between *rapture* and *transport* is that in rapture the soul only gradually dies to these exterior things and loses its senses and lives to God. The transport comes swiftly through some knowledge the Lord gives in the soul's intimate depths that makes it seem to the soul that its higher part is being carried away; for in its opinion this higher part leaves the body" (ST 59.9).

The description of these extraordinary experiences of various types and degrees must not obscure the fact that it is the union itself that is central. Since others may undergo similar experiences in their spiritual journeys without adequate spiritual direction to reassure and guide them, Teresa wants to provide description and counsel. But again, the experiences—no matter how extraordinary and sublime—are secondary to the union that produces or is manifested by them.

Teresa also addresses the experience of locutions—what seem like divine words that are intimately spoken to the person (IC 6.3). Some of these might be heard by the ears, others seem to be heard within without passing through normal hearing, and still others seem directly implanted within the person's depths. She herself had this experience, and she gives some counsel about discerning their authenticity. But she advises that generally they are best ignored, because such experiences can also come from the devil or from the imagination. Later, Teresa speaks of visions (IC 6.8–9), some of which involve images that are received deep within and others which can only be called "vision" by a kind of analogy since they do not really involve images at all.

Sufferings of This Stage

Teresa begins the eleven chapters of the sixth dwelling places in *The Interior Castle* with a chapter on the unique sufferings of this stage. The title of the first chapter begins: "Discusses how greater trials come when the Lord begins to grant greater favors. This chapter is good for souls undergoing interior trials." As sublime and delightful as the extraordinary experiences can be, this period is also marked by suffering. In the same chapter, she goes on to describe the pain that results from gossip, ridicule, and misunderstanding even from friends caused by these extraordinary experiences coming to be known (though the person ultimately gets beyond any concern about what others think). But, at the same time, praise is also a trial since the person feels a profound sense of being unworthy of any. Such persons suffer the inability to express what is being experienced even to their spiritual directors. As Teresa had detailed in the *Life*, directors for their part can bring on even greater confusion and doubt when they fail to understand or give bad counsel. The person begins to doubt that he or she really has—or ever had—an authentic love for God, fearing that everything already experienced was either a result of deception by the devil or a profound self-deception. Any kind of effort at earlier prayer forms seems empty, useless, completely lacking in consolation. There are physical illnesses and pains. But, more, as divine favors multiply and become more advanced, there comes forms of suffering, physical and spiritual, that Teresa cannot even describe.

The title of chapter seven of the sixth dwelling places "discusses the kind of suffering those souls to whom God grants the favors mentioned feel concerning their sins." Teresa is not speaking here of holding on to guilt from past sins that have already been repented. Rather, she is describing an abiding sense of the ingratitude of our past sins. Having been so blessed by God in having journeyed so far in one's intimate friendship with Christ, one recalls how many invitations, opportunities, and graces were neglected. Even at this advanced state, the person recognizes that the possibility of sin yet remains.

But the most profound form of suffering is created by the felt tension between assurance of the divine presence deep within and, at the same time, a wounded yearning for the loving fulfillment of which current experience is still merely a foretaste (IC 6.2.3). As Teresa describes it, it comes to be felt as a yearning to depart this life in order to enjoy the fullest union with God in the life to come. She writes: "As a result of these wonderful favors the soul is left so full of longings to enjoy completely the One who grants them that it lives in a great though delightful torment. With the strongest yearnings to die, and thus usually with tears, it begs God to take it from this exile. Everything it sees wearies it" (IC 6.6.1). Having tasted union with God in this life, the things of this world seem superficial and unsubstantial. The experience is succinctly portrayed in the refrain of one of her poems: "I die because I do not die."[6] The person feels left hanging between the passing things of life and the joys of heaven:

> . . . nor can the soul think of anything else than of why it is grieving, of how it is absent from its Good, and of why it should want to live. It feels a strange solitude because no creature in all the earth provides it company, nor do I believe would any heavenly creature, not being the One whom it loves; rather, everything torments it. But the soul sees that it is like a person hanging, who cannot support himself on any earthly thing; nor can it ascend to heaven. On fire with this thirst, it cannot get to the water; and the thirst is not one that is endurable but already at such a point that nothing will take it away. Nor does the soul desire that the thirst be taken away save by that water of which our Lord spoke to the Samaritan woman. (IC 6.11.5)

Teresa's use of the analogy of human love can allow the reader to remember that love poetry and music are full of references to the painful yearnings of those who are "dying with love" until they can be fully united with their human beloved.

Being wounded with love can be experienced as an arrow that pierces the heart, causing a delightful, burning pain. Again, following the analogy of human love, we recall that secular

---

6. Poem 1 ("Aspirations toward Eternal Life") in *The Collected Works of St. Teresa of Avila*, vol. 3, 375.

Valentine's Day cards are full of little cupids with their arrows ready to pierce the heart of the beloved. Speaking of being wounded by the divine love experienced in the prayer of union that is sublime but remains passing, Teresa writes: "Another type of prayer quite frequent is a kind of *wound* in which it seems as though an arrow is thrust into the heart, or into the soul itself. Thus the wound causes a severe pain which makes the soul moan; yet, the pain is so delightful the soul would never want it to go away. This pain is not in the senses, nor is the sore a physical one; but the pain lies in the interior depths of the soul without resemblance to bodily pain" (ST 59.17; see also L 29.10; IC 6.2.4; 6.11.2). Teresa herself experienced this mystical piercing of the heart—called the "transverberation"—on several occasions, as she describes in the *Life* (L 29.13).

Some authors view Teresa's descriptions of the trials of this period to be her form of describing what John of the Cross calls the dark night of spirit—the passive purifications of the person in his or her depths—which is the final, deepest purgation of the person as preparation for full union.[7] Just as the experiences themselves reflect the need to fully accommodate the body to receive the divine inflow deep within, so the sufferings are invitations to embrace a deeper purification and surrender in preparation for what, with God's gift, will come.

Effects of Spiritual Betrothal

Although it can be difficult for the reader to get past Teresa's description of the extraordinary experiences, she is more concerned with their effects. There is a profound knowledge of

7. See, for example, Kavanaugh's comments in Teresa of Avila, *The Interior Castle: Study Edition*, 205.

God, not based on study or reflection: "It happens that within an instant so many things together are taught him that if he were to work for many years with his imagination and mind in order to systematize them he wouldn't be able to do so, not with even one thousandth part of one of them" (IC 6.5.7). Further, the person gains a deeper self-knowledge and humility before this God and a still greater sense of the passing value of anything that is merely of this life: "Three things, especially, are left in it to a very sublime degree: knowledge of the grandeur of God, because the more we see in this grandeur the greater is our understanding; self-knowledge and humility upon seeing that something so low in comparison with the Creator of so many grandeurs dared to offend Him (and neither does the soul dare look up at Him); the third, little esteem of earthly things save for those that can be used for the service of so great a God" (IC 6.5.10). The authentic prayer of union with God does not yield a sense of pride or being better or more advanced than others, but rather wonder, humility, and detachment from what is infinitely less than God.

Do Not Abandon the Humanity of Jesus

Teresa's whole spirituality and understanding of the Christian journey is profoundly Christocentric. In the earlier stages of prayer, regular meditation on the life of Jesus is essential to grow in discipleship and prayer. Since prayer is shared intimacy with the divine friend, we must come to know him and draw close to him. But Teresa insists that, even as prayer passes well beyond any forms of meditation and acquired prayer, the person should never feel that he or she can move beyond Jesus in his sacred humanity. The time comes to pass beyond active meditation, and in infused forms of prayer, it becomes impossible. But Jesus must remain the focus of our silent interior gaze.

Jesus Christ remains, for Teresa, at each and every stage, the mediator between God and humanity and the way into union with God.

In the title of the twenty-second chapter of the *Life*, Teresa writes: "Treats of how safe a path it is for contemplatives not to raise the spirit to high things unless the Lord raises it and of how the humanity of Christ must be the means to the most sublime contemplation." Teresa expresses the same challenge in the seventh chapter of the sixth dwelling places of *The Interior Castle*, though at greater length and based on more mature experience. In part, the title of the chapter reads: "Tells what a great mistake it is, however spiritual one may be, not to practice keeping the humanity of our Lord and Savior Jesus Christ present in one's mind; also His most sacred Passion and life, His glorious Mother, and the saints." Recognizing that there are those who teach that the humanity of Christ must be left behind, she states firmly: "They will not make me admit that such a road is a good one" (IC 6.7.5).

Jesus, Teresa reasons, is the sure guide and mediator. To leave aside focus on him is to risk going astray:

> How much more is it necessary not to withdraw through one's own efforts from all our good and help which is the most sacred humanity of our Lord Jesus Christ. I cannot believe that these souls do so, but they just don't understand; and they will do harm to themselves and to others. At least I assure them that they will not enter these last two dwelling places. For if they lose the guide, who is the good Jesus, they will not hit upon the right road. It will be quite an accomplishment if they remain safely in the other dwelling places. The Lord Himself says that He is the way; the Lord says also that He is the light and that no one can go to the Father but

> through Him, and "anyone who sees me sees my Father." They will say that another meaning is given to these words. I don't know about those other meanings; I have got along very well with this one that my soul always feels to be true. (IC 6.7.6)

Jesus is the true way, guide, and light, not only of beginners, but of every person at every stage of prayer. The manner of our encounter and the intimacy of our sharing change and deepen, but Jesus must always remain the principal focus of our faith and prayer.

Teresa acknowledges that, after a certain point, contemplatives can find that they are unable to engage in discursive meditation as they did before: "There are some souls—and there are many who have spoken about it to me—who brought by our Lord to perfect contemplation would like to be in that prayer always; but that is impossible. Yet this favor of the Lord remains with them in such a way that afterward they cannot engage as before in discursive thought about the mysteries of the Passion and life of Christ. I don't know the reason, but this inability is very common, for the intellect becomes less capable of meditation" (IC 6.7.7).

But the answer, she writes, is not to give up on the humanity of Jesus but to rather to leave behind discursive meditation about him. Remaining focused on the humanity of Jesus means keeping the mysteries of his life in mind and mostly especially maintaining a silent, interior gazing on him:

> This prayer [discursive meditation] is the kind that those whom God has brought to supernatural things and to perfect contemplation are right in saying they cannot practice. As I have said, I don't know the reason, but usually they cannot practice discursive reflection. But I say that a person will

> not be right if he says he does not dwell on these mysteries or often have them in mind, especially when the Catholic Church celebrates them. Nor is it possible for the soul to forget that it has received so much from God, so many precious signs of love, for these are living sparks that will enkindle it more in its love for our Lord. But I say this person doesn't understand himself, because the soul understands these mysteries in a more perfect manner. The intellect represents them in such a way, and they are so stamped on the memory, that the mere sight of the Lord fallen to the ground in the garden with that frightful sweat is enough to last the intellect not only an hour but many days, while it looks with a simple gaze at who He is. (IC 6.7.11)

The mysteries of our faith are so "stamped" on the person of deep prayer that, even without active meditation, the focus on Christ in his sacred humanity remains.

Spiritual Marriage

(IC 7; SS 7; ST 46 and 31)

Teresa describes the spiritual marriage in the seventh and final dwelling places of *The Interior Castle.* The intimate sharing between the person at his or her depths with God reaches its greatest depths possible in this life. The experience of union with God in now abiding, without the experience of the absorption of one's consciousness. Although the person carries on with the normal realities of daily human living and continues to feel the full range of human emotions, deep within, the person is always in union with God. She cautions: "Don't think by this, daughters, that a person fails to remember to eat and sleep—doing so is no small torment—and to do all that he is obliged to in conformity with his state in life. We are speaking of interior matters" (IC 7.3.3). This continued grounding in normal human life and activity is obvious from the many letters written by Teresa after she herself had attained the spiritual marriage—as reported in a testimony that she wrote in 1572 (ST 31) about ten years before her death—in which she carried on the business of the reform, instructed and counseled others, and complained of her ill health.

In the abiding union, God is present and active—in fact, the principal agent—of every conscious thought and action. But, since union with God is the fulfillment of authentic human living, the person is not somehow less human but rather more fully and completely human. It is from the pinnacle of the spiritual journey that Teresa reflects on and teaches about all that has gone before in *The Interior Castle*. Or, following her image of marriage, we might say that she reflects on the history of a relationship, a friendship, deepening intimacy, more intimate encounters, communion, and becoming one.

All of the infused forms of prayer that Teresa has described have been, to some extent, ineffable. Despite her gift for the use of metaphors and her magisterial teaching thus far, she recognizes that she has not been able to fully describe or explain the experiences about which she is writing. But in the seventh dwelling places, she feels that she has reached the end of any ability to even approach an adequate sense of what has occurred: "What God communicates here to the soul in an instant is a secret so great and a favor so sublime—and the delight the soul experiences so extreme—that I don't know what to compare it to. I can say only that the Lord wishes to reveal for that moment, in a more sublime manner than through any spiritual vision or taste, the glory of heaven. One can say no more—insofar as can be understood—than that the soul, I mean the spirit, is made one with God" (IC 7.2.3). The person who regularly experiences union with God gains a profound knowledge of God but not in the form of concepts and categories that can be grasped by ordinary reflection or explained to others by those means.

Contrast with Spiritual Betrothal

Arriving at the spiritual marriage, the extraordinary phenomena of the earlier stages cease. The depths of the person's being has now been fully prepared to receive the divine inflow and union. The body has become accommodated to what is happening, and the divine union no longer overflows into the body in such a dramatic way: "I am amazed as well to see that when the soul arrives here all raptures are taken away. . . . Perhaps the reason is that the Lord has now fortified, enlarged, and made the soul capable" (IC 7.3.12).

Teresa attempts to describe the difference between the union with God in the previous stages and the abiding union in the seventh dwelling places using a number of different images:

> The spiritual betrothal is different, for the two often separate. And the union is also different because, even though it is the joining of two things into one, in the end the two can be separated and each remains by itself. We observe this ordinarily, for the favor of union with the Lord passes quickly, and afterward the soul remains without that company; I mean, without awareness of it. In this other favor from the Lord, no. The soul always remains with its God in that center. Let us say that the union is like the joining of two wax candles to such an extent that the flame coming from them is but one, or that the wick, the flame, and the wax are all one. But afterward one candle can be easily separated from the other and there are two candles; the same holds for the wick. In the spiritual

> marriage the union is like what we have when rain falls from the sky into a river or fount; all is water, for the rain that fell from heaven cannot be divided or separated from the water of the river. Or it is like what we have when a little stream enters the sea, there is no means of separating the two. Or, like the bright light entering a room through two different windows; although the streams of light are separate when entering the room, they become one. (IC 7.2.4)

In using the image of rainwater joining the water of a river or the water in a stream entering the sea, Teresa is speaking of the *experience* of union with God. She is not offering a theological statement about the *nature* of union—as if the distinction between creature and Creator has been dissolved.

In previous encounters and experiences of God, it had seemed to some degree as if the divine presence had come from outside. But, with abiding union, the encounter is experienced entirely within one's depths:

> In the spiritual marriage, there is still much less remembrance of the body because this secret union takes place in the very interior center of the soul, which must be where God Himself is, and in my opinion there is no need of any door for Him to enter. I say there is no need of any door because everything that has been said up until now seems to take place by means of the senses and faculties, and this appearance of the humanity of the Lord must also. But that which comes to pass in the union of the spiritual marriage is very different. The Lord appears in this center of the soul, not in an imaginative vision but in an intellectual one, although more delicate than those mentioned, as He appeared to the apostles without entering through the door when He said to them *pax vobis*. (IC 7.2.3)

The person in the abiding union remains always with God who dwells at the heart, as the ground, or in the very center of the soul.

Both Trinitarian and Christocentric

The experience of the abiding union is both Trinitarian and Christocentric. The person has a profound sense of the presence of the triune God in all three Persons. This comes to be known in what Teresa describes as an intellectual vision—that is, a profound and enduring experience and certainty of the triune presence with something analogous to normal vision, though it involves no real images at all:

> When the soul is brought into that dwelling place, the Most Blessed Trinity, all three Persons, through an intellectual vision, is revealed to it through a certain representation of the truth. First there comes an enkindling in the spirit in the manner of a cloud of magnificent splendor; and these Persons are distinct, and through an admirable knowledge the soul understands as a most profound truth that all three Persons are one substance and one power and one knowledge and one God alone. It knows in such a way that what we hold by faith, it understands, we can say, through sight—although the sight is not with the bodily eyes nor with the eyes of the soul, because we are not dealing with an imaginative vision. Here all three Persons communicate themselves to it, speak to it, and explain those words of the Lord in the Gospel: that He and the Father and the Holy Spirit will come to dwell with the soul that loves Him and keeps His commandments.
>
> Oh, God help me! How different is hearing and believing these words from understanding their truth in this way! Each

> day this soul becomes more amazed, for these Persons never seem to leave it any more, but it clearly beholds, in the way that was mentioned, that they are within it. In the extreme interior, in some place very deep within itself, the nature of which it doesn't know how to explain, because of a lack of learning, it perceives this divine company. (IC 7.1.6–7)

To experience the indwelling of the triune God is to enter into a profound, loving knowledge of the inner life of God and of the interaction of the three Divine Persons with us.

In her own journey, the experience of the presence of the triune God—even in this deepest of union—was mediated through a vision of the humanity of Christ. But even while recognizing that the experience of others may differ, she is making a more fundamental point of the continuing central place of Christ in bringing the person into the deepest union with the Trinity:

> The first time the favor is granted, His Majesty desires to show Himself to the soul through an imaginative vision of His most sacred humanity so that the soul will understand and not be ignorant of receiving this sovereign gift. With other persons the favor will be received in another form. With regard to the one of whom we are speaking, the Lord represented Himself to her, just after she had received Communion, in the form of shining splendor, beauty, and majesty, as He was after His resurrection, and told her that now it was time that she consider as her own what belonged to Him and that He would take care of what was hers. (IC 7.2.1)

Teresa further describes her own experience in the *Spiritual Testimonies*: "He appeared to me in an imaginative vision, as at other times, very interiorly, and He gave me His right hand

and said: 'Behold this nail; it is a sign you will be My bride from today on. Until now you have not merited this; from now on not only will you look after My honor as being the honor of your Creator, King, and God, but you will look after it as My true bride. My honor is yours, and yours Mine'" (ST 31: "Spiritual Marriage"). For Teresa, Christ remains always the way into the life of the triune God—not merely embraced in a conceptual way but rather experienced in the person's depths.

Transformed in Christ

Teresa's explicit focus is often on the experience of prayer. One of her driving purposes in writing is to help and counsel people to maneuver and walk the journey of prayer, especially in its most advanced stages. But prayer, as we have seen, is never her exclusive focus or concern. She is concerned, too, with the necessary preparation for deepening prayer—for example, in the three essential virtues and in the image of the little caterpillar weaving the cocoon in which it will be transformed, as described in the fifth dwelling places. And she consistently reports on the effects that follow upon encounters and union with God, especially in the growth of virtues. The same is true even in the seventh dwelling places. What she is describing is not only the deepest intimacy with the triune God in and through Christ but also the profound transformation of the whole person in Christ. The journey through the dwelling places has also been a path into deeper self-knowledge and the more profound transformation that God has especially been accomplishing. In the seventh dwelling places, the person truly discovers and awakens the authentic self in Christ, totally filled and immersed in God. The spiritual marriage is an abiding and transforming union.

Referring again to the transformation of the silkworm into a beautiful little butterfly after freeing itself of the cocoon in which it has "died," she writes: "Now, then, we are saying that this little butterfly has already died, with supreme happiness for having found repose and because Christ lives in it" (IC 7.3.1). And, using the same image, she writes: "Perhaps this is what St. Paul means in saying *He that is joined or united to the Lord becomes one spirit with him*, and is referring to this sovereign marriage, presupposing that His Majesty has brought the soul to it through union. And he also says: For me to live is Christ, and to die is gain. The soul as well, I think, can say these words now because this state is the place where the little butterfly we mentioned dies, and with the greatest joy because its life is now Christ" (IC 7.2.5).

The deepest prayer of abiding union together with a true transformation in Christ brings with it a profound and durable peace in the center of the soul, whatever may happen. But this does not free the person from the normal struggles of everyday human living: "It should not be thought that the faculties, senses, and passions are always in this peace; the soul is, yes. But in those other dwelling places, times of war, trial, and fatigue are never lacking; however, they are such that they do not take the soul from its place and its peace; that is, as a rule" (IC 7.2.10). Later, she adds: "I tell you, sisters, that the cross is not wanting but it doesn't disquiet or make them lose peace" (IC 7.3.15).

The person in the deepest union with God has not passed into some kind of angelic state but remains a child of Adam and Eve and thus still capable of sin: "Nor should it pass through your minds that, since these souls have such determination and strong desires not to commit any imperfection for anything on earth, they fail to commit many imperfections, and even sins. Advertently, no; for the Lord must give souls such as these very particular help against such a thing. I mean venial sins, for from what these souls can understand they are free from mortal sins, although not immune. That they might have some sins they don't know about is no small torment to them" (IC 7.4.3). Union with God in this life does not make us less human nor does it remove our freedom to sin. For Teresa, self-knowledge and self-vigilance remain important.

The Challenge: Works of Love

As we saw in an earlier chapter, Teresa frequently refers to the gospel story of the sisters Martha and Mary who, in the tradition, are often seen to represent the active, or apostolic, life and the contemplative life. But Teresa consistently insists on the need for both—that each of us must be both the apostolic Martha and the contemplative Mary at the same time, responding to what God calls for in any particular moment. In short, Martha and Mary are sisters who must walk hand-in-hand. This is so even and perhaps especially when the person has passed into the seventh dwelling places. The title of chapter four is "Concludes by explaining what she thinks our Lord's purpose is in granting such great favors to the soul and how it is necessary that Martha and Mary join together" (IC 7.4 title).

It is easy to see that a person in union with a God of love—in whom this God is the principal partner in the person's conscious thoughts and actions—must, by necessity, direct his or her attention to works of love for others: "This is the reason for prayer, my daughters, the purpose of this spiritual marriage: the birth always of good works, good works" (IC 7.4.6). We recall that Teresa follows her definition of prayer as an intimate sharing with the friend who loves us by saying: "In order that love be true and the friendship endure, the wills of the friends must be in accord" (L 8.5). Here in the final dwelling places, where the wills of the friends have been truly united, love expressed in active works of self-giving are the necessary fruit. United with God and yet remaining in ordinary flesh-and-blood human bodies, the divine love that rules the person's depths must be expressed and lived in relationship with the people around us. The transforming union seeks to pursue God's loving and transforming work in the world.

Epilogue

Is Everyone Called to Infused Contemplation?

Did Teresa of Jesus believe that every Christian is called to infused contemplative prayer and even divine union in this life? It's actually a little hard to say. She certainly encouraged her readers to continue to strive, to the degree that it is in our power, to prepare ourselves for contemplation and union. She believed that true contemplation can only be attained by divine gift, but she also knew that God likes to give: "What will He not give, who is so fond of giving and who can give all that He wants?" (IC 5.1.5) and "His Majesty never tires of giving" (W 32.12). She addresses God: "Who is more fond than You of giving, or of serving even at a cost to Yourself, when there is someone open to receive?" (F 2.7). But God always remains free to give if and when and to whom God wills. Still, Teresa would like to believe—and recommends that we act with the belief—that God will give contemplative gifts to those who do not give up: "for it is He who must bestow supernatural prayer, and He will grant it to you if you do not stop short on the road but try hard until you reach the end" (W 25.4).

Looking again at some texts cited earlier in other contexts, we will examine Teresa's efforts to respond to the question of what might be called a "universal invitation to contemplation."

Some Never Receive Infused Prayer

Teresa knew people of dedicated faith and mature Christian living—even among her own nuns—who, even after many years of faithful prayer and sincere longing—had never received these infused gifts. She writes, for example: "I know an elderly person who lives a good life, is penitential and an excellent servant of God, who has spent many hours for many years in vocal prayer, but in mental prayer she's helpless; the most she can do is go slowly in reciting the vocal prayers. There are a number of other persons of this kind. If humility is present, I don't believe they will be any the worse off in the end but will be very much the equals of those who receive many delights" (W 17.3). Her most focused response to this reality is found in *The Way of Perfection* (W 16–18). The title of chapter seventeen encapsulates her response: "Not all souls are suited for contemplation, and some reach it late. The truly humble person must be content with the path along which God leads him."

All of her nuns were called to prayer, but receiving the gift of contemplation is out of their control: "So, not because all in this house practice prayer must all be contemplatives; that's impossible. And it would be very distressing for the one who isn't a contemplative if she didn't understand the truth that to be a contemplative is a gift from God; and since being one isn't necessary for salvation, nor does God demand this, she shouldn't think anyone will demand it of her. So, you will not fail to be very perfect if you do what has been mentioned" (W 17.2).

If the nuns practice the essential and other virtues faithfully, they have nothing to be ashamed of nor to complain of: "In humility, mortification, detachment, and the other virtues there is always greater security. There is nothing to fear; don't be afraid that you will fail to reach the perfection of those who are very contemplative" (W 17.4). Speaking of the two gospel sisters, Teresa notes that, although Mary may have been a contemplative, Martha was not disadvantaged if she was not. She is a saint in any case: "St. Martha was a saint, even though they do not say she was contemplative" (W 17.5).

Holiness is not measured by any particular spiritual experiences, no matter how sublime they may seem. If we are looking for authentic evidence of sanctity, we must look elsewhere:

> A prioress should not think that since a sister has experiences like these she is better than the others. The Lord leads each one as He sees is necessary. This path is a preparation for becoming a very good servant of God, provided that one cooperate. But sometimes God leads the weakest along this path. And so there is nothing in it to approve or condemn. One should consider the virtues and who it is who serves our Lord with greater mortification, humility, and purity of conscience; this is the one who will be the holiest. Yet, little can be known here below with certitude; we must wait until the true Judge gives to each one what is merited. In heaven we will be surprised to see how different His judgment is from what we can understand here below. (IC 6.8.10)

As we have seen, Teresa insists that it is greater conformity with the divine will, whatever it may be, that is the true mark of someone who is advanced in the Christian life: "The highest perfection obviously does not consist in interior delights or in great raptures or in visions or in the spirit of prophecy but in having our will so much in conformity with God's will that there is nothing we know He wills that we do not want with all our desire, and in accepting the bitter as happily as we do the delightful when we know that His Majesty desires it" (F 5.10). We may legitimately hope and even actively aspire—to the degree that it is in our power—to the infused prayer of contemplation and union, but we must always remember that it is complying with and surrender to the divine will that is essential.

The Two Manners of Union

In *The Interior Castle*, Teresa distinguishes two different forms or modes of union: the union attained in mystical prayer and the union of the human will with the divine will. It is the second form in which true holiness is found and which, with God's help, is within reach of every Christian. The person at any and every stage of the journey of prayer must always seek the union of wills:

> The whole aim of any person who is beginning prayer—and don't forget this, because it's very very important—should be that he work and prepare himself with determination and every possible effort to bring his will into conformity with God's will. Be certain that, as I shall say later, the greatest perfection attainable along the spiritual path lies in this conformity. It is the person who lives in more perfect conformity who will receive more from the Lord and be more advanced on this road. Don't think that in what concerns perfection there is some mystery or things unknown or still to be understood, for in perfect conformity to God's will lies all our good. (IC 2.1.8)

She wanted her readers to pursue mystical union to the degree that it was in their power, but Teresa was insistent that authentic prayer served the uniting of our will with God's and that the deepest union could not be attained without arriving at the union of wills. In a text that we noted in an earlier chapter, Teresa writes:

> True union can very well be reached, with God's help, if we make the effort to obtain it by keeping our wills fixed only on that which is God's will. Oh, how many of us there are who will say we do this, and it will seem to us that we don't want anything else and that we would die for this truth, as I believe I have said! Well I tell you, and I will often repeat it, that if what you say is true you will have obtained this favor from the Lord, and you needn't care at all about the other delightful union that was mentioned. That which is most valuable in the delightful union is that it proceeds from this union of which I'm now speaking; and one cannot arrive at the delightful union if the union coming from being resigned to God's will is not very certain. Oh, how desirable is this union with God's will! Happy the soul that has reached it. (IC 5.3.3)

First things first, Teresa is insisting: strive to fulfill and surrender to the divine will, and you will have laid the proper foundation for receiving the "delightful union" in prayer, if God so chooses.

Mystical experiences, extraordinary phenomena, and advanced "degrees" of prayer—if authentic—bear fruit in bringing us into greater conformity with the divine will, but they do not replace or surpass this more fundamental goal of every Christian life. Every Christian must strive for transformation in Christ and, with him, a true union of our wills. This involves great and sustained efforts, with the help of grace, to bring about this change in ourselves; but this process is greatly helped by the gifts of infused prayer. Teresa uses the image of the silkworm to illustrate the difference:

> Nonetheless, take careful note, daughters, that it is necessary for the silkworm to die, and, moreover, at a cost to yourselves.

> *In the delightful union*, the experience of seeing oneself in so new a life greatly helps one to die; *in the other union*, it's necessary that, while living in this life, we ourselves put the silkworm to death. I confess this latter death will require a great deal of effort, or more than that; but it has its value. Thus if you come out victorious the reward will be much greater. But there is no reason to doubt the possibility of this death any more than that of true union with the will of God. This union with God's will is the union I have desired all my life; it is the union I ask the Lord for always and the one that is clearest and safest. (IC 5.3.5, emphasis added)

Union with the divine will takes great effort on our part, but it is the sure road to what must be the ultimate and essential goal of our lives: union with God in the next life, whether or not we experience the prayer of union in this life.

According to the Divine Plan

Teresa knew and accepted the traditional teaching that ascetical preparation and the determined effort to grow in prayer are necessary preparation for contemplation. This is apparent, as we have seen, in her insistence on the essential virtues and in the progression laid out in *The Interior Castle*. And yet, at the same time, she felt that God had given her mystical prayer when she had not yet engaged seriously in such preparation. In the *Life* (L 4.7), she tells us that, shortly after beginning the prayer of (acquired) recollection, she felt drawn into the prayer of quiet and even had passing experiences of union with God (and we recall that she was writing after having advanced in her prayer and thus was able to reflect on her past experience with a mature sense of what was happening at the time). Still, she subsequently passed through a long period of instability in her prayer due largely to what she perceived as the lack of coherence between her prayer and her manner of living. In fact, one of her early directors tried to convince her that she could not really be receiving infused gifts of prayer in light of her current manner of living: "Since he was getting to know my very great imperfections, and they would even be sins—although after I spoke with him I made greater amends—and since I mentioned to him the favors granted me by God so that he could give me light, he told me that my imperfections were incompatible with the favors and that these gifts were bestowed on persons who were already very advanced and mortified" (L 23.11).

In *The Way of Perfection*, even while challenging her readers to attend to her teaching about the essential virtues, she acknowledges that God sometimes gives people gifts of infused prayer precisely in order to challenge or invite them out of their current manner of living:

> I now want to explain—because some of you don't know—what mental prayer is, and please God we shall practice this as it ought to be practiced. But I fear that mental prayer also involves much labor if the virtues are not obtained—although it's not necessary that they be possessed in as high a degree as is required for contemplation. I say that the King of glory will not come to our soul—I mean to be united with it—if we do not make the effort to gain the great virtues. . . . *I want to say, then, that there are times when God will want to grant some great favor to persons who are in a bad state so as to draw them by this means out of the hands of the devil.* (W 16.6, emphasis added)

Growth in virtue is the normal foundation for growth in prayer and for the reception of infused forms of prayer, but God can sometimes give spiritual gifts precisely in order to encourage conversion on our part.

At times, the deeper communion with God that comes in infused forms of prayer, even when given despite the absence of adequate preparation, provides in itself the help needed to prepare the way for sustained growth in deeper prayer. Speaking of receiving raptures, Teresa writes:

> Why His Majesty does this is because He wants to, and He does it in the way He wants to; and even though the soul may not be ready, His Majesty prepares it to receive the good He gives it. Wherefore he doesn't always give raptures because souls have merited them through good cultivation of the garden (although it is very certain that anyone who does take good care of the garden and strives to be detached will not fail to be favored), but sometimes it is His will to show His greatness on very wretched soil, as I have said. (L 21.9)

The preparation for infused contemplation that would normally take great and sustained effort on our part can be accomplished by God very quickly by divine gift according to God's own sometimes inexplicable plans. Again, referring to the gift of raptures, Teresa writes:

> I don't deny that someone with the help of God, making use of the means mentioned by authors who have written about prayer, its principles, and properties, will by means of many efforts reach perfection and great detachment. But they will not do so in as short a time as it takes for the Lord to accomplish it in this stage, without anything done on our part. He definitely draws the soul up from the earth and gives it dominion over every earthly thing, even though there may be no more merits in it than there were

> in me—and I cannot overstress this absence of merit in me, because I had hardly any. (L 21.8)

Teresa insists that the amazing divine gifts that she has received despite what she believes to be her lack of merit should encourage her readers not to let their own lack of deserving hold them back.

God is not bound by our expectations or by our usual limitations. In the end, contemplation, union, and mystical gifts are a completely gratuitous gift of God, not a required reward for our best efforts to prepare ourselves. God's ways are often mysterious to us, but they do not therefore reflect any capriciousness on God's part. In fact, Teresa believes that God would give such gifts to everyone who truly loves him: "Even though it is true that these are blessings the Lord gives to whomever He wills, His Majesty would give them all to us if we loved Him as He loves us. He doesn't desire anything else than to have those to whom to give" (IC 6.4.12). In the *Life*, she concludes: "Let us understand most clearly the real fact: God gives them to us without any merit on our part" (L 10.4).

Remain Determined

Contemplation and union are gifts of God. We must generally do our part diligently and faithfully, even for years, to prepare to receive such gifts. Sometimes it might seem as if God does not intend to give them, and we must be prepared to accept that possibility. The most important thing, insists Teresa, is the union of our will with God's. Salvation and sanctity do not require infused gifts. But, at the same time, God can give it at any time, and we must not give up on doing our part to be ready to receive. Writing explicitly for her nuns, Teresa says: "Keep in mind that

I say we should all try to be contemplatives, since we are not here for any other reason. And we should try not for just a year, nor for only two, nor even for just ten; otherwise we leave the impression that we are giving up as cowards; and it is good for the Lord to know we are doing our best" (W 18.3).

If God chooses not to give divine union in prayer in this life, it is what awaits us in heaven. Meanwhile, we must continue to do what is in our power: "I don't say that we shouldn't try; on the contrary, we should try everything. What I am saying is that this is not a matter of your choosing but of the Lord's. . . . Be sure that if you do what lies in your power, preparing yourselves for contemplation with the perfection mentioned, and that if He doesn't give it to you (and I believe He will give it if detachment and humility are truly present), He will save this gift for you so as to grant it to you all at once in heaven" (W 17.7). We must hold together an insistent "very determined determination" with the trusting acceptance of the divine wisdom in choosing to whom and when infused gifts in prayer are given.

The Complete Gift of Self is Required

Teresa challenges us never to give up, but she is insistent that the reception of infused prayer and especially divine union require nothing less than the complete gift of self: "The whole point is that we should give ourselves to Him with complete determination. . . . And since He doesn't force our will, He takes what we give Him; but He doesn't give Himself completely until we give ourselves completely" (W 28.12). We have to give ourselves to God completely so that God is truly and fully free to act in us.

This total gift of self is another face of uniting our wills with the divine will, because without surrendering to God's will, we will never be able to be prepared to rest deeply in the divine presence and receive the divine self-giving. In *The Way of Perfection*—in which Teresa addresses contemplative prayer by commenting on the petitions of the Our Father—she titles chapter thirty-two: "Discuss the words of the Our Father, *Fiat voluntas tua sicut in caelo et in terra* [May your will be done on earth as in heaven]; the great deal a person does when he says them with full determination; and how well the Lord repays this." In the chapter, she writes: "Because everything I have advised you about in this book is directed toward the complete gift of ourselves to the Creator, the surrender of our wills to His, and detachment from creatures. . . . Unless we give our wills entirely to the Lord so that in everything pertaining to us He might do what conforms with His will, we will never be allowed to drink from this fount. Drinking from it is perfect contemplation, that which you told me to write about" (W 32.9). Although *The Way of Perfection* was written as a book about contemplative prayer, Teresa insists that its teaching is fundamentally directed toward the total gift of ourselves to God.

Conclusion

Is everyone called to infused contemplation? It appears that Teresa of Jesus wanted to respond, "Yes!" Teresa believed that true contemplation is a gift, and God gives it to whom God wills. But she knew from experience that God is fond of giving and never tires of doing so. At the same time, she knew good people of committed prayer and lives of virtue who never seemed to receive it. Nonetheless, for our part, we can and should do what we can to prepare to receive infused gifts of prayer. And we should do so with great determination. Sometimes God will give contemplative gifts to people even without the usual preparation as a way to spur them on. But in the end, it is God who decides.

Our principal task in this life, Teresa assures us, is to conform our wills to the divine will. That was her great goal in life—the conformity, surrender, and union of her will with God's. Contemplative prayer and mystical gifts advance that goal, but they do not replace or surpass it.

Perhaps not everyone will receive divine union in this life or even true contemplation. But all of us are called to intimate sharing with the divine friend who we know loves us. We are invited into prayer and into the friendship with Christ which it manifests, savors, and deepens. Christ, Teresa assures us, is a true friend and will never fail us. Remembering, pondering, resting in, and deepening the good news that he first loved us, we do what awakens and nurtures our love for him in return—not principally as a feeling or emotion but as a decision and commitment to frequently take time to be alone with him. The intimate sharing of prayer—in whatever form that it takes, consoling or dry—manifests and feeds a friendship with God become flesh.

Whether or not we are contemplatives in the classical sense, we can all live as true friends of Christ committed to spending time with him in prayer and to living lives increasingly consistent with being true friends of Christ. All of us can seek to nurture a spirit of recollection in our lives, attentive and present to the divine presence. Whether our prayer is contemplative according to a traditional understanding or not, we can seek to make all of our prayer—vocal, meditation, or according to some practice of recollection—truly a prayer of presence and recollection. This will make us contemplatives in a broader but true sense, living with an abiding contemplative spirit—whatever form our prayer might take. Teresa of Jesus invites all of us to a life of prayer that is nothing other than a life of intimate sharing and walking with our Savior.

Select Bibliography

IN ENGLISH

Álvarez, Tomás. *Prayer: Journeying to God with St. Teresa.* Translated by Anne Harriss. Oxford, England: Teresian Press, 2019.

[Devos], Gabriel of St. Mary Magdalen. *The Way of Prayer: A Commentary on Saint Teresa's Way of Perfection.* Translated by Baltimore Carmel. 2nd ed. San Francisco: Ignatius, 2017.

Dubay, Thomas. *Fire Within: St. Teresa of Avila, St. John of the Cross, and the Gospel on Prayer.* San Francisco: Ignatius, 1989.

Egan, Keith J. *Teresa, Teach Us to Pray: Study Guide* (CD lecture series). Rockville, Md.: Now You Know Media, 2011.

Kavanaugh, Kieran. "How to Pray: From the Life and Teachings of Saint Teresa." In *Carmel and Contemplation: Transforming Human Consciousness*, Carmelite Studies 8, edited by Kevin Culligan and Regis Jordan, 115–35. Washington, D.C.: ICS Publications, 2000.

Lantry, Jerome. *Praying with St. Teresa: Through the Way of Perfection.* Oxford, England: Teresian Press, 2015.

Larkin, Ernest E. "The Carmelite Tradition and Centering Prayer/ Christian Meditation." In *Carmelite Prayer: A Tradition for the 21st Century*, edited by Keith J. Egan, 202–22. Mahwah, N.J.: Paulist Press, 2003.

———. "St. Teresa of Avila and Centering Prayer." In *Carmelite Studies 3: Centenary of Saint Teresa*, edited by John Sullivan, 191–211. Washington, D.C.: ICS Publications, 1982.

O'Donoghue, Noel. *Adventures in Prayer: Reflections on St. Teresa of Avila, St. John of the Cross and St. Thérèse of Lisieux.* London: Burns and Oates, 2004.

O'Keefe, Mark. *In Context: Teresa of Ávila, John of the Cross, and Their World*. Washington, D.C.: ICS Publications, 2020.

———. *Learned, Experienced, and Discerning: St. Teresa of Avila and St. John of the Cross on Spiritual Direction*. Collegeville, Minn.: Liturgical Press, 2020.

———. *The Way of Transformation: Saint Teresa of Avila on the Foundation and Fruit of Prayer*. Washington, D.C.: ICS Publications, 2016.

Payne, Steven. "The Tradition of Prayer in Teresa and John of the Cross." In *Spiritual Traditions for the Contemporary Church*, edited by Robin Maas and Gabriel O'Donnell, 235–58. Nashville, Tenn.: Abingdon, 1990.

Ros García, Salvador. *St. Teresa's Manner of Prayer*. Translated by Kieran Kavanaugh. Alba de Tormes, Spain: Carmelitas Descalzas, 2003.

Seelaus, Vilma. *Distractions in Prayer: Blessing or Curse? St. Teresa of Avila's Teachings in The Interior Castle*. Staten Island, N.Y.: St. Paul's, 2005.

Tyler, Peter. *Christian Mindfulness: Theology and Practice*. London: SCM Press, 2018.

Welch, John. "Prayer in the Carmelite Tradition." In *Prayer in the Catholic Tradition: A Handbook of Practical Approaches*, edited by Robert J. Wicks, 209–34. Cincinnati: Franciscan Media, 2016.

In Spanish

Álvarez, Tomás. "Grados de oración." In *Diccionario de Santa Teresa: Doctrina e historia*, 2nd ed., edited by Tomás Álvarez, 317–20. Burgos, Spain: Editorial Monte Carmelo, 2006.

———. "Oración." In Álvarez, *Diccionario de Santa Teresa*, 469–74.

Caballero, Nicolás. *Cómo enseñaba a orar Santa Teresa*. Burgos, Spain: Editorial Monte Carmelo, 2003.

Castellano, Jesús. "Espiritualidad teresiana: experiencia y doctrina." In *Introducción a la lectura de Santa Teresa,* 2nd. ed., edited by Alberto Barrientos, 157–281. Madrid: Editorial de Espiritualidad, 2002.

Castro, Secundino. "Jesucristo y su misterio." In *Teresa de Jesús: mujer, cristiana, maestra.* 2nd. ed., edited by Secudino Castro, 137–56. Madrid: Editorial de Espiritualidad, 2013.

———. *Ser cristiano según Santa Teresa: teología y espiritualidad.* 2nd. ed. Madrid: Editorial de Espiritualidad, 1985.

Cuartas Londoño, Rómulo. "De la Dispersión al Recogimiento." In *La meditación teresiana: características fundamentales y su práctica,* edited by Francisco Javier Sancho Fermín, 11–49. Ávila, Spain: Centro Internacional Teresiano-Sanjuanista, 2012.

———. "Meditación discursiva y oración de recogimiento." In *Meditación y contemplación: Caminos hacia la paz (Budismo Theravada y mística teresiana),* edited by Javier Sancho Fermín, 255–71. Burgos, Spain: CITeS/Grupo Editorial Fonte (Monte Carmelo), 2019.

Gómez, Navarro, Eusebio. *Una mujer en camino: Teresa de Jesús.* Burgos, Spain: Editorial Monte Carmelo, 2012.

González, Luis Jorge. *Mindfulness y Santa Teresa: Estar con Quien sabemos nos ama.* Mexico City: Ediciones Duruelo, 2017.

Guerra, Augusto. "Oración teresiana." In Castro, *Teresa de Jesús: mujer, cristiana, maestra,* 157–79.

Herráiz García, Maximiliano. "Características de la oración teresiana" In *A zaga de tu huella: escritos teresiano-sanjuanistas y de espiritualidad,* 143–56. Burgos, Spain: Editorial Monte Carmelo, 2004.

———. "Oración, diálogo de amistad posible en todo lugar." In *A zaga de tu huella,* 157–73.

———. *La oración, historia de amistad.* 6th ed. Madrid: Editorial de Espiritualidad, 2003.

———. "Teresa de Jesús, teología de la amistad." In *Santa Teresa de Jesús: testigo y maestra de oración desde el libro de su "Vida,"* edited by Javier Sancho Fermín and Rómulo Cuartas Londoño 39–88. Burgos, Spain: CITeS/Editorial Monte Carmelo, 2011.

Marcos, Juan Antonio. *Un viaje a la plenitud: El Camino de Perfección de Teresa de Jesús*. Madrid: Editorial de Espiritualidad, 2010.

Maroto, Daniel de Pablo. *El carmelo teresiano en oración: vida y doctrina*. Burgos, Spain: Editorial Fonte, 2016.

———. *Dinámica de la oración: acercamiento del orante moderno a Santa Teresa de Jesús*. Madrid: Editorial de Espiritualidad, 1973.

———. *Teresa en oración: historia, experiencia, doctrina*. Madrid: Editorial de Espiritualidad, 2004.

Márquez, Miguel. "Teresa, pedagogía de la oración." In Fermín and Londoño, *Santa Teresa de Jesús*, 9–37. Burgos, Spain: CITeS/Editorial Monte Carmelo, 2011.

Martín del Blanco, Mauricio. *Catecismo de la oración según Santa Teresa de Jesús*. Burgos, Spain: Editorial Monte Carmelo, 2014.

Pérez, María José. "La oración vocal y mental: La religiosidad en la escuela de Teresa de Jesús." In Fermín, *Meditación y contemplación*, 235–54.

Sancho Fermín, Francisco Javier. "La oración 'mística' y sus grados a la luz del *Castillo Interior* de Teresa de Jesús." In Fermín, *Meditación y contemplación*, 273–308.

———. *Orar con Santa Teresa de Jesús*. Bilbao, Spain: Editorial Desclée Brouwer, 2014.

Valentín de San José. *Oración mental según Santa Teresa*, 5th ed. Seville, Spain: Apostolado Mariano, 1969.

Other Books by Mark O'Keefe, O.S.B

In Context: Teresa of Ávila, John of the Cross, and Their World
ICS Publications, 2020

Learned, Experienced, and Discerning: St. Teresa of Avila and St. John of the Cross on Spiritual Direction
Liturgical Press, 2020

The Way of Transformation: Saint Teresa of Avila on the Foundation and Fruit of Prayer
ICS Publications, 2016

Love Awakened by Love: The Liberating Ascent of Saint John of the Cross
ICS Publications, 2014

Deciding to Be Christian: A Daily Commitment
Liguori, 2012

Priestly Wisdom: Insights from St. Benedict
Abbey Press, 2004

Priestly Prayer: Reflections on Prayer in the Life of the Priest
Abbey Press, 2002

Priestly Virtues: Reflections on the Moral Virtues in the Life of the Priest
Abbey Press, 2000

The Ordination of a Priest: Reflections on the Priesthood in the Rite of Ordination
Abbey Press, 1999

In Persona Christi: Reflections on Priestly Identity and Holiness
Abbey Press, 1998

Becoming Good, Becoming Holy:
On the Relationship of Christian Ethics and Spirituality
Paulist Press, 1995; St. Pauls/India, 1997; St. Pauls/Philippines, 1997

What Are They Saying About Social Sin?
Paulist Press, 1990

Index

A

acquired recollection *vs.* infused recollection, 82, 95–96, 110–11
aids. *See* helps to prayer
alumbrados (enlightened ones), 124–25
Álvarez, Tomás, 90
Anthony of the Desert, 130
apophatic spirituality, 17
Ascent of Mt. Carmel, The (John of the Cross), 130
ascetical practice, 128–32
attentiveness to the presence of Christ
  overview, 84–85
  in contemplative attitude in life, 90–91
  in contemporary contemplative practice, 116
  dwelling within the soul, 41–42, 91–95, 251–52
  in every stage of prayer, 87
  interiorization and, 54–55
  in meditation, 71–72, 76–77, 80–81
  receptivity and, 55–56
  recollection as, 80–81, 88–90
  as "representing" Christ, 85–87, 99–100, 117
  solitude and, 46
  in vocal prayer, 63
Augustine, *Confessions*, 13, 93, 97–98

B

Bernard of Clairvaux, 50
betrothal imagery, 236, 250
busyness, 150–53, 198–200

C

Cassian, John, 120, 134
  Conferences, 115, 129
Catherine of Siena, 50
Centering Prayer
  Christ in, 120, 134
  practice of, 115–19
  recollection equated with, 113–14
  self-knowledge in, 126, 140
  transformation in, 126, 130–31
  wide audience for, 123
challenges. *See* trials in prayer
Christ
  as friend, 35–36
  humanity of, 48–52, 132–33, 245–48, 253–54
  images of, 86, 102, 156–57
  "representing," 85–87, 99–100, 117
  suffering of, 30, 48, 49, 70–71, 81, 87, 89–90, 145
  transformation into, 184, 254–56
  See also attentiveness to the presence of Christ; God
Christian Meditation (John Main)
  Christ in, 120–21, 133–34

practice of, 115–19
recollection equated with, 113–14
transformation in, 126
wide audience for, 123
Cloud of Unknowing, The, 115, 120, 129–30
cocoon and silkworm imagery, 127–28, 184, 255, 263–64
commitment. *See* determination and perseverance
Communion (Eucharist), 49, 81, 163–65
Conferences (Cassian), 115, 129
Confessions (Augustine), 13, 93, 97–98
consolations
determination despite lack of, 178
expecting, 143–44, 145, 146–48, 188
vs. spiritual delights, 149–50, 209–10
contemplation
contemporary practices (*see* Centering Prayer; Christian Meditation)
disposition for, 205–6
distractions and, 118
as gift, 82–83, 259, 260, 265–67
meditation as difficult after, 79–80, 247
transition to, from recollection, 82, 108–11, 208–9
as unattainable for many, 260–61
vocal prayer and, 64–66
See also quiet, prayer of; transformation; union; union, prayer of conversion
Teresa's experience of, 13
transformation and, 128–32, 183
courtship imagery, 225, 228–29, 233

D

Dark Night, The (John of the Cross), 130
death imagery, 227–28, 243, 263–64
desert tradition, 128, 129, 130
detachment
as essential virtue, 187–88
prayer of quiet and, 218
prayer of union and, 233–34, 245
determination and perseverance
as characteristic of prayer, 30–32, 176–79
moving forward and aiming high with, 180–81, 267–68
in Teresa's prayer journey, 11–13, 31
as virtue, 188
See also trials in prayer
devil
fear of determined souls, 178–79
temptations from (*see* trials in prayer)
difficulties. *See* trials in prayer
discursive meditation, 15, 68
See also meditation
distractions, 103–5, 118, 138–42, 214, 216–17, 224
drawing inward, 208
dryness, 142–50
dwelling of God, within the soul, 41–42, 91–95, 251–52

dwelling places. *See* progression of prayer
dynamism, as essential aspect of prayer, 44–45, 53

E

Eastern Christianity, Jesus Prayer, 116, 120, 129
ecstasy/rapture, 235, 238–39, 266
effort of prayer, 55–56, 167–68
Egan, Keith, 90–91
Eucharist, 49, 81, 163–65
Evagrius Ponticus, 128, 134
excessive practices, 214–15

F

faithfulness
  in dry prayer, 144–48
  effort and, 55–56, 167–68
  as essential to prayer, 45
  hope and, 175–76
  in recollection, 106–8
  See also determination and perseverance
false humility, 172–75
fasting and penance, 214–15
Feldmeier, Peter, 124, 129n26
Francis of Assisi, 50
Freeman, Laurence, 115, 121, 133n35
Frenette, David, 117
frequency. *See* determination and perseverance; faithfulness
friendship
  as aid to prayer, 157–58
  mutuality of, 42, 47, 183, 206, 256–57
  prayer as, overview, 38–40, 123–24
  See also love

G

garden imagery. *See* water and garden imagery
gazing
  with love, 57, 81, 100
  silent, 117
gentle words, 117–18, 217
God
  as active and principal agent in prayer, 28–29, 42–43, 56, 191–93, 249
  contemplation as gift of, 82–83, 259, 260, 265–67
  dwelling within the soul, 41–42, 91–95, 251–52
  humanity created in image of, 43
  knowledge of, 233, 244–45
  love of/for, 55, 196–97, 200–201, 256–57
  spiritual delights from, 150, 210
  in the Trinity, 121, 252–53
  will of, union with, 46–47, 152, 162, 181, 186, 187, 192, 197–98, 230–32, 261–64, 268–69
  See also Christ
González, Luis Jorge, 113n1

H

Hail Mary, 63
Haughton, Rosemary, 131
helps to prayer
  books, 153–55
  Eucharist, 163–65

friends and community, 157–58
images of Christ, 86, 102, 156–57
nature, 156
solitude, 46, 160–63
spiritual direction, 22–24, 159–60
heretical movements, 124–25
Herráiz, Maximiliano, 26–27, 54n1
Holy Communion, 49, 81, 163–65
Holy Spirit
as spiritual director, 22
in the Trinity, 121, 252–53
hope, 175–76
humanity of Christ, 48–52, 132–33, 245–48, 253–54
humility
defined, 172
determination and, 180–81
in dry prayer, 146–48
as essential virtue, 188
false, 172–75
prayer of quiet and, 215, 219
prayer of union and, 234, 245

I

Ignatian meditation, 15
Ignatius of Loyola, 17
images of Christ, 86, 102, 156–57
imagination. *See* intellect and imagination
indwelling of God, 41–42, 91–95, 251–52
infant nursing imagery, 203, 229–30
infused recollection
vs. acquired recollection, 82, 95–96, 110–11
transition to, 207–8
transition to contemplation from, 82, 108–11, 208–9
Inquisition, Spanish, 4, 5, 49–50, 155
intellect and imagination
in deepened union, 224–25, 248
distractions and, 103–5, 140–42, 216–17, 224
in meditation, 15–16, 68, 74–75
prayer as more than, 40–42, 76–78, 81, 100–101
quieting of, 213–14, 224
interiorization, 54–55

J

Jesus Christ. *See* Christ
Jesus Prayer (Eastern Christianity), 116, 120, 129
John of the Cross, 17, 68–69, 110, 135
Ascent of Mt. Carmel, The, 130
Dark Night, The, 130

K

kataphatic spirituality, 17
Kavanaugh, Kieran, 44, 85, 86–87, 215n2
Keating, Thomas, 113, 115, 117, 119, 120, 123, 130–31, 134
knowledge of God, 233, 244–45
See also intellect and imagination; self-knowledge

L

Larkin, Ernest, 113–14, 119, 131, 135
Lawrence of the Resurrection, *The Practice of the Presence of God*, 91

lectio divina, 15, 68, 80, 120, 123, 134
life, manner of
  congruence between prayer and, 18–22, 47, 182–83, 265
  love for others, 55, 196–97, 200–201, 256–57
  tension between life of prayer and life of action, 150–53, 162, 198–200
  and union with the divine will, 46–47, 152, 162, 186, 187, 192, 197–98
  while in the abiding union, 248–49, 256–57
  See also transformation; virtues
locutions, 238, 241
love
  betrothal imagery, 236, 250
  courtship imagery, 225, 228–29, 233
  as essential virtue, 187
  gazing with, 57, 81, 100
  humility and, 188
  vs. intellect in prayer, 41, 78, 101
  marital imagery, 249, 250–51
  mutual, 43, 201, 206, 222
  of/for God and neighbor, 55, 196–97, 200–201, 256–57
  prayer as expression of, 195
  yearning, 242–44

M

Main, John, 113, 115, 117, 119, 120–21, 133–34
marital imagery, 249, 250–51
Martha and Mary (biblical figures), 200–201, 256, 261
Martín del Blanco, Mauricio, 27n11
martyrs, 179
Mary Magdalene, 49
meditation
  after reaching contemplation, 79–80, 247
  challenges of, 16–18, 79
  defined, 69
  intellect and imagination in, 15–16, 68, 74–75
  methods of, 15, 68–70
  vs. recollection, 98–99, 100–101
  self-knowledge and, 72–74
  subjects/themes for, 70–72
  value of, 69–70
  See also contemplation; recollection
mental prayer, 37, 67–68, 217–18, 265
milk imagery, 203, 229–30
mind. *See* intellect and imagination
mindfulness. *See* attentiveness to the presence of Christ
monastic environment, 25–26
morality. *See* life, manner of; virtues

N

neighbor, love of, 55, 196–97, 200–201, 256–57
nursing infant imagery, 203, 229–30

O

obstacles. *See* trials in prayer
Ó Madagáin, Murchadh, 133n34
Osuna, Francisco de, *The Third Spiritual Alphabet*, 10, 23, 93, 97
Our Father, 63, 64, 65, 164, 269

P

pain, 243–44
palace imagery, 57, 92, 94–95
Paul (apostle), 50, 255
penance and fasting, 214–15
Pennington, Basil, 121n18
perseverance. *See* determination and perseverance
Peter of Alcántara, 106
Pius XI, Pope, 33
poverty of spirit, 146
Practice of the Presence of God, The (Lawrence of the Resurrection), 91
prayer
- characteristics of Teresa's, 26–33
- defined, 37
- as dynamic, 44–45, 53
- environments conducive to, 25–26
- essential elements of, 38–47
- spiritual direction in, 22–24, 159–60
- Teresa's writings on, 2–9
- *See also* helps to prayer; progression of prayer; trials in prayer

presence. *See* attentiveness to the presence of Christ
progression of prayer
- degrees/stages of, 59–63, 122–23
- dynamism and, 44–45, 53
- interiorization, 54–55
- many paths in, 58–59, 204–5
- mental prayer, 37, 67–68, 217–18, 265
- receptivity, 55–56
- simplification, 56–57
- vocal prayer, 37, 63–66, 67, 217–18
- *See also* attentiveness to the presence of Christ; contemplation; meditation; quiet, prayer of; recollection; union, prayer of

Q

quiet, prayer of
- experiences of, 211–15
- fruits of, 218–19
- *vs.* infused recollection, 209
- moving beyond, 211
- nursing infant imagery, 203
- response to, 215–18
- sleep of the faculties and, 219–21
- spiritual delights in, 149–50, 209–10
- *See also* union, prayer of

R

rapture/ecstasy, 235, 238–39, 266
receptivity, 55–56
recollection
- acquired *vs.* infused, 82, 95–96, 110–11
- as attentiveness to the presence of Christ, 80–81, 88–90
- contemporary contemplative practice, distinction from, 121–29, 131–33, 134–35
- contemporary contemplative practice, equated with, 113–14
- distractions and, 103–5, 141
- effort in, 168
- faithfulness in, 106–8
- in heretical movements, 124–25

vs. meditation, 98–99, 100
as method of prayer, 95–97
nursing infant imagery, 203
practice of, 99–102
reading as aid to, 154–55
in solitude, 161–62
spiritual communion and, 165
Teresa's discovery of, 97–98
transition to contemplation from, 82, 108–11, 208–9
transition to infused, 207–8
See also contemplation; quiet, prayer of; union, prayer of
relationship. *See* friendship
rewards. *See* consolations

S

Samaritan woman at the well, 49, 243
Seelaus, Vilma, 140
self, gift of, 268–69
self-knowledge
distractions and, 140
humility and, 188
interiorization and, 55
meditation and, 72–74
prayer as essential to, 43–44
prayer of quiet and, 219
prayer of union and, 245
sin and, 43–44, 73, 118
silence. *See* attentiveness to the presence of Christ; quiet, prayer of
silkworm and cocoon imagery, 127–28, 184, 255, 263–64
simplification, of prayer, 56–57
sin
after reaching union, 255–56
distractions and, 105
ingratitude of past, 242
prayer after falling into, 169–72
psychological interpretation of, 133, 134
salvation from, 132–33
self-knowledge and, 43–44, 73, 118
sleep imagery, 219–21, 227–28
sleep of the faculties, 219–21
solitude, as essential to prayer, 46, 160–63
See also contemplation; meditation
Spanish Inquisition, 4, 5, 49–50, 155
spiritual communion, 165
spiritual delights, 149–50, 209–10
spiritual direction, 22–24, 159–60
struggles. *See* trials in prayer
suffering of Christ, 30, 48, 49, 70–71, 81, 87, 89–90, 145

T

temptation. *See* trials in prayer
Teresa of Ávila
prayer characteristics, 26–33
prayer journey, overview, 9–14
prayer journey, challenges, 14–26, 137–38
writings on prayer, 2–9
Thérèse of Lisieux, 33
thinking. *See* intellect and imagination
Third Spiritual Alphabet, The (Osuna), 10, 23, 93, 97
Thomas Aquinas, 188, 201

Tomás de Jesús, 96n14
transformation
 into Christ, 184, 254–56
 cocoon and silkworm imagery, 127–28, 184, 255, 263–64
 in contemporary contemplative practice, 126, 130–31
 conversion and, 128–32, 183
 as measure of prayer, 193–94
 prayer as transformative, 190–93
 See also life, manner of; virtues
transport, 240
 See also rapture/ecstasy
trials in prayer
 busyness, 150–53, 198–200
 distractions, 103–5, 118, 138–42, 214, 216–17, 224
 dryness, 142–50
 false humility, 172–75
 giving up on prayer, 169–72
 in the sixth dwelling places, 241–44
 Teresa's experience with, 14–26, 137–38
 See also determination and perseverance; helps to prayer; sin
Trinity, 50, 120–21, 252–53
Tyler, Peter, 113n1

U

union
 abiding, 248–52
 certitude about, 232–33
 as Christocentric, 50, 245–48, 253–54
 with the divine will, 46–47, 152, 162, 181, 186, 187, 192, 197–98, 230–32, 261–64, 268–69
 ecstasy/rapture and, 235, 238–39, 266
 locutions and, 238, 241
 transforming, 254–55
 with the Trinity, 252–53
union, prayer of
 experiences of, 223–25, 226, 236–41, 248–50
 fruits of, 232–35, 244–45
 humanity of Christ as focus of, 245–48
 images and analogies, 203, 225, 227–30, 236
 progression of, 225–26, 235–37, 248–51
 sleep of the faculties as transition to, 219–21
 trials of, 241–44, 255–56

V

Venancio dello Spirito Santo, 95n12
virtues
 as essential preparation for contemplation, 126–27, 131, 135, 184–86, 189–90, 264–66
 prayer of quiet and, 218
 prayer of union and, 234–35, 245
 See also detachment; faithfulness; humility; life, manner of; love; transformation
visions, 50, 56–57, 238
vocal prayer, 37, 63–66, 67, 217–18
Vogüé, Adalbert de, 115n9, 129n27

W

water and garden imagery
  in degrees of prayer, 14, 60, 122, 227
  dryness in prayer, 143, 145–46, 147
  God's action, 192
wordless prayer. *See* contemplation; recollection
works. *See* life, manner of; virtues

Y

yearning, 242–44

About Us

ICS Publications, based in Washington, D.C., is the publishing house of the Institute of Carmelite Studies (ICS) and a ministry of the Discalced Carmelite Friars of the Washington Province (U.S.A.). The Institute of Carmelite Studies promotes research and publication in the field of Carmelite spirituality, especially about Carmelite saints and related topics. Its members are friars of the Washington Province.

The Discalced Carmelites are a worldwide Roman Catholic religious order comprised of friars, nuns, sisters, and laity—men and women who are heirs to the teaching and way of life of St. Teresa of Ávila and St. John of the Cross, dedicated to contemplation and to ministry in the church and the world.

Information about discerning a Carmelite vocation is available from the Discalced Carmelite Friars vocation directors at the following addresses:

Washington Province:
1525 Carmel Road, Hubertus, WI 53033

California-Arizona Province:
P.O. Box 3420, San Jose, CA 95156

Oklahoma Province:
906 Kentucky Avenue, San Antonio, TX 78201

Visit our websites at:

www.icspublications.org and *www.discalcedcarmel.org*